Goethe's Werther *and the Critics*

Studies in German Literature, Linguistics, and Culture:
Literary Criticism in Perspective

About *Literary Criticism in Perspective*

Books in the series *Literary Criticism in Perspective* trace literary scholarship and criticism on major and neglected writers alike, or on a single major work, a group of writers, a literary school or movement. In so doing the authors — authorities on the topic in question who are also well-versed in the principles and history of literary criticism — address a readership consisting of scholars, students of literature at the graduate and undergraduate level, and the general reader. One of the primary purposes of the series is to illuminate the nature of literary criticism itself, to gauge the influence of social and historic currents on aesthetic judgments once thought objective and normative.

Wake Tech. Libraries
9101 Fayetteville Road
Raleigh, North Carolina 27603-5696

Goethe's *Werther* and the Critics

Bruce Duncan

CAMDEN HOUSE

Copyright © 2005 Bruce Duncan

All Rights Reserved. Except as permitted under current legislation,
no part of this work may be photocopied, stored in a retrieval system,
published, performed in public, adapted, broadcast, transmitted,
recorded, or reproduced in any form or by any means,
without the prior permission of the copyright owner.

First published 2005
by Camden House

Camden House is an imprint of Boydell & Brewer Inc.
668 Mt. Hope Avenue, Rochester, NY 14620, USA
www.camden-house.com
and of Boydell & Brewer Limited
PO Box 9, Woodbridge, Suffolk IP12 3DF, UK
www.boydellandbrewer.com

ISBN: 1–57113–284–8

Library of Congress Cataloging-in-Publication Data

Duncan, Bruce, 1942–
 Goethe's Werther and the critics / Bruce Duncan.
   p. cm. — (Studies in German literature, linguistics, and
 culture)
 (Literary criticism in perspective)
 Includes bibliographical references and index.
 ISBN 1–57113–284–8 (hardcover: alk. paper)
  1. Goethe, Johann Wolfgang von, 1749–1832. Werther.
 2. Goethe, Johann Wolfgang von, 1749–1832—Appreciation.
 I. Title. II. Series. III. Studies in German literature, linguistics,
 and culture (Unnumbered)

PT1980.D86 2005
833'.6—dc22
                                                    2004029194

A catalogue record for this title is available from the British Library.

This publication is printed on acid-free paper.
Printed in the United States of America.

Contents

Introduction	1
1: First Responses	7
2: Religious Interpretations	29
3: Psychological Approaches	39
4: Political Interpretations	73
5: Goethe, Werther, Reading, and Writing	107
6: Lotte, Sex, and Werther	135
Bibliography	155
Index	191

Introduction

WHEN SHE HEARD the plans for this book, my 91-year-old mother remarked that "it doesn't sound like much of a page-turner." She's right, of course. Few people will take *Goethe's* Werther *and the Critics* along to the beach. Students and scholars, on the other hand, might find it a useful tool. As part of the Camden House series *Literary Criticism in Perspective,* it seeks to trace the critical reception of Goethe's first novel. "One of the primary purposes of the series," the editors state, "is to illuminate the nature of literary criticism itself, to gauge the influence of social and historic currents on aesthetic judgments once thought objective and normative." Goethe's *Werther,* which has inspired well over two centuries' worth of criticism, turns out to be a particularly good subject for just such an investigation. The book's age, textual richness, and sustained popularity, combined with its author's canonical, even mythical status, have invited a broad range of interpretations by critics of all stripes.

When it appeared in 1774, *Die Leiden des jungen Werther,* traditionally translated as *The Sorrows of Young Werther,* created a possibly unique sensation in the history of publishing. "Werther-Fever," a phenomenon that included not just enthusiasm for the novel, but also a desire to emulate its hero, spread throughout Europe and then to America. There was even a translation into Chinese, a first for a German book. So influential was *Werther* that nineteenth-century social critics later designated any romantic overindulgence as "Werther-sickness" or "Wertherism," and twentieth-century psychologists adopted the term "Werther effect" to describe imitative suicides. This last assertion, that the book inspired numerous people to take their own lives, is largely a fiction invented by overly zealous social guardians, but one that still clings stubbornly to the novel's history and underscores its cultural significance. Undeniable, on the other hand, is that a whole generation of young men adopted Werther's blue swallow-tail coat, high boots, and yellow waistcoat and breeches, not to mention his emotionality, while young women donned Lotte's white dress with pink bows and sought to emulate her feminine virtues. Even after such clothing fads passed, *Werther* continued to function as an icon. Forty-four years after its original publication, it was the first book that Dr. Frankenstein's monster read in order to learn what it means to be human.

The novel succeeded commercially, as well, although the absence of effective copyrights meant that much of the profit went to the rogue publishers of pirated versions. Indeed, the first edition to identify Goethe as the author was the unauthorized "first volume" of Goethe's works, printed by Christian Friedrich Himburg in Berlin in 1775 — the original edition of 1774, published by Weygand in Leipzig, appeared anonymously. It is telling that when Goethe set about writing the second version of 1787, the only copy that he could find to work from was a pirated one full of errors. Nor did the author benefit financially from products like *Eau de Werther* or the images of Werther and Lotte that were sold as porcelain figures or on fans, gloves, bread boxes, and jewelry.

The novel did bring Goethe lasting fame, however. When Napoleon visited him in 1808, it was to meet the author of *Werther*, a book he claimed to have read seven times. Over the past two and a quarter centuries, the novel has also spawned countless imitations, parodies, and sequels, including nine Italian operas, in addition to Jules Massenet's more famous French one. The best-known modern retelling, Ulrich Plenzdorf's *Die neuen Leiden des jungen W.* (The New Sufferings of Young W., 1973), caused a major sensation in the German Democratic Republic, where it seemed to define the longings of yet another generation. Even the travel industry still benefits from *Werther;* tourists continue to flock to Wetzlar to view the home of Charlotte Buff, who inspired the figure of Lotte, while visitors to Goethe's house in Frankfurt want to see the desk at which he composed his first novel. In another measure of continuing interest, a recent web search on "Die Leiden des jungen Werther" turned up 51,000 hits.

Perhaps most extraordinary of all, however, is *Werther*'s enduring popularity with readers. There are still twenty-eight German editions and nine English translations in print, not to mention various audiocassettes and on-line versions. Commercial interest in the novel has moved with the times, of course. Eighteenth-century illustrators took some liberties with the plot by showing, for example, Lotte distributing bread to her siblings in a garden setting (see Göres 1972, 183–200; Assel 1984), but the cover on the latest American translation (Pike 2004) features a close-up of a young man kissing a woman's bare midriff — something that Werther never even dreamed of doing, despite what some of the studies discussed below in chapter 6 might claim.

The present volume, however, is concerned not with reception in the broader sense, but with the history of literary criticism. Here, too, various trends come into play. Scholars, like booksellers and other purveyors of fiction, are creatures of their times, and their methods and results reflect social forces and literary tastes. Not only do the many interpreters discussed here choose to focus on different elements in the text — or, in some instances, *not* in the text — they also approach these elements in different ways and arrive at surprisingly different conclusions. This observation could easily lead to a cynical dismissal of the whole enterprise of literary criticism as a branch of the fashion industry. And, as we will see, it is not difficult to find interpreters so given to one vogue or another that they become cavalier about the finer points of evidence and logic. But the bulk of the studies considered here lead to just the opposite conclusion: both Goethe's novel and the history of its criticism are extraordinarily rich; the variety of responses is less an example of fashion than a testimony to the novel's genius and its interpreters' fertility of mind.

A strictly chronological ordering of these interpretations would require a crisscrossing of themes that would soon become chaotic; I have instead chosen to organize each chapter around a particular approach, or set of approaches. Within those categories, the various investigations then appear roughly in the order of their composition. This means that some multi-faceted studies are treated more than once, often in different chapters. In such cases, readers should use the index in order to assure complete coverage of individual interpretations. This listing of names provides some historical orientation by adding dates of birth and death or, when the exact information was not readily available, at least the century in which the person was born.

As prescribed by the publisher, each chapter is followed by its own alphabetically arranged bibliography. A comprehensive chronological listing of sources is found at the end of the book. This chronology is based upon the year of a study's first appearance, which often differs from the date of the edition cited. Georg Lukács's essay on *Werther*, for example, was originally published in 1936 and reissued many times. I consulted and cite the version in Hans Peter Herrmann's 1994 anthology, but the bibliographical entry appears under 1936. This arrangement seemed to be the best way to establish the essay's historical context. For the same reason, I have included the original year of publication when first citing a reference within the text; for example, "(Lukács 1936, 42)." I have not, however, attempted to list every edition of these studies. Thomas Mann's essay on "Goethes Werther," for example, began as a talk in 1939, was broadcast on the radio in 1940, and is now available in at least five subsequent printings. I have listed only the one from which I cite (again, Herrmann), while still referring to it as "Mann 1939." Sometimes, however, the original source seems to deserve its own mention; I include, for example, the information that Matthias Claudius's review of *Werther* appeared in his periodical, *Wandsbecker Bote* (Wandsbeck Messenger), even though my citations come from a modern anthology. In other words, students using the bibliography will find what are intended to be useful, but not complete, listings of each study. Finally, I should add that the final bibliography contains some works that I consulted but did not specifically cite.

References to *Werther* itself include the dates of his letters, on the assumption that readers might be consulting any of a number of editions. References to other works by Goethe are from the Hamburg edition, here designated as *HA*. I assume, by the way, that readers are already familiar with Goethe's story, and so I make no attempt to summarize scenes within it.

To accommodate readers who do not know the language, I have used German quotations sparingly and then included translations in parentheses, usually my own. In several cases, I refer directly to readily available translations, citing, for example, Thomas Burger's translation from 1989 when discussing Jürgen Habermas's *Strukturwandel der Offentlichkeit* (1965).

A further caveat: this survey may seem exhausting, but it is not exhaustive. Neither the publisher's guidelines nor my own endurance has permitted a truly comprehensive review. It was with gratitude that I acceded to the editors' request that I limit myself primarily to publications written in German and English. There are, of course, a great many French, Italian, Japanese, and Slavic contributions to *Werther* scholarship, but even within the German and Anglo-American traditions there is far too much material to treat fully. I have therefore included those items that seem to illustrate the major critical approaches to *Werther*, although I frequently try to point readers to still others that deserve attention. The most daunting prospect of all, however, has been to try to do justice to each study that is treated: to present its arguments fairly, without too much reduction. Encountering others' distortions of my own prior investigations of *Werther* has been both a humbling and an irksome aspect of this research. I have tried especially hard not to be vindictive in such cases.

This history of *Werther* studies, then, attempts to achieve two purposes: on the one hand, to serve as a useful first stop for those planning research on *Werther* by characterizing for them what their predecessors have already chosen to tackle; on the other hand, to provide what I hope is an instructive diachronic slice of literary criticism. In this latter role, the survey reveals some dross, but mostly it shows a rich tradition in which recent studies continue to break new ground, and older ones prove to be worth a further visit.

I would like to thank those who aided me in this undertaking. Dartmouth's Presidential Scholars program enabled me to employ two undergraduate assistants: Alexia O. Huffman, who combed nineteenth-century literary histories for discussions of *Werther*, and Peter C. Hughes Jr., who gathered information for the index. Patricia A. Carter and Reinhart Sonnenburg, Dartmouth librarians, helped to locate elusive resources. Professors Lynn A. Higgins, Susannah Heschel, and Konrad Kenkel shared their erudition and interest, and Steven P. Scher and Ellis Shookman, always important sources of support, read the manuscript and provided valuable editorial advice. I am also grateful to Jim Hardin and Jim Walker of Camden House for their patient guidance and Susan Innes for her superior copy editing.

Finally, I dedicate this study to Wat and Max.

Works Cited

Assel, Jutta. 1984. "'Werther'-Illustrationen: Bilddokumente als Rezeptionsgeschichte." In *Leiden des alten und neuen Werther: Kommentare, Abbildungen, Materialien zu Goethes "Leiden des jungen Werther" und Plenzdorfs "Neuen Leiden des jungen W.,"* ed. Georg Jäger, 57–105, 190–208. Munich: Hanser.

Claudius, Matthias. 1774. "'Die Leiden des jungen Werthers.'" In *Der junge Goethe im zeitgenössischen Urteil*, ed. Peter Müller, 163–64. Berlin: Akademie Verlag, 1969. Originally published in the *Wandsbecker Bote* 169 (October 22, 1774).

Göres, Jörn, ed. 1972. *"Die Leiden des jungen Werthers": Goethes Roman im Spiegel seiner Zeit: Eine Ausstellung des Goethe-Museums Düsseldorf, Anton- und-Katharina-Kippenberg-Stiftung, in Verbindung mit der Stadt Wetzlar; Katalog*. Düsseldorf: Goethe-Museum.

Goethe, Johann Wolfgang von. 1775. *J. W. Goethens Schriften, erster Band*. Berlin: Himburg.

———. 1961–62. *Goethes Werke,* ed. Erich Trunz. Hamburg: Wegner.

Habermas, Jürgen. 1965. *The Structural Transformation of the Public Sphere: An Inquiry into a Category of Bourgeois Society*. Trans. Thomas Burger. Cambridge, MA: MIT UP, 1989.

Herrmann, Hans Peter, ed. 1994a. *Goethes "Werther": Kritik und Forschung*. Darmstadt: Wissenschaftliche Buchgesellschaft.

Lukács, Georg. 1936. "'Die Leiden des jungen Werther.'" In Herrmann, 1994a, 39–57.

Mann, Thomas. 1939. "Goethes 'Werther.'" In Herrmann, 1994a, 85–97.

Pike, Burton, trans. 2004. *"The Sorrows of Young Werther," by Johann Wolfgang von Goethe*. New York: Modern Library.

Plenzdorf, Ulrich. 1973. *Die neuen Leiden des jungen W.* Ed. Richard A. Zipser. New York: Wiley, 1978.

1: First Responses

*W*ERTHER'S EXPLOSIVE EFFECT, wrote Goethe thirty-eight years after the fact, was a matter of timing: at this particular point in history, a disaffected but inarticulate younger generation suddenly found its concerns expressed (*HA* 9: 589–90[1]). As Peter Hohendahl reports, the novel uncovered a rift between the adherents of the optimistic-sentimental doctrine of virtue and the exponents of *Weltschmerz* (world-weariness; 1977, 81). The novel's appearance coincided with another less dramatic but nevertheless significant schism that marked the tail end of a profound paradigm shift in German literary criticism. Pre-Enlightenment critics had assessed a work's literary value on the basis of classical models, invoking what were considered timeless and immutable rhetorical prescriptions that conformed to courtly expectations. Wit and power of expression were of course crucial ingredients, but these qualities, too, had to match the fixed standards of cultivated learning. That way, a literary work exemplified its author's erudition and inventiveness; it also reflected these qualities back onto the author's patron. Readers, too, in appreciating a work appropriately, were giving public witness to their own refinement and good breeding.

Over the course of the eighteenth century, German critics gradually developed a new notion of criticism's purpose.[2] Many of the former desiderata remained, but they received a radically new basis: the authority of tradition was now replaced by an inductively defined efficacy. The new theories might still give traditional poetics the benefit of the doubt, but even established judgments ultimately had to withstand the scrutiny of reason. Another new consideration was the growing recognition that evaluative criteria once thought to be universal were in fact influenced by historical context: as readers' expectations changed over time, so did the notions of how to meet them. Enlightened critics, for all their differences, shared an assumption that the location of a work's value, the source of its legitimacy, had migrated from a set of supposedly timeless rules to the emotional effect that it exercised on contemporary recipients. With this shift came an increased emphasis on an individual reader's experience. When older critics speak of a work's "truth," they mean either its representation of external reality or its articulation of acknowledged verities — such as the unacceptability of suicide. For the younger critics, on the other hand, "truth" refers to individual readers' encounter with something in the text that seems to mirror a part of themselves (Flaschka 1987, 253–54).

This new emphasis on emotional reception still devoted primary attention to the author, who was seen as speaking from the heart, but the reader's role as an active recipient grew in importance. Critics increasingly stressed that the connection between novelist and reader was a private, individual, and necessarily sincere bond. Although reading aloud in groups was still common, eighteenth-century readers now tended to consume literary works in isolation, feeling as they did so that they were engaged in a privileged relationship with the author. And it was from this perspective that the earliest enthusiasts judged *Werther*.[3] An anonymous review in the *Neueste critische Nachrichten* (The Latest Critical Reports; May 20, 1775), for example, describes the novel as a product of Goethe's genius, "das ganz aus der Fülle eines warmen, gefühlvollen Herzens entsprungen sich wieder ans Herz drängt, allmälig eine jede Sehne erreicht, und zuletzt alles mit Jammer und Herzleid erfüllt" (P. Müller 1969, 162; which, springing forth from a warm heart full of feeling, in turn presses itself upon [another] heart, eventually reaching each of its fibers and finally filling everything with lament and heartache). Goethe, according to such critics, has fulfilled his part of the literary bargain; it is now up to his readers to open their hearts to his. As Johann Jakob Wilhelm Heinse writes in *Iris*, the women's literary quarterly that he and Johann Georg Jacobi published from 1774 to 1776, it is inappropriate to subject *Werther's* literary features to analysis, much less to suggest any deficiencies; it is not a novel, says Heinse, but rather a simple, natural expression of its hero's sufferings, originating from its author's innermost heart (Heinse 1774, 209). Readers who fail to appreciate this genuine emotion and instead get tangled up in tertiary questions of literary form or merit simply disqualify themselves as judges by revealing their own lack of heart. The book, he stresses, was not written for those young ladies who consider Werther's overflowing heart to be immature, or who join the philosophers in condemning his suicide. It is intended for nobler hearts, those who will savor the novel more than once. Heinse claims to speak for such readers when he extends heartfelt thanks to the genius that gave them this gift of Werther's sufferings (210).

As these reviews assume, the reading experience establishes an individual connection between author and reader; but there is a further effect that is produced among readers themselves, creating a group of kindred souls who partake of the general fervor for the work, its characters, and its author. Werther's and Lotte's shared enthusiasm for the poetry of Friedrich Gottlieb Klopstock (letter of July 16) is an obvious example, but the phenomenon extended beyond *Werther* and constituted a widespread and even self-conscious attempt to form a literary public. An enthusiasm for Goethe — or Rousseau or Klopstock or Shakespeare — brought together people of feeling who were eager to join hearts (see Lenz 1775, 673). In welcoming Goethe's sudden influence on the national literature,

Christian Heinrich Schmid describes him as eschewing theoretical issues and instead forging sympathetic bonds with Herder and others through a shared reverence for Shakespeare (1774, 61). This emotional affinity would then, such critics hoped, expand to embrace additional authors, a sense of nationhood, and ultimately bourgeois values in general. Jürgen Habermas tells how the "relations between author, work, and public changed. They became intimate mutual relationships between privatized individuals who were psychologically interested in what was 'human,' in self-knowledge, and in empathy" (1965, 50). Indeed, the whole literary enterprise justified itself in the end by its goal of educating, even creating, a republic of readers that would form the new public sphere.

Literature assumed this role not only because a true political forum for the rising middle class was lacking, but also because the later eighteenth century assumed that human worth in general, and morality in particular, lay in the emotions (Duncan 2003). The traditional dual purpose of literature, *prodesse et delectare*, now gained a new emphasis; a work's pleasure derived from the reader's empathetic response, but its utility stemmed from tying its reader emotionally to communal values. In this model, the arousal of fear and pity became a training session in moral sensibilities. Literature educated the heart and in doing so created a community of readers who were sensible — in both meanings of the term (see Schings 1980).

The enlightened critic's goals changed accordingly: now the point was to encourage works that would speak to readers through profound emotion, and conversely, to open up readers to such aesthetic experiences. The ultimate hope was to produce an enlightened literary public that would be ready to assume the role of advancing the human condition. These ambitions had a national component, as well, for reading German works both required and promoted a German sensibility. An explicit appeal to nationalism, so prominent in the critical response to Goethe's *Götz von Berlichingen* (1772), is largely missing from the published reviews of *Werther*, but the critics' personal correspondence shows that the novel, too, exerted a patriotic appeal (Flaschka 1987, 256).

Christian Friedrich Daniel Schubart was particularly devoted to encouraging such feelings. His journal, *Deutsche Chronik* (German Chronicle), begun in 1774, promoted Klopstock and the Sturm und Drang writers because he hoped that an emotional identification with these geniuses, as he saw them, would help to build a German national character (see Honolka 1985). Schubart's rhapsodic review of *Werther*, which addresses readers familiarly and employs colloquial elisions, is an especially clear appeal to a community of feeling — note that in his ecstasy, he does not forget to tell his audience where to buy the book:

> Da sitze ich mit zerfloßenem Herzen, mit klopfender Brust, und mit Augen aus welchen wollüstiger Schmerz tröpfelt, und sag dir, Leser, da

ich eben *die Leiden des jungen Werthers* von meinem lieben *Göthe* — gelesen? — Nein, verschlungen habe. Kritisieren soll ich? Könnt ichs, so hätt ich kein Herz. [. . .] Kauf's Buch, und lies selbst! Nimm aber dein Herz mit! — Wollte lieber ewig arm seyn, auf Stroh liegen, Wasser trinken, und Wurzeln essen, als einem solchen sentimentalischen Schriftsteller nicht nachempfinden können. Ist bey Stage zu haben. (Schubart 1774, 205–6)

[Here I sit with melted heart, with pounding chest, and with eyes from which tears of voluptuous pain fall, and tell you, Reader, that I have just read *The Sorrows of Young Werther* by my beloved Goethe — read? — no, devoured. I should write a critique? If I could, I'd have no heart. [. . .] Buy the book, and read it yourself! But take your heart along! — I'd rather be poor, lie on straw, drink water and eat roots than not be able to empathize with such a sentimental writer. Can be bought at Stage's.]

The anonymous reviewer in the *Frankfurter gelehrte Anzeigen* (Frankfurt Learned Reviews) on November 1, 1774, similarly congratulates those readers who can emotionally identify with Werther or Lotte: "Glücklicher Mann! der du mit Werther sympathisiren — fühlen kannst, [. . .] sey mir gegrüßet unter den wenigen Edeln! — Und du verehrungswürdige Schöne, die du mit Lotten den ganzen Werth unsers Werthers zu schätzen weist, [. . .] mögest du doch in den Armen deines Gatten, jetzt oder in Zukunft, alle die Seligkeiten einathmen, die Dein und mein unglücklicher Freund nur in der Ferne schimmern sah" (P. Müller 1969, 193–94; Happy man! you who can empathize — feel — with Werther, [. . .] I bid you welcome among those few noble souls! And you, admirable, beautiful woman, who shares with Lotte an appreciation of Werther's complete worth, [. . .] may you, in your husband's arms, now or in the future, breathe in all of those blessings that your and my unhappy friend only saw shimmering in the distance).

Enthusiasm for Werther was far from universal, however. Two weeks after the *Frankfurter gelehrte Anzeigen* printed its review, its publisher, J. K. Deinet, stepped in to announce that he had only now read the novel himself and was definitely *not* among the fortunate few who identified with its hero. Another presumed ally, Matthias Claudius, whose journal *Wandsbecker Bote* (Wandsbeck Messenger) was normally open to newer writings, was even more critical, skewering Werther's emotionality with sarcasm, mocking his style and labeling him weak (1774, 163–64).

These contemporary critics tend to divide along generational lines that also separate attitudes toward suicide. While younger enthusiasts revel in Werther's rich inner life and express understanding for the forces that led to his death, older defenders of the social order protest against the book's apparent justification, even encouragement, of suicide. These detractors managed to get it banned in Denmark and Leipzig — although not always effectively; Weygand's second edition of 1775 was featured at the Leipzig book fair that year (see Hertling 1963, 404). Students of Gotthold Ephraim Lessing will not be surprised to learn that the Hamburg pastor Johann Melchior Goeze led the way, excoriating not only the novel itself, but also those critics who gave it so much as faint praise. Even he, however, subscribes in his own way to the new critical assumptions. While convinced that any reasonable reader who is sufficiently girded with a knowledge of Scripture will find *Werther* at best ridiculous, he recognizes the power of its emotional appeal and fears the sympathy of inadequately equipped enthusiasts who, like Werther, feel warm blood in their young hearts (1775, 122).

Goeze's fellow cleric in Hamburg, Christian Ziegra, voices a similar complaint:

> Alles dieses wird mit einer, die Jugend hinreissende Sprache, ohne die geringste Warnung oder Misbilligung erzählt: vielmehr schimmert die Zufriedenheit und Achtung des Verfassers für seinen Helden allenthalben durch. Natürlich kann die Jugend keine andre als diese Lehren daraus ziehen: Folgt euren natürlichen Trieben. Verliebt euch, um das Leere eurer Seele auszufüllen. Gaukelt in der Welt herum; will man euch zu ordentlichen Berufsgeschäften führen, so denket an das Pferd, das sich unter den Sattel bequemte, und zu schanden geritten wurde. Will es zuletzt nicht mehr gehen, wohlan ein Schuß Pulver ist hinlänglich aller eurer Noth ein Ende zu machen. (1775, 128)
>
> [All this is told without the least warning or approbation in a language that overwhelms the young; indeed, the author's satisfaction with and admiration for his hero shine through everywhere. Young people can of course draw only one lesson from it: follow your natural drives. Fall in love to fill up the emptiness in your souls. Flit about the world; if someone tries to lead you to take up a proper career, just think about the horse that grew used to a saddle and was ridden to death. If things don't work out in the end, then a bit of gunpowder is all it will take to end your misery.]

When, from the perspective of 1970, Klaus Scherpe characterizes such criticisms as ignoring questions of the novel's literary value, he somewhat simplifies the case (1970, 16). Even Goeze's and Ziegra's attacks, however benighted they seem today, address central aesthetic issues of the time: the relationship between feeling and reason and the consequences of that relationship for the social order. The earliest critics' quarrel about *Werther,* as Hans-Jürgen Schings points out, was in important ways an extension of the ongoing struggle between "rationalists" and "enthusiasts" that had been fought on many fronts since the late seventeenth century (1977, 270–78). Even the moralists who took strong exception to Werther's suicide accepted certain nuances and did not necessarily object in principal to that act's portrayal in literature. Numerous plays, including Lessing's *Miss Sara Sampson* and Schiller's *Kabale und Liebe,* employed suicide without controversy as a convention to usher in the traditional conciliatory death scene (see Meyer-Kalkus 1977, 114–19). What disturbed these critics most was Goethe's effective depiction of suicide from within, a portrayal that could arouse similar feelings in his readers.

Friedrich Nicolai, normally a reliable supporter of new literature, shared Goeze's and Ziegra's concern and in 1775 published a short alternative version entitled *Die Freuden des jungen Werthers* (The Joys of Young Werther), together with a sequel, *Leiden und Freuden Werthers des Mannes* (The Sorrows and Joys of Werther, the Man). In Nicolai's version, Albert foils Werther's attempt to kill himself and then, moved by the depth of the young man's despair, steps aside to allow the two lovers to marry. This union almost founders on Werther's emotional instability, but Albert helps out again. All turns out well when Werther finally achieves maturity by accepting the boundaries of reason. Nicolai was appalled when a number of contemporaries, including Goethe himself, took this piece to be a malevolent parody. Indeed, their reaction, strengthened by Goethe's own later counter-parodies, has colored most literary historians' views of Nicolai, unfairly denigrating his important contributions to the development of eighteenth-century literary culture. Nicolai in fact intended no diminution of the novel's worth. He wrote *Die Freuden des jungen Werthers* not to discredit the entire original, but only to remind more fragile souls not to follow Werther's example (Nicolai 1775, 146). As Eckhardt Meyer-Krentler reminds us, Nicolai adds only an alternative ending; he does not change Werther's character, just the nature of his friendship with Albert (1982, 83–91). Furthermore, he brackets this version with what is meant to be a humorous dialogue that acknowledges the greatness of Goethe's achievement. Other evidence suggests that this admiration was genuine, tempered only by a perceived need for societal concerns: "Darf ich meine Meinung nicht über eine wichtige moralische Frage sagen? Oder ist das Wohl der Gesellschaft gar nichts werth?" (Nicolai 1775, 145; May I not give my opinion on an important question? Or is society's well-being of no worth?). In 1775, while announcing a French translation in the *Allgemeine deutsche Bibliothek* (Universal German Library), the literary review that he published from 1765 to 1806, Nicolai describes *Werther* as possibly the only true German novel (Hertling 1963, 411). His own copy of the book is annotated with spontaneous expressions of delight (Müller 1965, 296), and his private correspondence also stresses his enthusiasm for the spirit, fire, and truth of the novel's characters. It should be noted, however, that not all modern commentators would agree with this assessment of Nicolai. Matthias Luserke, for example, considers his protestations disingenuous and calls *Die Freuden des jungen Werthers* and *Leiden und Freuden Werthers des Mannes* nasty parodies that mark the critic's general turn toward a reactionary literary stance (1995, 277–94).

Wieland, not normally inclined to take Nicolai's side in literary matters, did so in this case, pointing out that *Die Freuden des jungen Werthers* satirized only a certain kind of reader, not Goethe's novel itself. Picking up on Schubart's assertion that he had "devoured" *Werther*, rather than read it, Wieland writes, "Hr. Nicolai hat (. . .) dem Publikum bloß ein kleines Digestivpülverchen eingeben wollen, um den Folgen der Unverdaulichkeit zuvorzukommen, welche sich manche junge *Hansen* und *Hänsinnen* durch allzugieriges Verschlingen der Werke des Hrn. Goethe zugezogen haben möchten" (1775, 167; Mr. Nicolai [. . .] merely wanted to administer a little digestive powder to the public to combat the possible effects of indigestion that some Johnnies and Janies might suffer after all-too greedily devouring Mr. Goethe's works). The anonymous reviewer in the *Neueste Critische Nachrichten* also, after praising *Werther*, suggests that Nicolai's version has its virtues and calls upon those discussing the issue to use a more measured tone (Anonymous 1775, 162–63).

Despite such support, Nicolai was stung by the attacks mounted by *Werther's* more enthusiastic admirers. Most such assaults were in unpublished form, but Schubart, never one to shy away from controversy in his *Deutsche Chronik,* accused him in print of wanting to turn Werther into a bloodless fop and Goethe's genius into cold reason. Consistent with his own project of promoting a German sensibility, he describes Nicolai as lopping off Werther's head to set "ein französisches Milchgesichtlein" (a little French milksop) in its place (1775, 206).

Such rebukes led Nicolai to prevail on his friend Johann Heinrich Merck to defend him in the *Allgemeine deutsche Bibliothek*. Also a friend of Goethe, Merck found himself in a difficult position, and it took some prompting to get him to finish his essay. Hartmut Schmidt describes this undertaking as finding the lowest common denominator between the two quarreling parties (1988, 100). Merck prefaces his defense of Nicolai with a paean to Goethe's genius, which has not only imbued Werther's character with profound feeling, but has also given the work poetic shape. Only gossips and others of ill will, he says, will care whether or not the story is based on true events; of sole importance is the poetic truth that comes from within the author. At this point, however, Merck seems to become caught in a contradiction. On the one hand, he urges up-and-coming authors to take an example from Goethe's "unnachahmlich" (inimitable) art — advice that is itself an incongruity. On the other, they should find in it a warning not to write about even the most insignificant subject without having first viewed "a fixed point" [*einen festen Punct*] of its true existence in nature, whether in the outside world or within oneself (1775, 198). Does Goethe have such a point? Merck does not give a clear answer. He tells us that any writer incapable of recognizing "den Epischen und Dramatischen Geist" (198: the epic and dramatic spirit) in the most common scenes of domestic life and of capturing this spirit on paper has no business venturing out into idealized worlds of fantasy. "Ist er ein Mann, und hat sich seine eigene Denkart gebildet, so mag er uns die bey gewissen Gelegenheiten in seiner

Seele angefachte Funken von Gefühl und Urtheilskraft [. . .] wie helle Inschrift vorleuchten lassen" (199; If he is a man, and has developed his own way of thinking, then he may allow the feeling and power of judgment that have on certain occasions ignited in his soul [. . .] to shine forth to us like a bright script).[4]

Again Merck seems to be inviting us to ask: Is Goethe such a man? And again he remains ambiguous: "Der V. hat seinen Helden wahrscheinlicherweise zum Theil mit seinen eigenen Geistesgaben dotirt. Aus der Fülle des Gefühls, vereinbart mit dem natürlichen Trübsinn der Werthern von Jugend auf bezeichnete, entsteht das interessanteste Geschöpf, dessen Fall alle Herzen zerreißt." (199; The author has apparently invested his hero in part with his own gifts of spirit. From this fullness of feeling, combined with the natural melancholy that distinguished Werther from his early youth, emerges the most interesting creation, whose case tears apart all hearts.) But Merck's next sentence suddenly shifts the responsibility over to the reader: "Die Jugend gefällt sich in diesem Sympathetischen Schmerz, vergißt über dem Leben der Fiktion, daß es nur eine *Poetische Wahrheit* ist, und verschlingt alles im *Gefühl* ausgestoßene Säze als *Dogma*" (199; Youth takes pleasure in this sympathetic pain, and in the liveliness of this fiction forgets that it is merely a *poetic truth*, and devours as *dogma* all the sentences that are ejaculations of *feeling*). When such a text treats suicide positively, he goes on to say, reading it can become problematic for those hearts that already bear within themselves an inclination toward such an act. At this point, Merck begins his defense of Nicolai, suggesting that his *Freuden des jungen Werthers* was intended to give these immature readers of Goethe's novel aesthetic distance by reminding them that Werther was a fictional construct, not a real figure with which to identify uncritically. Nicolai himself, Merck assures us, was as sensitive as anyone else to Werther's emotional appeal. Any satirical impulses in his text are directed not toward the novel itself, but toward those readers and critics who are unable to distinguish between primitive self-identification and aesthetic experience.

Merck, in other words, in trying to defend both Goethe and Nicolai simultaneously, does not differentiate so much between their texts themselves as between the two types of people who will read them. To those readers who possess the necessary autonomy, Goethe's *Werther* offers a profound and uplifting emotional experience; to immature readers, however, Nicolai's *Werther* provides a corrective that militates against the deleterious effects of overenthusiasm.

The rest of Merck's review (200–201) defends *Werther* against those who call the book immoral. They have, he points out, at best confused a sympathetic portrayal of suicidal impulse with an apology for suicide. At worst — and here he reserves special venom for Goeze — they have engaged in self-righteous stupidity.

As one would expect, Jakob Michael Reinhold Lenz had no such interest in finding a middle ground when he composed his *Briefe über die Moralität der Leiden des jungen Werthers* (Letters on the Morality of The Sorrows of Young Werther) in 1775. Seeking to have the essay published, he sent it to Goethe, who passed it on to his friend the philosopher and critic Friedrich Heinrich Jacobi. Jacobi decided that the essay's eccentricities would appeal only to those who already agreed with it; otherwise, it would just stir up trouble. Goethe seems to have acquiesced in that view, and the tract remained unprinted for 150 years (see Damm's notes to Lenz 1775, 915). Nevertheless, we can assume that, as was quite usual with unpublished works of the time, a number of contemporaries were aware of the essay's contents. We know at least that he read it aloud to the literary society in Strasbourg in March of 1776 (Flaschka 1987, 261). Lenz's "Letters" are addressed to a fictional friend who has expressed concern over *Werther's* capacity to harm the moral order by stirring up strong emotions. Skewering Nicolai along the way, Lenz maintains that this arousal is in fact the real source of *Werther's* ethical value: "Laßt uns also einmal die Moralität dieses Romans untersuchen, nicht den moralischen Endzweck den sich der Dichter vorgesetzt (denn da hört er auf Dichter zu sein) sondern die moralische Wirkung die das Lesen dieses Romans auf die Herzen des Publikums haben könne und haben müsse." (1775, 676–77; Let us then examine the morality of this novel, not the moral goal that the author has set for himself [for there he stops being an artist], but rather the moral effect that reading this novel can and must have on the hearts of the public.) Literary works, he says, are not the place to look for philosophical or sociological truths. Instead, it is through the emotional perception of Beauty that we experience the Good quintessentially (674). Lenz modestly adds that the fact that his own works engendered so much discussion about issues of private education and religious reform is "ein trauriger Beweis" (sad proof) that he failed as an artist to engage his readers' hearts and imaginations sufficiently (675).

Lenz also explicitly rejects Nicolai's and Merck's argument that *Werther* might be suitable for discerning readers, but not for labile ones. In fact, he claims, the young and inexperienced person stands to benefit most from having such emotions transmitted by literature: *Werther's* merit — indeed, the merit of every literary work — derives from its making readers aware of sensations and passions that they otherwise feel only darkly and cannot name (682). On the one hand, Lenz is here advancing a conventional argument of the Enlightenment: practicing emotions in itself makes us more fully human (see Schings 1980). On the other, he is, like Merck, appealing to a notion of aesthetic distance in the context of a reader-response theory. *Werther* may articulate feelings to the reader, but this should not be reduced to the concept of rendering dark (or obscure) representations clear, as the conventional terminology of the day would describe it.[5] In fact, Lenz dismisses the notion that literature achieves anything through conscious appeals. Rather, it is the structure of the aesthetic experience itself that leads to reflection: the figure of Werther is a literary construct and as such cannot exist in real time. To enable us to enter Werther's being wholly, to take on his identity completely as our own, Goethe would have had to write an impossibly large novel, one that would take as long to read as Werther spent living and suffering — that is, the narrated time and the time of narration would have to be equal. In reality, however, a novel's scope is limited, so that the author can portray only those portions of a character's inner being that suit his purpose. The rest must be left to the reader's own mental faculties, which necessarily become engaged even as the reader identifies with the character (685). Lenz's defense of *Werther* thus anticipates modern reader-response theory in interesting ways.

In 1774, before having seen *Werther,* Christian Friedrich von Blankenburg published his *Versuch über den Roman* (Essay on the Novel), which describes the novel in general as a fresh and potentially valuable genre that up until that point had largely been expropriated by unworthy hacks (Wölfel 1968, 34–35). Blankenburg's study attempts to guide aspiring young novelists to a higher level, using Wieland's *Agathon* as its primary positive example. Blankenburg is much less enthusiastic about the epistolary novel, however, considering it a particularly unpromising form. But that was before he had read *Werther.* After that experience, in 1775, he corrected his earlier opinion while reviewing Goethe's work in the *Neue Bibliothek der schönen Wissenschaften und der freyen Künste* (New Library of Belles Lettres and the Liberal Arts). Eberhard Lämmert rightly calls this discussion the theoretically most assured treatment of *Werther* in the eighteenth century (1965, 545). Other than the change inspired by Goethe's novel, Blankenburg's second essay continues the ideas of the first. Both works commend the novel to young writers as a particularly flexible literary medium: not only can it impart information on any kind of subject and describe any kind of world — including the quotidian — but it can also include other literary genres, such as poetry (compare Herder 1796, 109–10). And while drama, for example, is limited to revealing character intensively in relatively discrete moments in time, the novel can do so extensively, showing transformations in depth and breadth (Blankenburg 1774, 391–92). Wieland, by the way, makes a similar point in describing our perception of Werther's suicide: in drama, a suicide always strikes us as a sudden act. But in the long succession of Werther's letters, we can follow the cumulative effect of a great number of small determinants upon his character and hence accompany him to the edge of the abyss (Wieland 1774, 166).

As a genre, says Blankenburg in both of his essays, the novel is particularly well suited to portraying character development because it can present both inner feeling and external circumstances. The skilled novelist creates a structure in which these two perspectives augment each other, providing the reader with a profounder experience and understanding of the world than would be available to reason alone (see Wölfel 1968, 56). This reciprocal process gains part of its power through the reader's active participation, for we are continually invited to discover and affirm the correspondences between the two realms and to take pleasure in the organic wholeness of the literary work. Readers experience Werther's development not just through his self-descriptions, but also through his changing responses to the seasons, the poetry of Homer, and so on. Blankenburg's review mirrors this process. Although he assumes that his audience has already read "diesen ausserordenlich rührenden *Roman*" (this extraordinarily moving novel; Blankenburg 1775, 168), he decides to walk us through it, calling attention to how the interactions between the novel's inner and outer worlds change, what kind of a through-composition the author has constructed, and why the reader eventually becomes Werther in order to understand him (176).

Because it primarily addresses would-be novelists, Blankenburg's review continually stresses Goethe's mastery in balancing *Werther's* elements. The novel is successful because nothing in it strikes us as gratuitous, nor do any of its elements seem to have been imported from outside the story to influence its development. From the very first scene until the end, every constituent part is simultaneously a cause and an effect of the narrative (180). The seasons of the year, to take just the most obvious example, both reflect and influence the developments in Werther's character. This novel, Blankenburg says, is so exquisitely constructed that each of its threads necessarily leads to the knot at the end, and this knot could have been created from these threads only (178). Or, using another image of organic wholeness, he says that the author has allowed a variety of characteristics and propensities to shoot forth from the roots and trunk of Werther's character according to their nature, so that in the end we have before us a complete growth with its branches spread, full and round from every perspective (170).

Before he had read *Werther*, Blankenburg had maintained in his *Versuch über den Roman* that the epistolary novel was particularly unlikely to produce this kind of organic wholeness, since any first-person narration restricts the author in essential ways (1774, 285–86, 520–25). When the narrator is also a character, and not identical with the author, the discrepancy compromises the illusion; readers cannot help but notice the novelist peeking through. Somewhat less significantly, conventions of modesty constrain the correspondent: the depiction of one's own positive traits strikes the reader as boastful. A letter format exacerbates this situation, since the purported writer is limited to reporting events in retrospect. And, Blankenburg adds, the mere act of composition is antithetical to the convincing portrayal of strong feeling. Setting out pen, ink, and paper and then deliberately composing one's thoughts militate against outpourings of emotion. He notes the tendency of epistolary novelists to begin their letters calmly and then unconvincingly turn passionate. This contrast between form and content, says Blankenburg, is fatal to the reader's necessary suspension of disbelief.

At the same time, he repeats that his study's purpose is to offer practical pointers to the budding novelist, not to issue immutable proscriptions: "Es sey ferne von mir, dem Genie Gränzen vorzeichnen zu wollen!" (1774, 525; Far be it from me to set constraints on genius!). Perhaps, he grants, there is a novelist out there who is capable of overcoming the limitations inherent in the epistolary form. And indeed, a year later, when reading *Werther,* he concludes that Goethe is just such a writer. This change of heart not only testifies to Blankenburg's flexibility; it also underscores the extent to which his critical approach centers on the reader. While his theory of the novel describes the novelist's creative process, as well as the characteristics of the ideal novel, its proof is in the reading. Blankenburg applauds both Goethe and *Werther* not because author and work conform to accepted prescriptions, but because they affect the recipient. Goethe's decision to reveal Werther's inner development in letters was right because it works: readers are drawn in by the convincing interplay of Werther's descriptions of his feelings and of the outer forces that affect him.

But Blankenburg does not assign readers a passive role. Like Schubart, he requires the reader to possess a heart that *Werther* can address. But he defines this potential less dramatically, as an active readiness to identify with the hero emotionally. The critics who maintain that Werther should have renounced Lotte at the time of Albert's return are readers "die hier von Lotten nur *erzehlen* hören, und wenn sie *Werthers* Leiden lesen und beurtheilen, immer *sie selbst* bleiben, und nicht einen Augenblick *Werther* werden wollen, — vermuthlich, weil sie es nicht können" (1775, 176; who at this point only hear Lotte's being *told* about, and, when they read and judge Werther's *sufferings,* remain only *themselves,* and never for a moment want to become *Werther* — presumably because they are incapable of it). In other words, readers are expected to be more than just kindred spirits; they are to be open to another being's inner world and willing to take it on as their own, at least temporarily.

Contrary to what Goeze might think, this expectation does not lead to an approval of Werther's suicide. Blankenburg agrees with the guardians of virtue that the act is reprehensible, but their condemnation of the novel misses the point of aesthetic experience. It is not the author's task to communicate moral positions nor any other kind of abstraction, because readers who accompany Werther's inner development are not doomed to imitate him. Rather, in empathetically experiencing an aesthetic totality, they enrich their souls in ways wholly unavailable to moralizing philosophy. Thus strengthened, they are later on far better prepared to deal with their own suicidal urges — although, Blankenburg stresses, that result is wholly tangential to the novelist's primary goal of engaging the reader.

Christian Garve, a professor of philosophy and mathematics in Breslau, may well embody Blankenburg's ideal reader. Reviewing *Werther* in Johann Jakob Engel's journal, *Der Philosoph für die Welt* (Philosopher for the World, 1775, 149–53), he praises Goethe's artistic achievement and sympathizes with Werther's perceptions of both the light and the dark sides of nature and human fate. But he also draws back from the totalism of Werther's feeling. He recognizes and even empathizes with the inevitability of Werther's suicide, but he views the progression toward it as specific to the hero's individual character. Garve himself sees no likelihood that other readers, no matter how empathetic, will be moved to follow Werther's example. He does add a somewhat anomalous ending to his review, however, suddenly taking Goethe to task for failing to show explicitly that Werther's actions are wrong. These last sentences are so inconsistent with the essay's former points and so weakened by adverbial modifiers and the subjunctive voice, that we suspect that he was throwing out a sop to the more militant defenders of moral virtue: "Aber nie muß er dabey den anderen Gesichtspunkt vergessen: das heißt, er muß mir die Fehlschlüsse als Fehlschlüsse, die irrigen Begriffe als irrig, die falschen Gründe als falsch, und die daher entspringenden verwerflichen Handlungen als wirklich verwerflich zeigen. Dieses nicht gethan oder nicht genug gethan zu haben, ist wohl der größte Vorwurf, den man dem Verfasser der Leiden Werthers machen kann, und gegen den er sich vielleicht am wenigsten rechtfertigen ließe" (153; But in all this he must never forget the other aspect: that is, he needs to show me the fallacies as fallacies, the erroneous concepts als erroneous, and the reprehensible actions that arise from them as truly reprehensible. Not to have done this, or not to have done it sufficiently, is surely the greatest reproach that one could make against the author of Werther's Sufferings, and against which he could perhaps least be defended).[6]

In a modern survey of *Werther's* earliest critics, Robert Ellis Dye reports that the "contemporary writers on *Werther* anticipated much of what is significant in later and more considered readings of the book" (1975, 314). One such topic that has endured is the novel's subversive effect (see chapter 4). Writing in 1979, Stefan Blessin interprets *Werther* as revolutionary — ultimately in a political sense — because it allows readers the freedom to come to terms autonomously with its problematic stance. "Im Widerstreit der Gefühle (. . .) emanzipiert sich die Sinnlichkeit" (1979, 271: In the conflict of emotions [. . .] the [reader's] sensuality is emancipated) in the dialogue between two affective urges: on the one hand to identify with Werther, on the other to renounce his suicide. In thus encouraging the reader's self-awareness without the guidance of didactic promptings, the novel, according to Blessin, represents a sharp break with the repressive Enlightenment tradition. Pastor Goeze would certainly agree with this assessment — even if he would deplore what it describes. Most of his contemporaries, however, would maintain that promoting such autonomy in fact falls squarely within the Enlightenment's compass.

The twentieth-century critic Hans Robert Jauss approaches the experience of *Werther's* eighteenth-century readers from another direction, defining the horizon of expectations (*Erwartungshorizont*) that the novel assumed in its audience. While critics have always been aware that *Werther* took much of its inspiration from Rousseau's *Nouvelle Héloïse*, Jauss shows how "Goethe followed his predecessor's basic model step by step and, in his response to Rousseau, took advantage of the expectations thus evoked in order to point the German reader of 1774 toward a new sort of experience — the tragic experience of an autonomous sense of self" (Jauss 1982, 178). To the extent to which Goethe challenged these expectations, he got ahead of much of his audience: "It was in *Werther* that the reversal of the traditional relationship between fiction and reality announced by Rousseau actually took place. The enhanced immediacy of 'writing to the moment,' the epistolary form that had reverted to monologue, the rejection of any moral commentary, and the generally subliminal social criticism required a reader who is already mature, one who is able to involve himself in an empathetic reading and nevertheless form his own aesthetic and moral judgments" (180). Such readers, as we have seen, were not always available. By dispensing with, or at least altering, the conventions of fictionality, Goethe "unintentionally led the imagination to an idealization of Werther's sorrows" (182). The enthusiastic readers who confused the imaginary with the real and naively identified themselves with Werther caused Goethe even more distress than did the moral watchdogs who attacked the book. "Along with the discrepancy between intention and effect there emerged a gap between the author and his public, one that Goethe noticed and lamented in his later comments about *Werther*" (182).

In examining German readers' horizon of expectations in 1774, Jauss thus comes to a surprising conclusion. He would agree with Blessin that *Werther's* effect was revolutionary, but he would not attach quite so much approval to that assessment. While he joins modern readers in finding the moralistic commentary in *La nouvelle Héloïse* tiresome, his awareness of the historical context leads him to judge the absence of such elucidation in *Werther* somewhat differently, "since such commentary was in no way reactionary in the eighteenth century" (181). By forgoing it, says Jauss, Goethe made demands on his contemporaries that could be "met only by a small group of readers of which Merck, Blankenburg and Lenz are representative. The wide majority of readers, who took up the book with edification in mind and who read it intensively, were misled into identifying literature and life" (181).

The early critical responses to *Werther* (often written *Werter*) in England and the United States echo the German concerns. The *Critical Review* saw Goethe as the "apologist of suicide," and others pointed out that when a certain Miss Glover died by her own hand, a copy of *Werther* was found under her pillow. In 1790, Charles Moore's *Full Inquiry into the Subject of Suicide* "gravely cited the evil tendency of *The Sorrows of Werter* and presented an unfavorable analysis of *Werter's* character" (Haney 1902, 145, 150–51). Nor was the book's threat to youth confined to actual suicide. As a writer for *The Analytical Review* complained in 1788, "I am sorry to see a taste prevail for novels which exhibit unnatural pictures of misery, and diffuse a kind of taste for the woeful. The novel entitled *Werther* is of a bad tendency, and cannot have failed to have given the falsely delicate, the over-refined, and the idolizers of themselves, additional encouragement in the affectation of misery" (151; for a review of English women writers' responses to *Werther*, see Conger 1986).

Other critics' assessments are more in line with the general public's enthusiastic reception, however. *The London Magazine* reports that "foreign criticks" accuse Goethe of being "an apologist for that cowardly crime. Setting aside this objection, his little work may be read with great pleasure, for he is a delicate painter not only of human nature, but of all the social joys of life, his descriptions of rural scenes are likewise animated, and his story is told in simple, unaffected and pathetick language" (Haney, 145). As in Germany, the onus resides with the reader to respond appropriately. As *The Monthly Review* says, "In this little work is drawn, by a masterly hand, a lively picture of the horrors of a mind disordered by the phrensy of a disappointed passion, and at length abandoning itself to despair, and seeking refuge from its sorrows in a voluntary death. An excellent moral may be deduced from it — if the reader pleases" (145–46).

The American vogue for *Werther* was especially strong between 1784 and 1809, despite the unavailability of anything but terrible translations. These early texts generally carried an added condemnation of Werther's character, and the very first American edition, published in Philadelphia in 1784, says that the novel reveals a "state of mind frequently to be seen in most countries 'where civilization and extravagant refinement of manners have attempted to abrogate the attachments of simple Nature'" (quoted by Long 1941, 88–89). The critics of this period were mostly negative, although *Massachusetts Magazine* did reprint an English review that admired "the fiery spirit of enthusiasm and overflowing sensibility which pervades the Sorrows of Werter" (Long, 108). More typical was the anonymous critic in Philadelphia, writing in *The Literary Magazine, and American Register for 1806*, who urged readers not to damn all novels only because of *Werther*, "which no parent should suffer to enter the hands of her child; which no bookseller should sell." It is "a book more read than any of its kind by the young, and which has proved the bane of more than one family." The critic hastens to assure us that "There are, however, numerous novels which tend rather to enlarge the heart and to produce only the most generous emotions" (1806, 451).

Later New England scholars were of course much more positive, especially those who had made the journey to Weimar while studying in Göttingen. Edward Everett and George Bancroft each praised the novel enthusiastically in the *North American Review* in 1817 and 1824 (Long 1941, 111), and, probably shortly before that time, George Ticknor completed a translation not published until the middle of the next century (see Ryder 1952). As a professor at Harvard, Henry Wadsworth Longfellow praised the original German in a lecture given in 1838 — "Above all the work should not be read in a translation" — and echoed some of the same judgments that we have seen so often: "Looked at as a work of art merely, the book deserves high praise. . . . As to the moral effect of the book, I cannot think it is bad, unless upon minds weak and willing to err" (Long 1941, 113). Finally, Margaret Fuller, writing in *The Dial* in 1841, applauded the novel's "fervid eloquence of Italian glow" but objected to Werther's response to the world's constraints: "The best or worst occasion in man's life is precisely that misused in Werther, when he longs for more love, more freedom, and a larger development of genius than the limitations of this terrene sphere permit. Sad is it indeed if, persisting to grasp too much at once, he lose all as Werther did" (Long 1941, 115).

By the middle of the nineteenth century, however, *Werther* had largely faded from view. An anonymous review in *Littell's Living Age* could treat it as a "Forgotten Novel" (1862) in America, where, until the twentieth century, only a few critics like Bayard Taylor continued to commend it to readers (1879, 310–15). In 1856, George Henry Lewes could also complain that "*Werther* is not much read now-a-days, especially in England, where it labors under the double disadvantage of a bad name and an execrable translation" (225–26). But even where translations were not an issue *Werther* suffered a popular decline: by 1845, according to Konrad Schwenck, *Werther* had ceased to be daily fare for readers in Germany as well (quoted by Bickelmann 1937, 30).

This survey of the early responses to *Werther* has confined itself to literary critics. There were also countless imitations, sequels, and parodies in every literary genre, including opera, and this production continues to the present day: the lists compiled by Stuart Atkins (1949; 1979) and Ingrid Engel (1986), are necessarily only partial. Ulrich Plenzdorf's *Die neuen Leiden des jungen W.* (The New Sufferings of Young W., 1973) is not even the most recent play to build on *Werther* (see Peter Parnell's *The Sorrows of Stephen*, 1980). In the visual arts, too, *Werther* gave rise to an extensive iconography (see Assel 1984). Other works in the history of literature have of course inspired successors, but the depth and intensity of *Werther's* immediate reception was perhaps unique (see Mandelkow 1980, 35). Also unique, or at least unusual, is the extent to which later critics consider this reception crucial to the novel's understanding. Stefan Blessin evokes no controversy when he claims that *Werther* not only *has* a reception history; "er selbst *ist* die Diskussion, die Anteilnahme und die Antipathie, die er entfacht" (1979, 269: it itself *is* the discussion, the sympathy and antipathy, that it arouses). As the following chapters show, interpreters of *Werther* typically rely not only on Goethe's text, but also on the contemporary reactions to it when they go about their work. Indeed, even the text that we now generally use is itself a product of this early reception: for the second printing in 1775, Goethe added verse mottoes before each of the novel's two parts, warning readers not to follow the hero's example, and the 1787 edition, now the standard one, contains even more substantial changes that, responding to earlier readers' reactions, seek to reshape the novel's effect. Goethe's 1796 prequel to *Werther,* the "Briefe aus der Schweiz" (Letters from Switzerland), were also, according to Hans Vaget, intended to be such a corrective (2004, 23–29).

Deirdre Vincent's recent study of the 1787 version reads it in a way that recalls some of the eighteenth-century controversies. She accuses other modern critics of allowing their own attitudes about suicide to skew their interpretations of Goethe's revisions. An unbiased reader or, as she argues, one sensitive to the state of mind in which Goethe composed the new version, would challenge the standard assumption that the changes he made were intended to distance his readers further from an emotional identification with Werther (1992, 243–58). She is of course not agreeing with Goeze that *Werther* frivolously endorses suicide, but instead arguing that each of the novel's versions reflects the author's inner turmoil at the time of composition.

Notes

[1] The abbreviation *HA* refers to the Hamburg edition (1961–64) of Goethe's *Werke,* edited by Erich Trunz.

[2] Countless studies trace the course of this complex process, which was international in scope but also, in several of its manifestations, peculiar to Germany. See, among many others, Berghahn 1985.

[3] Reprints of early responses to Werther are available in, among other publications: Appell 1896; Blumenthal 1935; Braun 1883; Gräf 1901; Jäger 1984; Mandelkow 1975; Scherpe 1974; P. Müller 1969; Scherpe 1970.

[4] Merck develops the idea further in his essay of 1778, "Ueber den Mangel des epischen Geistes in unserm lieben Vaterlande" (On the Lack of the Epic Spirit in Our Dear Fatherland), which holds up Shakespeare as an example of an author who wrote from genuine experience, not literary tradition (177).

⁵ For a summary of the terminology, see Barnouw 1995, 29–33.

⁶ For a modern theoretical description of the duality of the reader's response to *Werther*, see Haverkamp 1982, especially 245–47.

Works Cited

Anonymous. 1774. Review of *Werther: Frankfurter gelehrte Anzeigen* (November 1, 1774). In P. Müller, 1969a, 192–94.

———. 1775. "Die Leiden des jungen Werthers — Freuden des jungen Werthers. Leiden und Freuden Werthers des Mannes." In P. Müller, 162–63. Originally published in *Neueste Critische Nachrichten* (May 20, 1775).

———. 1806. "The Sorrows of Werter." *The Literary Magazine, and American Register* [Philadelphia] 6 (1806): 451.

———. 1862. "Forgotten Novels (Goethe, 'Werther')." *Littell's Living Age* 73 (1862): 237.

Appell, Johann Wilhelm. 1896. *Werther und seine Zeit: Zur Goethe-Litteratur.* Oldenburg: Schulze.

Assel, Jutta. 1984. "'Werther'-Illustrationen: Bilddokumente als Rezeptionsgeschichte." In Jäger, 1984, 57–105, 190–208.

Atkins, Stuart. 1949. *The Testament of Werther in Poetry and Drama.* Cambridge: Harvard UP.

Barnouw, Jeffrey. 1995. "The Cognitive Value of Confusion and Obscurity in the German Enlightenment: Leibniz, Baumgarten, and Herder." *Studies in Eighteenth-Century Culture* 24 (1995): 29–50.

Berghahn, Klaus L. 1985. "From Classicist to Classical Literary Criticism, 1730–1806." In *Geschichte der deutschen Literaturkritik (1730–1980)*, ed. Peter Uwe Hohendahl 1985a, 13–98. Stuttgart: Metzler.

Bickelmann, Ingeborg. 1937. *Goethes "Werther" im Urteil des 19. Jahrhunderts. (Romantik bis Naturalismus 1830–1880)*. Diss., Frankfurt am Main.

Blankenburg, Christian Friedrich von. 1774. *Versuch über den Roman.* Leipzig and Liegnitz: David Siegers Wittwe. Facsimile of the 1st edition, ed. Eberhard Lämmert. Stuttgart: Metzler, 1965.

———. 1775. Review of *Werther.* In P. Müller, 1969a, 168–92. Originally published in *Neue Bibliothek der schönen Wissenschaften und der freyen Künste*, 18 (1775): 46–95.

Blessin, Stefan. 1979. *Die Romane Goethes.* Königstein/Ts.: Athenäum.

Blumenthal, Hermann. 1935. *Zeitgenössische Rezensionen und Urteile über Goethes "Götz" und "Werther."* Berlin: Junker und Dünnhaupt.

Braun, Julius W. 1883. *Goethe im Urtheile seiner Zeitgenossen: Zeitungskritiken, Berichte, Notizen, Goethe und seine Werke betreffend, aus den Jahren 1773–1812.* Berlin: Luckhardt, 1883–1885.

Breidenbach zu Breidenstein, Karl Wilhelm, Freiherr von. 1775. *Berichtigung der Geschichte des jungen Werthers.* Freystadt, 1775; 2nd ed. Frankfurt and Leipzig.

Claudius, Matthias. 1774. "'Die Leiden des jungen Werthers.'" In P. Müller, 1969a, 163–64. Originally published in the *Wandsbecker Bote* 169 (October 22, 1774).

———. 1775. "Freuden des jungen Werthers: Leiden und Freuden Werthers des Mannes." In P. Müller, 1969a, 164–65. Originally published in the *Wandsbecker Bote* 15 (1775).

Conger, Syndy McMillen. 1986. "The Sorrows of Young Charlotte: Werther's English Sisters 1785–1805." *Goethe Yearbook* 3 (1986): 21–56.

Deinet, J. K. (1774). Review of *Werther.* In P. Müller, 1969a, 194. Originally published in the *Frankfurter gelehrte Anzeigen* (November 15, 1774).

Duncan, Bruce. 2003. "Sturm und Drang Passions and Eighteenth-Century Psychology." In *Literature of the Sturm und Drang,* ed. David Hill, 46–68. Rochester, NY: Camden House.

Dye, Robert Ellis. 1975. "Man and God in Goethe's 'Werther.'" *Symposium* 29 (1975): 314–29.

Engel, Ingrid. 1986. *"Werther" und die Wertheriaden: Ein Beitrag zur Wirkungsgeschichte.* St. Ingbert: Röhrig.

Flaschka, Horst. 1987. *Goethes "Werther": Werkkontextuelle Deskription und Analyse.* Munich: Fink.

Garve, Christian. 1775. "Aus einem Briefe." In P. Müller, 1969a, 149–53. Originally published in *Der Philosoph für die Welt,* ed. J. J. Engel, 1. Teil, 2. Stück (1775), 21–33.

Goethe, Johann Wolfgang von. 1772. "Gedichte von einem polnischen Juden." In *Frankfurter gelehrte Anzeigen vom Jahr 1772,* 461–64. Heilbronn: Henninger, 1882–1883.

———. 1813. *Dichtung und Wahrheit.* Ed. Erich Trunz. Vol. 9 of *Werke.* Hamburg: Wegner, 1961–64. (This Hamburg edition of Goethe's works is cited in the text as *HA*).

Goeze, Johann Melchior. 1775. Review of *Werther.* In P. Müller, 1969a, 119–26. Originally published in the *Freywillige Beyträge zu den Hamburgischen Nachrichten aus dem Reiche der Gelehrsamkeit* (April 7, 1775).

Gräf, Hans Gerhard. 1901. *Goethe über seine Dichtungen: Versuch einer Sammlung aller Äußerungen des Dichters über seine poetischen Werke.* Vol. 1. Frankfurt am Main: Literarische Anstalt.

Habermas, Jürgen. 1965. *The Structural Transformation of the Public Sphere: An Inquiry into a Category of Bourgeois Society.* Trans. Thomas Burger. Cambridge, MA.: MIT UP, 1989.

Haney, John Louis. 1902. "German Literature in England before 1790." *Americana Germanica* 4 (1902): 144–54.

Haverkamp, Anselm. 1982. "Illusion und Empathie: Die Struktur der 'teilnehmenden Lektüre' in den 'Leiden des jungen Werthers.'" In *Erzählforschung: Ein Symposium*, ed. Eberhard Lämmert, 243–68. Stuttgart: Metzler.

Heinse, Johann Jakob Wilhelm. 1774. Review of *Werther*. In P. Müller, 1969a, 208–10. Originally published in *Iris* (December, 1774): 78–81.

Herder, Johann Gottfried. 1774. *Übers Erkennen und Empfinden in der menschlichen Seele*. In *Sämmtliche Werke*, ed. Bernhard Suphan, 8:236–62. Berlin: Weidmann, 1902.

———. 1796. *Briefe zur Beförderung der Humanität, achte Sammlung*. Vol. 18.

Hertling, Gunter. 1963. "Die 'Werther'-Kritik im Meinungsstreit der Spätaufklärer." *German Quarterly* 36 (1963): 403–13.

Hohendahl, Peter Uwe. 1977. *Der europäische Roman der Empfindsamkeit*. Wiesbaden: Athenaion.

Honolka, Kurt. 1985. *Schubart: Dichter und Musiker, Journalist und Rebell; Sein Leben, sein Werk*. Stuttgart: Deutsche Verlags-Anstalt.

Jäger, Georg, ed. 1984. *Leiden des alten und neuen Werther: Kommentare, Abbildungen, Materialien zu Goethes "Leiden des jungen Werther" und Plenzdorfs "Neuen Leiden des jungen W."* Munich: Hanser.

Jauss, Hans Robert. 1982. *Question and Answer: Forms of Dialogic Understanding*. Trans Michael Hays. Minneapolis: U of Minnesota P, 1989.

Lämmert, Eberhard. 1965. "Nachwort." In *Friedrich von Blanckenburgs Versuch über den Roman*, ed. Eberhard Lämmert. Stuttgart: Metzler.

Lenz, Jakob Michael Reinhold. 1775. "Briefe über die Moralität der 'Leiden des jungen Werthers.'" In *Werke und Briefe*, ed. Sigrid Damm, 2:673–90. Leipzig: Insel, 1987.

Lewes, George Henry. 1856. *The Life and Works of Goethe: With Sketches of His Age and Contemporaries, from Published and Unpublished Sources*. Boston: Ticknor and Fields.

Long, O. W. 1941. "'Werther' in America." In *Studies in Honor of John Albrecht Walz*, 86–116. Lancaster, PA: Lancaster Press.

Luserke, Matthias. 1995. *Die Bändigung der wilden Seele: Literatur und Leidenschaft in der Aufklärung*. Stuttgart: Metzler.

Mandelkow, Karl, ed. 1975. *Goethe im Urteil seiner Kritiker: Dokumente zur Wirkungsgeschichte Goethes in Deutschland*. Vol. 1: 1773–1832. Munich: Beck.

———. 1980. *Goethe in Deutschland: Rezeptionsgeschichte eines Klassikers*. Vol. 1. Munich: Beck, 1980.

Merck, Johann Heinrich. 1775. Review of *Werther*. In P. Müller, 1969a, 198–201. Originally published in *Allgemeine deutsche Bibliothek* 26 (1775): 102–8.

———. 1778. "Ueber den Mangel des epischen Geistes in unserm lieben Vaterlande." In *Johann Heinrich Mercks ausgewählte Schriften zur schönen*

Literatur und Kunst, ed. Adolf Stahr, 175–80. Göttingen: Vandenhoeck & Ruprecht, 1965. Reprint of edition of 1840.

Meyer-Kalkus, Reinhart. 1977. "Werthers Krankheit zum Tode: Pathologie und Familie in der Empfindsamkeit." In *Urszenen: Literaturwissenschaft als Diskursanalyse und Diskurskritik,* ed. Friedrich A. Kittler and Horst Turk, 76–138. Frankfurt am Main: Suhrkamp.

Meyer-Krentler, Eckhardt. 1982. "'Kalte Abstraktion' gegen 'versengte Einbildung': Destruktion und Restauration aufklärerischer Harmoniemodelle in Goethes 'Leiden' und Nicolais 'Freuden des jungen Werthers.'" *Deutsche Vierteljahrsschrift für Literaturwissenschaft und Geistesgeschichte* 56 (1982): 65–91.

Müller, Peter. 1965. *Zeitkritik und Utopie in Goethes Roman "Die Leiden des jungen Werther": Analyse zum Menschenbild der Sturm- und Drang-Dichtung Goethes.* Berlin 1965 Diss. HU; Berlin: Rütten & Loening, 1969.

———. 1969. *Der junge Goethe im zeitgenössischen Urteil.* Berlin: Akademie Verlag.

Nicolai, Friedrich 1775. *Freuden des jungen Werthers: Leiden und Freuden Werthers des Mannes; Voran und zuletzt ein Gespräch.* In P. Müller, 1969, 130–45.

Parnell, Peter. 1980. *Sorrows of Stephen: A Comedy.* New York: French.

Plenzdorf, Ulrich. 1973. *Die neuen Leiden des jungen W.,* ed. Richard A. Zipser. New York: Wiley, 1978.

Ryder, Frank G., ed. 1952. *George Ticknor's The Sorrows of Young Werther.* Chapel Hill: U of NC P, 1952.

Scherpe, Klaus R. 1970. *"Werther" und Wertherwirkung: zum Syndrom bürgerlicher Gesellschaftsordnung im 18. Jahrhundert; Anhang: Vier Wertherschriften aus dem Jahre 1775 in Faksimile.* Bad Homburg: Gehlen, 1970.

———. 1974. "Natürlichkeit und Produktivität im Gegensatz zur 'bürgerlichen Gesellschaft': Die literarische Opposition des Sturm und Drang: Johann Wolfgang Goethes 'Werther.'" In *Grundkurs 18. Jahrhundert: Die Funktion der Literatur bei der Formierung der bürgerlichen Klasse Deutschlands im 18. Jahrhundert,* ed. Gert Mattenklott, Klaus Scherpe, 1:189–215; supporting materials: 2:113–35. Kronberg/Taunus: Scriptor.

Schings, Hans-Jürgen. 1977. *Melancholie und Aufklärung: Melancholiker und ihre Kritiker in Erfahrungsseelenkunde und Literatur des 18. Jahrhunderts.* Stuttgart: Metzler.

———. 1980. *Der mitleidigste Mensch ist der beste Mensch: Poetik des Mitleids von Lessing bis Büchner.* München: Beck.

Schmid, Christian Heinrich. 1774. "Fortsetzung der kritischen Nachrichten vom Zustande des teutschen Parnasses." In Braun 1883, 61–63. Originally published in *Der Teutsche Merkur* (November 1774): 179–83.

Schmidt, Hartmut. 1988. "'Werther' oder die Passion des Sturm und Drang." In *Sturm und Drang: Ausstellung im Frankfurter Goethe-Museum,* ed. Christoph Perels, 99–115. Frankfurt am Main: Freies Deutsches Hochstift.

Schubart, Christian Friedrich Daniel. 1774. Review of *Werther*. In P. Müller, 1969, 205–6. Originally published in *Deutsche Chronik* (December 5, 1774).

———. 1775. Review. In P. Müller, 1969, 206. Originally published in *Deutsche Chronik* (March 16, 1775).

Schwenck, Konrad. 1845. *Goethes Werke: Erklärungen von Konrad Schwenck*. Frankfurt am Main: Sauerländer.

Sulzer, Johann Georg. 1771. *Allgemeine Theorie der schönen Künste in einzeln, nach alphabetischer Ordnung der Kunstwörter auf einander folgenden, Artikeln abgehandelt*. 2 vols. Leipzig: Weidmann, 1771–74.

Taylor, Bayard. 1879. *Studies in German Literature*. New York: Putnam.

Vaget, Hans Rudolf. 2004. "Werther, The Undead." *Goethe Yearbook* 12 (2004): 17–29.

Vincent, Deirdre. 1992. *Werther's Goethe and the Game of Literary Creativity*. Toronto: U of Toronto P.

Wieland, Christoph Martin. 1774. "'Die Leiden des jungen Werthers.'" *Der Teutsche Merkur* (December, 1774): 241–43. In P. Müller, 1969, 166.

———. 1775. "Freuden des jungen Werthers: Leiden und Freuden Werthers des Mannes." In Müller 1969, 167–68. Originally published in *Der Teutsche Merkur* (March, 1775): 282–84.

Wölfel, Kurt. 1968. *Deutsche Romantheorien: Beiträge zu einer historischen Poetik des Romans in Deutschland*. Ed. Reinhold Grimm. Frankfurt: Athenäum.

Ziegra, Christian. 1775. Review of *Werther*. In P. Müller, 1969, 126–29. Originally published in *Freywillige Beyträge zu den Hamburgischen Nachrichten aus dem Reiche der Gelehrsamkeit* (April 7, 1775).

2: Religious Interpretations

IT SHOULD NOT NECESSARILY SURPRISE US that the earliest critical responses to *Werther* paid relatively little attention to its religious elements. As Albrecht Schöne observes, the eighteenth century was so steeped in biblical language and imagery that their presence does not necessarily point to religious feeling so much as to feeling itself (1958, 175–76, 248–49). Nevertheless, one might expect orthodox churchmen like Johann Melchior Goeze and Christian Ziegra to be disturbed by Werther's blasphemous appeals to God, not to mention his self-identification with Christ. Their objections, however, center far more on the novel's threat to the church's position on suicide. At least insofar as Protestant orthodoxy is concerned, Roland Barthes is incorrect when he claims that "Religion condemns in Werther not only the suicide but also, perhaps, the lover, the utopian, the class heretic, the man who is 'ligatured' to no one but himself" (1977, 210). In England the situation was somewhat different. The first translation, *The Sorrows of Werter: a German Story* (1779), deliberately elided many of the original's religious references, explaining in the preface that "Werter [*sic*] appears to have been strongly impressed with sentiments of religion: and it is not to be wondered at, that in his state of mind they should take an irregular form, and sometimes border on extravagance" (quoted by Rose 1931, 148). Even the translator's choice of "sorrows," rather than "sufferings," to render *Leiden* lessens the potential religious effect.

In Germany, by and large, critical interest in the novel's religious content did not surface until somewhat later, and then as part of a larger focus on intellectual history, Werther's psychological profile, or Goethe's own religious views. Heinrich Düntzer's approach is typical. He writes that nature itself is Werther's gospel and attributes that attitude to the hero's sensitivity to the surrounding world (1849, 120). At the same time, Düntzer excuses the "sophistic" appeals to God and scripture that Werther employs to justify his death; they are nothing more than a lost soul's desperate attempt to find some way to deal with his passions. In seeking solace from a paternal God, Werther is drawing sustenance from "the human relationship of a father to his children" and only coincidentally invoking a religiously charged image that is in fact devoid of religious content. This appeal, says Düntzer, should be seen as a psychologically justified expression of Werther's condition, not as a true statement of belief (152; see also Sørenson 1987, 126). Like many other apologists for

Werther's religious attitudes, Düntzer cites the hero's assurances in the letter of November 15 as evidence that he honors religion.

Georg Zimmermann, writing twenty years later, in 1869, is similarly inclined to excuse Werther's religious lapses, or at least to give them an acceptable context. Werther, he says, "hatte früher eine lebendige Religiösität in seinem Herzen getragen" (1869, 263: had earlier carried a lively religiosity in his heart), but his emotional confusions have now turned him into a doubter unable to reconcile his passions with his previous relationship to God. His attitude toward organized religion is particularly uncertain. Nevertheless, Zimmermann ascribes a strong underlying religious belief to Werther, albeit one that presents itself mostly in his imagination and "in *romantischer Vermischung* christlicher und subjektiver Elemente" (265: in a *romantic confusion* of Christian and subjective elements). Werther's strongest endorsement of religion is a respect for others' beliefs that he himself does not share.

The early twentieth-century interest in *Geistesgeschichte* (intellectual history) inclined critics of that time to identify Werther's beliefs with what they believed to be Goethe's own spiritual development. Hans Gose, writing in 1921, concludes that *Werther's* biblical allusions and references to God reflect both the pantheistic and pietist traditions that had occupied Goethe earlier. In fact, he finds that the religious elements, being mere echoes of issues that Goethe had previously considered in his own life, are of only secondary importance to the novel itself (1921, 22–24, 84–87). Herrmann August Korff adopts an even wider perspective, feeling that these elements bear witness to the "new paganism" that was freeing the German spirit from established Christian theology (1923, 276). Hans von Schubert, in contrast, finds that they resonate with Goethe's pietist experiences of 1768, which became the basis for his life-long personal relationship with religion (1925, 43).

The appearance of Herbert Schöffler's study of *Werther* in 1938, as most critics acknowledge, changed the way in which scholars view the novel's approach to religion. Until that point, Ingeborg Bickelmann's summary, written one year earlier, was typical of most interpretations: in the early part of the novel, she says, Werther's religiosity wholly coincides with his feeling for nature. By implication, his enthusiasm for Creation embraces the Creator, as well, without any institutional intervention. When societal pressures begin to interfere with this harmony, however, Werther turns to a personal God, one who lovingly accepts this reunion (1937, 14). Schöffler's 35-page monograph begins a new paradigm. The novel's allusions to the *Gospel According to John* now seem so obvious that it is hard to imagine that Schöffler was the first critic to point them out. This insight is part of his larger argument that *Werther's* appeal rests on its position in the last phase of the eighteenth century's shift from orthodox Protestant theology to a rationalistic deism and then finally to an extreme pantheism in which God's independent presence is indiscernible. *Werther*, Schöffler argues, embodies a radical vision of this new stage by retaining the forms of religion — and the power that they evoke — but by secularizing their content. Its hero reenacts Christ's passion, but his suffering, a result of frustrated love, assumes no transcendent moment. *Werther*, he says, is the first work in modern times in which secular values alone determine the outcome; it is "die erste nichtdualistische Tragödie (. . .) ohne Schuld, ohne Prinzip des Bösen. Kein Schurke fällt den Helden. Eine neue, viel tiefere Tragik ist erreicht, die Tragik einer ganz neuen Zeit. (. . .) Werther geht zugrunde an den besten Kräften seines Wesens, an allem, was gut ist in ihm, daran, daß er liebevoll und treu ist, daß er die Gesetze der Kirche und der Gesellschaft hält, daß die Ehe anderer ihm heilig ist" (86–87: the first non-dualistic tragedy [. . .] without guilt, without an evil principle. No villain brings the hero down. A new, far more profound tragedy is achieved, the tragedy of a wholly new era. [. . .] Werther is destroyed by the best powers of his being, by all that is good in him, by the fact that he is loving and true, that he honors the laws of the church and society, that he holds others' marriage sacred).

Such is Schöffler's influence that almost all subsequent studies that address the religious question have to come to terms with it, usually after some obeisance. In 1940, two years after its appearance, Herrmann Blumenthal salutes Schöffler's study, but he finds its focus on religion too limited. Werther's tragedy extends to many spheres of life in which the conflict between higher values and human realities can be played out: "Die unglückliche Liebe zu einer versagten Frau, die künstlerische Ohnmacht bei stärkster Erlebnisfähigkeit, die Preisgabe der amtlichen Laufbahn bei hochfliegenden Ideen von Wirksamkeit und Einfluß, die gesellschaftliche Isolierung bei größter Menschenliebe, die gedankliche Verstiegenheit bei klaren Wissen um das menschlich Richtige, die religiöse Entwurzelung bei innigem religiösen Bedürfnis — all das sind nur verschiedene Seiten des gleichen Verhängnisses, des Zusammenstoßes von unendlichem Streben und höchstem Anspruch mit den 'Grenzen der Menschheit'" (1940, 319; The unhappy love for an unavailable woman, the artistic impotence joined with heightened sensitivity, the failure of a career combined with exaggerated ideas of effectiveness and influence, the social isolation paired with the highest altruism, the notional eccentricity together with clear insight into what is humanly right, the religious uprootedness coupled with profound religious need — all these are simply different sides of the same fate, the collision of endless striving and highest goals with human limitation). That same year, Ernst Beutler respectfully takes issue with Schöffler's assertion that Ossian's appeal to eighteenth-century readers rested on the bard's intimate depiction of nature without a religious presence (1940, 151–52). Most of all, however, he draws on the young Goethe's other writings to insist that their author was at heart a theist, that the novel does in fact depict a dualism, at least at the end, when Werther's suicide "breaks through to the metaphysical" (153). Beutler also acknowledges pietist influences on the novel but is most interested in Werther's — and Goethe's — theism. The hero, he maintains, would not have committed suicide without the belief that a personal God awaited him in the afterlife, and Goethe's own assertions at the time suggest that he, too, shared this belief. Beutler draws on Goethe's early religious experiences to explain a specific incident in the novel: in his letter of September 15, Werther complains that the pastor's wife has chopped down his beloved walnut trees; he relates this atrocity to her interest "an der neumodischen, moralisch-kritischen Reformation des Christentumes" (in the new-fangled critical-moral reformation of Christianity), as well as to her coolness toward Lavater. Consistent with his interest in Werther's autobiographical aspects (see chapter 5), Beutler points out that the original model for this figure is Johanna Dorothea Griesbach, née Rambach, wife of the vicar of St. Peter's Church in Frankfurt. The daughter, wife, and mother of theologians, she subscribed to the emerging academic philological approaches to the Bible and, as Goethe later reported, had a disruptive effect on the pietist circle around Susanna von Klettenberg. Her negative portrayal, claims Beutler, is Goethe's statement in favor of belief (145–57).

The period following World War II saw a flurry of religiously oriented interpretations. Grete Schaeder, writing in 1947, tries to differentiate within the paradigm that Schöffler establishes. Although it antedates the German Democratic Republic, this study is still a surprising product of East German scholarship, which normally agrees with J. M. R. Lenz's characterization of Werther as a "crucified Prometheus" (for example, Müller 1965, 178). Like Beutler, Schaeder also draws on Goethe's own statements about religion, and assumes that the author and his fictional character share the same beliefs. She sees Werther's secular strivings as ultimately deriving from a religious longing: "Es geht letzten Endes nicht um Lotte und nicht um die Welt, sondern um Gott, um die Möglichkeit, Gott in der Seele lebendig zu erhalten; nicht die Gottesidee, aber die Gegenwart Gottes im Innern des Menschen ist der höchste Wert in Goethes Roman" (1947, 75; It is finally not a question of Lotte, nor of the world, but of God, of the possibility of keeping God alive in his soul; not the idea of God, but the presence of God within the human soul is the highest value in Goethe's novel). Werther's tragedy, she says, lies in the impossibility of uniting temporal and eternal values. She cites Goethe's later maxim that "Wir sind naturforschend Pantheisten, dichtend Polytheisten, sittlich Monotheisten" (68; In science we are pantheists, in poetry polytheists, in ethics monotheists) and adds that Werther's passion drives him to insist on combining all three experiences of God at once and on manifesting them both sensually and transcendentally. Despite such a combination's impossibility, Schaeder concludes that Werther's development is in the end positive: he cannot have Lotte, but the mere experience of love releases his inner genius and brings him closer to God. During his last few hours he is at peace, for he is convinced that in death he will be united with Lotte without sin. As evidence Schaeder cites what she considers Goethe's own belief in an afterlife and in the forgiveness of a loving God the Father. Goethe, she claims, has placed Werther's suffering next to Christ's passion, not in opposition to it (75–81). In a later study written in 1975, James Wilson also finds Werther's analogy with Christ to be apt: "Central to Christology is the understanding that Jesus is not some hybrid figure who is half human, half divine; rather he is wholly mortal and wholly God" (105). Werther analogously shares this contradiction, in that he simultaneously experiences the two extremes of the human condition, finite constraints on the one hand and infinite longings on the other. Both Christ and Werther, says Wilson, are released from this tension by death.

Jean-Jacques Anstett, by contrast, considers Werther's identification with Christ to be a destructive distortion: Werther not only fails to recognize Christ's ultimate submission to God's will, but he diminishes Christ's divinity in asserting his own. In general, says Anstett, Werther's appeal to the Christian tradition, like his illusory union with nature, is a desperate psychological attempt to fix upon something external to himself. At most he achieves an ultimately unsatisfactory pantheism (1949, 161–69). A later study from 1958 sees Werther's deviations from orthodox Christianity more positively: Johanna Graefe first assembles a catalogue of all the religious expressions and references to religion in *Werther* and discovers in it an unconventional creed that stresses the bond between human and divine creativity. This "natural" religion has its roots in the Christian tradition and so partakes of its symbols, but it differs from both Catholic and Protestant belief in important ways, most notably in its failure to accept salvation through the notion of God made flesh. Werther, says Graefe, seeks to be saved through his own harmony with God's feeling (1958, 97–98).

Stuart Atkins, in a seminal article also discussed in chapter 3, points in a new direction by stressing the psychological component in Werther's religiosity. He is, says Atkins, a theist, but a highly subjective one: "Werther, who has rejected revealed Christianity, exemplifies in this theistic religious thinking a kind of voluntary fatalism favorable to temporization, inactivity, inertia, feelings of irresponsibility and frustration. . . . It is fascinating to see how Werther the theist convinces himself that what he desires is really only to perform God's will" (1948, 539). Hans Reiss agrees that Werther's faith is idiosyncratic: "Werther uses a mistaken analogy when he likens his suffering to that of Christ. It indicates the extent and nature of his pretension. . . . [I]n the last resort, his arrogant aspiration to suffering like Christ is an attempt to glorify his own feelings" (1963, 40). Paul Mog, however, emphasizes Werther's psychological motivation more strongly, equating his fantasy of being the Prodigal Son with the mad Heinrich's search for flowers in winter. He is grasping at straws, not expressing faith, when he seeks God's direct intervention (1976, 137).

While most subsequent critics follow Atkins and Mog into psychological explanations of Werther's religion (see chapter 3), another strain continues Beutler's and Blumenthal's attempts to build on Schöffler. Erich Trunz's commentary to the Hamburg edition of *Werther* emphasizes the book's position in the eighteenth century's religious development, calling it "der erste Roman, in welchem ein Mensch das Absolute sucht durch Erlebnisse in dieser Welt, durch Naturerleben und Liebe; es ist also der erste Roman der neuen Weltfrömmigkeit" (1951, 558; the first novel in which someone seeks the absolute in worldly experiences, in the experiences of nature and of love; it is thus the first novel of the new "world-piousness"). Albrecht Schöne (1958), August Langen (1963), and Ludwig Kahn (1964) all add various nuances to Schöffler's thesis, and the latter two attempt to show that Werther's secularization of the Gospels is in fact part of a larger tradition in a period of religious crisis (see especially Kahn, 124). Rolf Christian Zimmermann points to Goethe's own fragmentary verse epic, *Der ewige Jude* (The Wandering Jew, 1774), as evidence of the author's approach to the figure of Christ, who is seen in both texts as a lovingly empathetic outsider fated to act in the world. In this context, says Zimmermann, we encounter Christ as Werther's brotherly companion (1979, 183; see also Brinkmann 1976). Hermann Zabel uncovers even more Biblical allusions, but, picking up on a topic introduced by Schöne, he assigns them a different significance: while all of these echoes and references have their origin in the language of the Bible and the Church, they have been extended to portray feelings and concepts that address the whole of human existence. They become general symbols for human suffering and for the compulsion to seek liberation through death (1972, 64–65).

Christoph Perels identifies *Werther's* evocations of the Bible at every narrative level and comes to a conclusion opposite from Zabel's. Up until 1774, he points out, the only available source of salvation was the story of Christ's passion. Within this tradition, and especially in pietism, Christ appears as the "friend" with whom the lost soul intimately communicates (1990, 58). *Werther* taps into this iconography, beginning with the editor's opening appeal to the reader, which recalls the beginning of the *Gospel According to Luke* (57) — indeed, the whole structure of *Werther* echoes the gospels, which, like the novel, tell not the whole life of a hero, but a "Passionsgeschichte mit ausführlicher Einleitung" (a passion story with an extended introduction; 56). Perels cites further biblical allusions, adding to Schöffler's and Zabel's collections, and also shows linguistic similarities between Jesus and Werther. In discussing the morality of suicide with Albert, for example, Werther argues in parables and even sounds like the preaching Christ when he uses the second-person plural *ihr* (58–60).

Perels argues that *Werther* was thus read at the time of its publication as a kind of alternative, secularized gospel, one that consoled a younger generation and offered, if not a path to salvation, at least a way out of crisis (63–64).

Matthias Luserke also identifies an intended secularization of Christ's passion in the novel (1995, 240–41). After summarizing the important biblical references and parallels in *Werther*, he adds the insight from Horst Flaschka's study that the word *Leiden* in *Werther's* title is ambiguous. Although traditionally translated into English as "sorrows," *Leiden* can mean either "suffering" or "passion." Admittedly, the plural form (*die Leiden*) to be found in the title before 1777 can refer only to Werther's sufferings or his emotions, but the fictional editor's forward uses the singular form (*das Leiden*), which can also denote passion in the sense of *passio*. Subsequent editions, including the one of 1787, omit the first article, thus creating the ambiguous *Leiden des jungen Werthers,* and leaving open which kind of passion or suffering is being presented (Flaschka 1987, 209–10). Luserke, whose greater project is to identify the discourses of passion at work in the novel (see chapter 3), sees this ambiguity as a structural device. It seems to promise a story of salvation, and when this expectation is disappointed in the end, the effect is to withdraw the metaphysical dimension and to collapse the two secular meanings of "passion" and "suffering" together. To have human passions is thus to suffer.

Works Cited

Anstett, Jean-Jacques. 1949. "Werthers religiöse Krise." In *Goethes "Werther": Kritik und Forschung,* ed. Hans Peter Herrmann, 163–73. Darmstadt: Wissenschaftliche Buchgesellschaft, 1994.

Atkins, Stuart P. 1948. "J. C. Lavater and Goethe: Problems of Psychology and Theology in *Die Leiden des jungen Werther.*" *PMLA* 63 (1948): 520–76.

Barthes, Roland. 1977. *A Lover's Discourse: Fragments.* Trans. Richard Howard. New York: Hill & Wang, 1978.

Beutler, Ernst. 1940. "Wertherfragen." *Viermonatsschrift der Goethe-Gesellschaft* 5 (1940): 138–60.

Bickelmann, Ingeborg. 1937. *Goethes "Werther" im Urteil des 19. Jahrhunderts. (Romantik bis Naturalismus 1830–1880).* Diss., Frankfurt am Main.

Blumenthal, Herrmann. 1940. "Ein neues Wertherbild?" *Viermonatsschrift der Goethe-Gesellschaft* 5 (1940): 315–20.

Brinkmann, Richard. 1976. "Goethes 'Werther' and Arnolds 'Kirchen- und Ketzerhistorie.' Zur Aporie des modernen Individualitätenbegriffs." In *Versuche zu Goethe: Festschrift für Erich Heller zum 65. Geburtstag am 27.3.1976,* ed. Volker Dürr und Géza v. Molnár, 167–89. Heidelberg: Stiehm.

Düntzer, Heinrich. 1849. *Zu Goethe's Jubelfeier: Studien zu Goethe's Werken.* Elberfeld und Iserlohn: Baedeker.

Flaschka, Horst. 1987. *Goethes "Werther": Werkkontextuelle Deskription und Analyse.* Munich: Fink.

Gose, Hans. *Goethes "Werther."* 1921. Halle an der Saale: Niemeyer, 1921. Reprint Walluf bei Wiesbaden: Sändig, 1973.

Graefe, Johanna. 1958. "Die Religion in den 'Leiden des jungen Werther': Eine Untersuchung auf Grund des Wortbestandes." *Jahrbuch der Goethe-Gesellschaft* 20 (Weimar, 1958): 72–98.

Kahn, Ludwig W. 1964. *Literatur und Glaubenskrise.* Stuttgart: Kohlhammer.

Korff, Hermann August. 1923. *Geist der Goethezeit: Versuch einer ideellen Entwicklung der klassisch-romantischen Literaturgeschichte.* Vol. 1. Leipzig: Weber.

Langen, August. 1963. "Zum Problem der sprachlichen Säkularisation in der deutschen Dichtung des 18. und 19. Jahrhunderts." *Zeitschrift für deutsche Philologie.* Sonderheft zum 83. Band (1964): 24–42.

Luserke, Matthias. 1995. *Die Bändigung der wilden Seele: Literatur und Leidenschaft in der Aufklärung.* Stuttgart: Metzler.

Mog, Paul. 1976. *Ratio und Gefühlskultur: Studien zur Psychogenese und Literatur im 18. Jahrhundert.* Tübingen: Niemeyer.

Müller, Peter. 1965. *Zeitkritik und Utopie in Goethes Roman "Die Leiden des jungen Werther": Analyse zum Menschenbild der Sturm- und Drang-Dichtung Goethes.* Diss. HU, Berlin; Berlin: Rütten & Loening, 1969.

Perels, Christoph. 1990. "Auf der Suche nach dem verlorenen Vater. Das 'Werther'-Evangelium noch einmal." In *Goethe in seiner Epoche,* 49–64. Tübingen: Niemeyer, 1998.

Reiss, Hans S. 1963. *Goethes Romane.* Bern, Munich: Francke, 1963. In English: *Goethe's Novels.* London: Macmillan; New York: St. Martin, 1969.

Rose, William. 1931. "The Historical Background of Goethe's 'Werther.'" In *Men, Myths, and Movements in German Literature: A Volume of Historical and Critical Papers,* 125–55. New York: Macmillan.

Schaeder, Grete. 1947. *Gott und Welt: Drei Kapitel goethischer Weltanschauung.* Hamlen: Seifert.

Schöffler, Herbert. 1938. *"Die Leiden des jungen Werther": Ihr geistesgeschichtlicher Hintergrund.* In *Goethes "Werther": Kritik und Forschung,* ed. Hans Peter Herrmann, 58–87. Darmstadt: Wissenschaftliche Buchgesellschaft, 1994.

Schöne, Albrecht. 1958. *Säkularisation als sprachbildende Kraft: Studien zur Dichtung deutscher Pfarrersöhne.* Göttingen: Vandenhoeck & Ruprecht.

Schubert, Hans von. 1925. *Goethes religiöse Jugendentwicklung.* Leipzig: Quelle & Meyer.

Sørensen, Bengt Algot. 1987. "Über die Familie in Goethes 'Werther' und 'Wilhelm Meister.'" *Orbis Litterarum* 42 (1987): 118–40.

Trunz, Erich. 1951. "Anmerkungen des Herausgebers zu *Die Leiden des jungen Werther*." In *Goethes Werke*, 6:514–95. Hamburg: Wegner, 1951.

Wellek, René. 1965. *A History of Modern Criticism: 1750–1950*. Vol. 4: *The Later Nineteenth Century*. New Haven: Yale UP.

Wilson, James D. 1975. "Goethe's 'Werther': A Keatsian Quest for Self-Annihilation." *Mosaic* 9/1 (1975): 93–109.

Zabel, H. 1972. "Goethes 'Werther' — eine weltliche Passionsgeschichte?" *Zeitschrift für Religions- und Gesitesgeschichte* 24 (1972): 57–69.

Zimmermann, Georg. 1869. "Werther's Leiden und der literarische Kampf um sie." *Herrigs Archiv* 45 (1869): 241–98.

Zimmermann, Rolf Christian. 1979. "Die Leiden des jungen Werthers." In *Das Weltbild des jungen Goethe: Studien zur hermetischen Tradition des 18. Jahrhunderts*, 2: 167–212, 312–20. Munich: Fink.

3: Psychological Approaches

THE EARLIEST CRITICAL responses to *Werther*, as we have seen, tend to define its hero psychologically. Many factors continue to encourage this approach. Goethe himself invites it by asserting in his autobiography that *Werther* describes a sick delusion (*HA* 9, 583[1]) and by reporting on the therapeutic effect that the story's composition had on his own youthful preoccupation with suicide. Later, in 1824, he confessed to Eckermann that he hesitated to look at the book again, fearful that he would be forced to revisit the pathological condition from which it sprang (Eckermann 1824, 28–29 [January 2]); and his poem "An Werther" (To Werther), composed that same year, indicates how the feelings associated with the novel had persisted throughout his life (*HA* 1, 380–81). But *Werther* itself, not just the author's memory of its genesis, also asks us to look at the book as a psychological portrait. As Karl Viëtor claims, "Among European novels *Werther* is the first in which an inward life, a spiritual process and nothing else, is represented, and hence it is the first psychological novel" (1949, 31; see also Siebers 1993, 16; Wellbery 1994, 180). It contains, according to Max Diez's quantitative analysis of its metaphors, an overwhelming preponderance of "psycho-physical" images (1936, 1006), and its one-sided epistolary form structurally supports Werther's inclination to focus on his emotional state. The novel is a kind of "psychological monodrama" (M. Herrmann 1904: vi) in which everything, except perhaps the accounts of Werther's last few days, has been sifted through his subjectivity. Even Werther himself suggests a psychological reading, as well as a biblical one, when he refers to his "Krankheit zum Tode" ("sickness unto death"; letter of August 12). All of these features, especially since they culminate in Werther's suicide, compel us to try to understand his motivations, regardless of whether he inspires sympathy or outrage. Even those critics who eventually trace Werther's problem to larger social, economic, or intellectual forces or to the inherent frustrations of artistic genius are inclined to begin with the question of what makes him tick. Recent scholarship has added a historical dimension to this perspective by focusing on how eighteenth-century literary theory and popular culture defined emotions in general, and the ways in which *Werther* and the critical response that it evoked conform to Enlightenment psychological discourse.

"Psychological," however, is an especially protean term. It can designate anything from vague ideas about emotionality to speculations about the relationship between mind and body, notions of "national psychology" (Wellek 1965, 358), practical methods of clinical therapy, and the specific theories of various psychoanalytical schools. All of these meanings can be found throughout the history of *Werther* studies. In fact, a collection of the psychologically oriented critical responses to *Werther* comes close to providing a complete history of the speculations about human behavior since 1774. While reporting on "Goethe as a Psychologist" for the Goethe Society in Weimar in 1901, Richard Meyer attempts such a review, but his survey goes back only to the middle of the previous century. Naive readings of character, Meyer admits, are of course as old as humankind, but self-consciously theoretical psychology is relatively young, having started with the nineteenth century's empirical approach. Before this, Meyer claims, the field of psychology indulged in speculation and concerned itself merely with types, not individuals. Goethe, however, is an exception. He anticipates later developments by creating unique, rounded figures that are based on more than just a single characteristic. Their many facets not only make them more interesting as characters, but they also offer almost every reader some feature with which to identify (1901, 3*–11*; see also Bickelmann 1937, 9).

Present-day psychologists would agree with Meyer that their field began in Germany in the mid-nineteenth century, when psychology first became a science in the modern sense.[2] But psychology actually dominated eighteenth-century philosophical discourse, often under the rubrics of *Seelenkunde* (science of the soul) or *Anthropologie* (see Duncan 2003), and the theories prevalent at that time necessarily played an important role in formulating Werther's sufferings (see especially Renner 1985).

The first critical reactions to *Werther,* as we discovered in chapter 1, confine themselves largely to descriptions of Werther's "nature," seeing him either as admirably sensitive or as appallingly weak and self-centered. Subsequent commentators from the early nineteenth century tend to subscribe to the latter judgment, viewing him as emblematic of an effete period in German history (see Bickelmann 1937, 15–22). Both Wolfgang Menzel (1828, 90) and Joseph Freiherr von Eichendorff (1851, 79–80), for example, despite coming at Werther from opposite ends of the political spectrum, describe him as a Narcissus to whom the outside world represents nothing more than either a mirror or else a frustrating hindrance to selfish pleasure. His suicide, they claim, results merely from the kind of weakness that one would expect of his generation. Karl Hillebrand, himself a frustrated revolutionary who spent much of his life in exile, characterized the youth of Goethe's generation as having been reduced by societal repression to a whining, effeminate passivity and neurotic hypersensitivity that culminated in melancholy (1885, 288). By implication, nineteenth-century Germans, nurtured by nationalist feelings of whatever stripe, were made of sturdier stuff.

The academic psychiatrists of the mid-nineteenth century who interpret the novel share some of these assumptions, but they differentiate more carefully among the various deleterious effects that history caused Werther's generation to suffer. In fact, Carl Gustav Carus, in 1843 the first academic physician to consider Goethe's novel,[3] sees Werther's problem more from a developmental standpoint than an historical one. Werther, he says, is the direct outcome of the *taedium vitae* (tedium of life) and melancholia from which Goethe himself suffered, like so many other young men. In this regard, Carus agrees with most of his contemporaries, who feel that Werther, in contrast to the author who created him, lacks the mental and moral strength to combat his "sickness of the heart" (see, for example, Heinrich Düntzer 1849, 122). But Carus seeks a medical explanation for this phenomenon. When Goethe's "disease" reached crisis proportions, says Carus, he was compelled by an "organic necessity" to purge it from his own inner being by composing the novel (Carus 1843, 175, 81). The difference between Goethe and Werther is one of *Organisation,* what we would now call brain structure. Carus, who knew Goethe personally, offers a phrenological analysis based on the poet's portraits and death-mask to show that he was not only "healthy," but was also "ein eigentümlich 'schön und mächtig Organisierter'" (possessed of a "singularly beautiful and powerful [brain] structure"; 85). Werther, in contrast, is naturally weak.

Georg Zimmermann, professor of medicine at the University of Giessen, sounds more like Nicolai — whom he specifically applauds (1869, 275–80) — when he distinguishes between the hardy souls who can emerge intact from reading *Werther* and those immature people, especially women, who lack the psychological starch and firm moral principles needed to interpret the novel correctly. Like Nicolai, Zimmermann praises Goethe's artistic achievement but feels that the author of a publicly available book, indeed, a "national possession" (248), is obligated to eliminate possible moral ambiguities by taking a clear stand against suicide. While Zimmermann ultimately worries about *Werther's* effect on readers, he directs most of his attention toward understanding the young hero's behavior. Some of the blame for Werther's condition, he says, lies with the political and social structures that frustrate the realization of his legitimate passions. Here Zimmermann, a liberal democrat, is referring not to the institution of marriage that makes Lotte unavailable, but rather to the prevailing class system and a general malaise that inhibit Werther's overall personal development. His forbidden love for Lotte simply exacerbates the problem. More importantly, however, Zimmermann decides that *Werther* needs to be treated as an individual case history.[4] After all, he points out, every human being necessarily struggles with society's obstacles, and there are those who possess sufficient strength and optimism to achieve personal fulfillment. Werther, in contrast, is psychologically too weak to enter the real world. Instead of easing his torment through useful engagement in public affairs, he chooses an indolence that only compounds his difficulties. Zimmermann agrees that Werther's resignation from his post with the ambassador is an appropriate response to an objectively bad situation, but when the young man then fails to look for another position, he shifts the blame onto Werther himself (271–73). As a psychiatrist, Zimmermann has pretensions to scientific objectivity, but he displays here the same ambivalence that we so often find among lay readers: on the one hand, he recognizes Werther's malady as something beyond his control; on the other, he is irritated by the hero's unwillingness to get a grip on himself and find some useful occupation. Here Zimmermann has more in common with Robert Eduard Prutz, a professor of literature at Halle, who, despite his own strongly liberal views, cites Goethe's moral superiority to Werther as the reason that the former can rise above the condition that dooms the latter (1856; see Bickelmann 1937, 44).

Ludwig Wille, too, brings a therapist's perspective to *Werther*. In 1877, while director of the psychiatric department of Basel's municipal hospital, he presented a "psychiatric-literary study of Werther and his times." It traces Werther's problems back to eighteenth-century Germany's paralyzing lack of national consciousness, which, Wille says, made it impossible for its people to assert their proper rights and human worth. More precisely, Werther's condition derives from the first clumsy stirrings of the German spirit as it began to awake from this malaise. The Sturm und Drang, says Wille, brought a period of awkward, if welcome, upheaval; its burgeoning life force produced vital creations, but its immaturity informed these works with an unhealthy, pathological character (1877, 4–5). *Werther* is the result. Like Zimmermann, however, Wille points out that such historical forces are not the only determinant. After all, Goethe, "wie die übrigen deutschen Jünglinge litten an einer epidemischen Melancholie, die naturgemäss zu vielerlei Nachdenken und Gesprächen über den Selbstmord führte" (12; like the other German youths suffered from an epidemic melancholy that naturally led to all sorts of contemplation of and discussions about suicide), but his strength of character enabled him to rise above these emotions. The congenitally weak Werther, in contrast, would have had trouble in any era; he essentially resembles many of Wille's own mentally ill patients, suffering from an egoism, as Wille labels it (19), that produces a vicious cycle: a lack of self-control and a fixation on sensual stimuli together feed his agitation; the resulting emotional extremes isolate him from other people, which further increases his obsession with his subjective feelings. While a normal ego constructs a reciprocal relationship between the self and world over time, Werther's kind of sickness subverts this process, and its victims fail to engage in morally-defined undertakings with others, instead developing only superficial bonds. Unable to empathize with individuals — or to identify with national entities (19) — such patients enthuse about ultimately meaningless utopian abstractions that they label humankind, nature, or religion. They become increasingly frustrated by their encounters with reality and often turn destructive, either toward others or themselves. The farmhand in *Werther* who murders his rival is responding to the same impulse as the hero who kills himself (21–22).

While Werther's pathology is a universal psychiatric phenomenon, says Wille, the novel's earliest reception was affected by the particular spirit of its time. In 1774, a whole generation was subject to the same affliction and was inclined to view the hero's condition as something to admire and cultivate. Wille finds it understandable that Goethe's contemporaries would want to call for added warnings to discourage imitators, even if the novel was never intended to be a moral tract. Readers a century later, in the more robust Wilhelminian Germany, are fortunate in not needing to fear such contamination. They can safely appreciate *Werther* as a great artistic achievement. Aware that its hero is sick, they require no additional caveats from the author; the story itself contains sufficient cautions for the modern young enthusiast (25–29).

Paul Julius Möbius, an academic neurologist and practicing psychiatrist in Leipzig, has a particular ax to grind in his 1898 study *Über das Pathologische bei Goethe* (On the Pathological in Goethe). Throughout his career Möbius advocated against incarcerating the insane in all but the most extreme cases, arguing that the difference between mental health and illness is largely one of degree, rather than of kind (Möbius 1898, 81–103). Almost all people, especially artists, are pathological to some extent, and Goethe is no exception. In fact, Möbius asserts, the first half of *Werther* is largely Goethe's self-portrait, assembled before the author has "rehabilitated" himself (113). In contrast to Goethe, however, Werther does not have the benefit of a timely intervention. Had he received help, like the countless other young people who share his condition but do not commit suicide, he could have continued to live, even though his underlying pathology was probably not curable (115). Möbius is even more interested in the figure of Heinrich, the scribe who has been driven insane by his love for Lotte and, after a violent period of being restrained in an institution, now lives gently in his own hallucinatory world (115–17). Perhaps Goethe has drawn this figure so trenchantly, Möbius speculates, because he had a model in the hebephrenic Johann David Balthasar Clauer, who lived in the Goethe family's house for many years. Only the etiology is wrong; such a condition does not result from tragic love, but from an inherently faulty brain structure (*Gehirn-Organisation*).

These early analyses display one of the methodological difficulties inherent in all psychological interpretations: Werther is a fictional construct, not a real human being, yet practicing therapists in particular tend to consider him just another patient. Wille and Möbius do acknowledge Werther's fictionality in passing, but they draw no consequences from it. Hubertus Tellenbach, a clinical and academic psychopathologist writing 100 years later, explicitly dismisses the problem, "trusting" that art "is not a mere imagination, but [rather] a condensation of reality" (1977, 16);

having thus dispensed with the distinction between art and the real world, he then draws on his clinical experiences and his own theoretical formulations (Tellenbach 1960) to describe Werther as an example of endogenic melancholia and to compare him specifically with two of the patients he has treated in real life.

Sylvia P. Jenkins comes to the same conclusion as Tellenbach about Werther's diagnosis, concluding that by book 2 of the novel, when "the depression takes over completely, it reduces Werther to despair and derangement and ultimately drives him to self-destruction" (1992, 97). But at the same time she stresses that Werther is *not* a real person, and that to speculate about the causes of his condition is — or should be — a problematic undertaking. As Victor Lange reminds us, literary works are not reducible to the direct articulation of inner impulses; artistic expression necessarily partakes of conventions of genre, language, and so forth, and the interpreter cannot ignore these elements (1970, 154–56). Admittedly, however, it is part of the novel's structure to invite us to see Werther as real, presenting us with dated letters purportedly gathered by an editor intent on getting at the truth. Indeed, the book derives much of its power from the reader's ready acceptance of Werther's objective existence. Even its ironic devices, which simultaneously undercut such an identification, work precisely because they call into question a structure that otherwise seems so credible.

In addition to asking if it is possible to diagnose a fictional character, however, we might also wonder why especially these early psychotherapists attempt such an undertaking in the first place. Their analyses seem neither to add insight into his character nor to further an understanding of psychotherapeutic practices. One possible answer is that they hope to exploit Goethe's canonical status to add legitimacy to psychiatry in general or their own theories in particular. Another is that the figure of Werther seems to offer insight into Goethe himself, either as a person or as a creative artist. This notion, shared implicitly or explicitly by most psychologically oriented critics, is also fraught with methodological concerns, since it rests on particularly questionable assumptions about the relationship between an author and a text.

This desire to approach Goethe through his hero is of course not new. As we saw in chapter 1, even the earliest critics treat *Werther* as a conduit to Goethe's heart. To read the novel is to partake of its author's inner emotional life, to feel the fullness of his passion. As Anton Matthias Sprickmann wrote in 1776, "Die Dichtkunst soll schöne Seelen schildern, und die Stimmung, die eine Seele schön macht, ist Kraft, Leidenschaft, ist, was in der Grundlage des Dichters eigene Seele ist; daher auch selten ein großer Dichter, der sich nicht einmal selbst in seinen Werken geschildert hätte" (Literature should portray beautiful souls, and what determines a soul's beauty is power, passion, that which lies at the foundation of the poet's soul; thus rare is a great poet who has never portrayed himself in his works; quoted in Luserke 1995, 247). Even Carus, despite his interest in an objective brain science, ultimately supports this purpose of literature. Werther's story, he claims — like *Stella, Faust, Tasso,* and many of Goethe's poems — reflects its author's need to come to terms with an otherwise cripplingly passionate temperament (1843, 75–76). Read together, says Carus, these works offer us a view into the author's great soul, provided that we approach them with empathy, diligence, and a reverence for the mystery of genius. Even then, however, we never see the whole of the artist's spirit; we are like scientists trying to understand a planet's fiery inner core by examining its surface (200–201).

This approach is more complex than Schubart's admonition, "Nimm aber dein Herz mit!" (Take your heart along!) when reading *Werther* (1774, 205–6). Carus is introducing an important new strain in Goethe scholarship, one that most notably Wilhelm Dilthey defined somewhat later. It treats Goethe's works as a route to understanding not just his heart but his whole being, as well as the creative process itself (see Lange 1970, 142–45). Although biographically oriented, this approach eschews an easy equivalence between work and author. It assumes that each literary creation springs from, but does not wholly define, its author's character. In Dilthey's terminology, the basis of genuine literature is the author's *Erlebnis* (Dilthey 1887, 128), a particular kind of experience distinguished by "its relation to the mind. It must be intensely felt; it must not merely be perceived passively, but transformed actively; it must engage the whole man" (Wellek 1965, 322).

Friedrich Gundolf extends this interpretive tradition into the twentieth century. *Werther,* he writes in 1916, only superficially portrays an individual psychological development; it gains its substance by investing Werther's story with the titanic conflict that characterizes all of Goethe's creative works. Like Faust, Werther is tragically torn between losing himself in a total union with the Universal and asserting his individual self by taking possession of the immediate moment. Faust renounces the "beautiful moment," but Werther retreats into a passivity that dooms him to dissolution in the All — in other words, death (1916, 162–84). What Werther does share with Faust, however, is a direct line to Goethe. Gundolf, who reflects the aesthetics of the circle around Stefan George, has no trouble with seeing *Werther* as a genuine expression of Goethe's own psychological makeup, its artistry serving only to distill the projected image into something more intense. Goethe, according to Gundolf, is a titanic genius, and "Bei solchen Naturen sind die Äußerungen des formenden Bewußtseins nur der getreue Index dessen, was in der dunklen Mitte und Tiefe vorgeht, die Helle ihrer Glut, der Logos ihres Eros. (...) Darum ist der Werther ebenso echt Goethisch wie die Briefe an Lotte Buff und ihren Bräutigam, aber zugleich intensiver und monumentaler Goethisch" (13; With such natures, the expressions of their formative consciousness are nothing other than the true index of what transpires in their dark core and depths, the brightness of their fire, the logos of their eros. [...] *Werther* is therefore as genuinely Goethean as the letters to Lotte Buff and her fiancé, only at the same time more intensively and more monumentally Goethean).

A number of other critics also approach Werther as a "titan" whose frustrations mirror Goethe's. In one of his earliest studies, Dilthey describes both the young Goethe and Werther as men of genius constrained by a world that allows them little room for action. But in contrast to Goethe, Werther by nature lacks the means to defend himself against the demands of his society and is doomed to destruction (1867, 20). Viëtor, too, asserts that "Qualities which might have raised [Werther's] being to a pinnacle in friendlier times and under more favorable circumstances become his doom" (1949, 32).

Helene Herrmann's 1904 dissertation on *Die psychologischen Anschauungen des jungen Goethe und seiner Zeit* (The Psychological Views of the Young Goethe and His Times, 1904), directed by Dilthey and Erich Schmidt, similarly describes Werther as a quintessential Sturm und Drang figure bursting with vitality but prevented by the repressive structures of his era from finding a creative outlet for his energies. He thus turns inward and becomes self-destructive. Herrmann actually published only her dissertation's first chapter, which deals with Goethe's Leipzig period. The second, which treats *Werther*, did not appear in print, but it nevertheless achieved influence when her husband, Max, quoted extensively from it in his edition of the novel that same year (1904: xix–xxvi). It also, according to Stuart Atkins, has the virtue of employing "dynamic and relative" terms to describe *Werther*, rather than the "static and absolute" ones with which many critics reduce the novel to sterile theory (1948, 575).

One unique study takes the notion of *Erlebnis* to an even greater level of abstraction. Using concepts developed by Hermann Pongs (1927), Josef Michels attempts a stylistic analysis of *Werther* that reveals a higher order of "poetic experience" that is produced at the intersection of artist, symbol, and language and represents a kind of metapsychology. It is a "geistige Wirklichkeit, die wirksam ist, auch wenn sie nicht vom Individuum 'erlebt' wird" (spiritual reality that exerts an effect even if it is not 'experienced' by the individual; 1936, 11–13). Michel's "existentialist style-analysis" takes the form of detailed descriptions of stylistic devices, but these seemingly objective characterizations lead him to speculative generalizations, as here in his conclusion:

> Im "Werther" erhalten diese Erscheinungen aus der dichterischen Tiefe und Formkraft ihren besonderen Ausdruckswert. Trotz der starken Gefühlssteigerung haben die schlichten Sätze in ihrer einfachen Nebenordnung ein Ausströmen des inneren Ich, wo sich die Wirkung der

Ergriffenheit in einem Satzgefüge von vorwiegend lyrischem Eigenleben ausspricht. Die gliederreichen Perioden und feierlich ansteigenden Vordersätze, das Vorwegnehmen und neue Einsetzen, die steigende Spannung, die durch das leise Andeuten und betonte Wiederaufnehmen eines Satzteils erreicht wird, zeigen deutlich, wie der Satz über seine äußeren Grenzen hinwegklingt und in der Bewegung des inneren Ich seine Einheit findet. Durch die Mannigfaltigkeit der syntakten Verknüpfungen wird das Eigenleben des Satzgliedes betont, das hinwieder durch die besondere Lebendigkeit seiner rhythmischen Bewegung über das Inhaltlich-Gemeinte hinausführt und im dichterischen Sagen seinen Gehalt neu formt. (Michels 1936, 59–60)

[In *Werther* these phenomena derive their particular expressive value from the poetic depths and creative power of form. Despite the increasing intensity of emotion, these plain sentences, with their simple parataxis, exhibit an effusion of the inner psyche, in which the emotional effect expresses itself in a sentence constellation with a largely lyrical life of its own. The sentences, with their many protases and the emotionally augmented antecedents, the anticipations and then ensuing new beginnings, the rising tension achieved through the muted intimation and then accentuated resumption of syntactical elements all show clearly how the sentence resonates beyond its outermost borders and finds its unity in the movement of the inner psyche. The multiplicity of syntactic concatenations emphasize the clause's independent existence, which, through the vibrancy of its rhythmic movement, simultaneously leads beyond its explicit meaning and forms a new significance in the poetic utterance.]

Hans Gose, who wrote in 1921, would surely find it odd to see his monograph listed among the psychological studies of *Werther*. He himself stresses that his reading of the novel intends to extract its "Gedankengehalt" (intellectual content). Gose's sense of that term, however, brings his study closer to a portrait of Werther's psychological development than to an elucidation of the novel's ideas. While Hermann Hettner had already touched on the idea half a century earlier (1869, 142), Gose was one of the first critics to explore in detail the notion that Werther's condition is already apparent in his earliest letters, and that its origins can be traced back to events that took place before the novel begins. We are by now so accustomed to noticing the disturbing contradictions in the early letters' reports of Werther's memories, hopes, and resolves that it is hard to imagine that earlier critics largely agreed that he was a contented, if somewhat impulsive, individual until love's frustrations entered. Gose's study is the first to point out that even before Werther meets Lotte, his poor relationship with his mother, the traumatic deaths of his father and of the "friend of his youth," his guilt over his relationship with Leonore, and a general emotional mutability all have already undermined his existence (1921, 12–34). The terminology that Gose employs to make these points is misleading, however; he claims to be probing Werther's *Weltanschauung* (philosophy of life) and repeatedly refers to Werther's *dynamische* or *naturalistische Lebensauffassung* (dynamic, naturalistic concept of life) or even his religious beliefs, but these terms actually indicate a psychological structure that in some ways resembles a Freudian model: "Werthers dynamische Lebensauffassung kennt also keine dualistische Scheidung von Leib und Seele, sondern betrachtet das Menschenleben als einen organischen, körperliche und seelische Erscheinungen einheitlich umfassenden Ablauf, der allein durch das Zusammen-, Gegeneinander- und Wechselwirken mannigfaltiger Kräfte natürlich bedingt ist" (46; Werther's dynamic concept of life is thus unaware of any dualistic separation of body and mind; rather it views human life as an organic process that uniformly encompasses both corporeal and mental phenomena and whose nature is determined solely by manifold forces that are working with, against, and in alternation with one another).

Despite referring to Werther's *Denkart* (way of thinking), Gose depicts non-intellectual processes when he demonstrates how Werther seeks to fill his emotional emptiness with pantheistic feelings, imagined worlds, and attachments to children and uneducated people who, he believes, are unspoiled by self-consciousness. These "natural" environments bring him temporary but unstable happiness. His relationship with Lotte is initially satisfying, but his growing passion, fired by increasing sexual desire, eventually drives him to despair. Internal emotional forces overcome his compunctions and his sense of reality, so that his suicide is the natural outcome of these forces, rather than an act of free will or of ethical consideration (63).

Since he does not intend a rigorous psychological theory, it would be unfair to criticize Gose for failing to articulate one. In fact, if we ignore his terminology, he offers a more useful formulation than that provided by some of the earlier therapists. Still, his study does suffer from a tendency to consider Werther an objective reporter and to take what he says at face value. Much of Gose's reading of Werther's letters paraphrases them without questioning their reliability, uncritically accepting the young man's assurances that he is appreciated by the common folk, adored by children, admired by people of learning, and loved by Lotte — all shaky assumptions that, as Gose's own conclusions about Werther later suggest, rely on a problematic informant.

Robert Clark, in contrast, aims at methodological rigor. Defining the psychological novel as a "genre whose chief characteristic is the fact that the action, however symbolically or lyrically conceived, is analyzable according to the organized body of observations and principles of a consistent system of psychology" (1947, 273), he tries to relate *Werther* to an already existing system of analysis. Unaware that Georg Lukács (1936) had already done so a few years before, Clark turns to an early writing of Johann Gottfried Herder, *Übers Erkennen und Empfinden in der menschlichen Seele* (On Perception and Sensation in the Human Soul).

Herder's essay was published after *Werther*, but it existed in manuscript form in 1774, and Clark reasonably assumes that Goethe became familiar with its ideas when spending time with its author in Strasbourg in 1772. The essay proposes that, in the state of nature, the soul's three functions — sensation, cognition, and volition — act in concert. Society's need for specialization disrupts this harmony, however, unlinking the three functions and bringing them into conflict with one another. Especially introverted individuals experience this fragmentation as an *Einschränkung* (constraint), a word that appears prominently in both Herder's essay and Goethe's novel. In the extreme, this disharmonious condition can lead to insanity, but healthy individuals, even naturally introverted ones, can come to terms with this frustration through activity (*Handeln*) in the real world. Practical engagement allows them to recognize "the symbolic nature of all sensation-cognition" and thus to gain a healing insight into the beneficence of God's creation (Clark 1947, 274–78). Werther, however, turns further inward and increasingly despairs of finding solace in society, nature, or religion. In linking Herder's theory with the novel, Clark stresses that it is only one of many conceptual frameworks that help to explain *Werther*, but he extends the modest hope that a knowledge of it will aid modern readers in understanding some of the assumptions that went into the work's composition.

Stuart Atkins, in what remains one of the most influential articles on *Werther*, calls on still another eighteenth-century articulation of psychological theory. At the time he wrote his novel, Goethe was acquainted with at least two texts by the Swiss theologian, social reformer and physiognomist Johann Caspar Lavater: the third volume of *Aussichten in die Ewigkeit* (Views of Eternity, 1773) and *Predigten über das Buch Jonas* (Sermons on the Book of Jonah, 1773). Goethe discussed the first book — unfavorably — in the *Frankfurter gelehrte Anzeigen* and then later included ideas from his review in the novel (Atkins 1948, 522–26). Lavater's book of sermons had an even more important effect. When Werther's letter of July 1 reports on a discussion about the "vice" of "üble Laune" (ill humor), the fictional editor adds a footnote to tell us that we now have an excellent sermon on this topic in Lavater's series on the Book of Jonah. Atkins claims that "the reader with access to a copy of the *Predigten* who put *Werther* aside for a moment to see what Lavater had to say [. . .] would take up the novel once again much enlightened about the character of its hero and well prepared to understand the patterns of conduct which Werther exhibits" (528). This is not to say that Lavater presents a coherent psychological theory; he does, however, articulate "certain patterns of thought current at the time that Goethe conceived and wrote the novel" (533). Furthermore, his twelfth sermon, which treats ill humor specifically, posits several psychological types who suffer from this "vice" and, Atkins points out, turn out to look a good deal like Werther. Atkins is not suggesting that Goethe followed some template in constructing his figure; his primary point is to demonstrate how eighteenth-century theory sees both theological and moral questions in psychological terms.

Recent critics have gone beyond Clark's and Atkins's more tentative investigations of the psychological theories that might have informed *Werther.* Building in part on Gerhard Sauder's studies, especially his monumental *Empfindsamkeit* ("Sentiment" or "Sensibility," 1974), scholars are continuing to examine the enormous amount of eighteenth-century literature on psychology. Matthias Luserke has been particularly active in this regard (see also Flaschka 1987, 222–37; Helene Herrmann offers an excellent short summary of eighteenth-century psychological theories, 1904: 1–9; on *Werther's* use of Lavater's theories of physiognomy, see Abbott 1992). Luserke's *Bändigung der wilden Seele* (Taming the Wild Soul, 1995) describes three distinct psychological discourses at work in the Enlightenment and compares their realizations in *Werther*, in Nicolai's parody of 1775, and in Albert Christoph Kayser's now-forgotten imitation of 1778, *Adolfs gesammelte Briefe* (Adolf's Collected Letters). According to Luserke, the Age of Sensibility (*Empfindsamkeit*) seeks to cultivate the emotions in a way that expands individual inner life while still remaining consistent with societal concerns. Cold reason and unbridled passion are extremes to be avoided. Luserke distinguishes the three approaches to this project that were available at the time of *Werther's* publication. Nicolai, although once a progressive force in the Enlightenment, begins in the mid-1770s to adopt a reactionary stance ("residual discourse"); his parody of *Werther* engages in a discourse that promotes the repression of strong feeling (1995, 277–94). Kayser's novel, *Adolfs gesammelte Briefe,* participates in the "dominant discourse," which seeks to moderate the emotions without repressing them. Consistent with prevailing psychological theory, Kayser's approach tries to set all of the passions in motion, so that no single one achieves dominion over the others. Virtue, so goes the theory, is then able to emerge from the resulting balance.

Goethe's *Werther,* in contrast, represents the dynamic interplay of various approaches that Luserke labels *progredient* ("progressive," but normally used in a medical, rather than a political sense). He reads *Werther* as a psycho-historical document of a societal process. Above all it concerns itself with the emancipation of the passions as a corollary to the socio-historical bourgeois emancipation (239). To achieve this reading, he examines a number of parallel discourses from which the novel draws, especially those involving religion and, above all, the control of emotion. One example of the latter is Luserke's discussion of the contemporary literature about the use of music and dance as emotional outlets (254–60; on dance in *Werther,* see also Kittler 1980, 299, 303–4; Wellbery 1994, 182–85).

Clark Muenzer's analysis of Werther's psychological development turns to yet another Enlightenment model of human cognition, suggesting that the novel anticipates the concept of moral awareness that Kant later proposes in his *Kritik der Urteilskraft* (Critique of Judgment, 1790). "Kant's analysis begins with the imagination, the aspect of judgment that alerts the mind (through its contemplation of an object of beauty as a unified presentation of the manifold) to its ability to order the phenomenal world through concepts" (1984, 29). This first stage corresponds to Werther's early responses to nature and to his experience of Lotte before Albert's arrival. "When the concept of unity falls short, however, and the imagination fails to order what the senses have perceived, the aesthetic faculty's work for the understanding is disrupted" (30). The resulting crisis in the mind's conceptual apparatus, says Kant, is ultimately beneficial, since it leads to the development of a higher faculty: "For in reflecting on the cause of its expressive collapse, the mind comes to recognize a superior dimension unknown to it before" (30). In Kant's model, a relatively short paralysis precedes this transition to a contemplation of the sublime. In Werther's case, says Muenzer, it is much more painful and represents a "nightmarish defeat" that threatens his very self (31); nevertheless it still yields the same positive transition. Werther's failure within the empirical world leads him to achieve a transcendent personal autonomy, an internal imperative. "Werther's suicide is, in this regard, not the consequence of his mind's final collapse, but an intermediate phase in his movement toward recognizing an independent purposefulness as the basis of self-definition" (152). Muenzer's reading requires us to credit Werther's final assurances that he is completely composed when he chooses death, that his suicide is "an affirmation of his life rather than its condemnation" (34). Indeed, not only we, but also the "skeptical editor" must become convinced in order that this death truly be "an intermediate phase," for, according to Muenzer, Werther achieves in the end one more transcendence: "he sets the stage for his own transformation from a person into a book" (35). As such, he will present future readers with a fictional model of sublime human possibility (We will return to this idea in chapter 5). Muenzer's analysis advances a theme also found in the more orthodox Marxist interpretations: that, while Werther fails on one level, he achieves a higher purpose in his transition to a fictional character that presents the reader with greater human possibilities.

Jill Anne Kowalik specifically examines the eighteenth-century discourse on grief, rage, and shame, especially as it is realized in the pietist tradition, and determines that *Werther* offers "a devastating critique of pietist psychology, by which I mean a model of the mind and a theory of experience that would later inform the psychology of *Empfindsamkeit*" (1999, 78). Tracing the history of this discourse with the aid of modern psychoanalytic insights, Kowalik shows its destructive ambivalence toward the emotions. The novel, she concludes, "documents the *internal* splitting of a character and the resulting demise of one who has transformed himself into his own antagonist with the help of decades of theological demonization of his own affective life. The tragedy of his suffering rests with his extraordinary, indeed astounding, articulateness about feelings, urges, emotions, fears, and fantasies that he, unlike most of his contemporaries, was able both to describe and to disavow at once" (114).

In a somewhat related vein, Caroline Wellbery compares *Werther* with Rousseau's *La Nouvelle Héloïse* and Sophie von La Roche's *Fräulein von Sternheim* to show how Goethe's work departs from "the traditional harmonizing model of sentimentalism and its conciliatory values" (1986, 231): "In the traditional sentimental novel, the emotions serve as a means of integrating the individual into the prevailing system of norms by subjectively mirroring a well-defined external order and securing the felt conviction that accompanies the internalization of values. In *Werther*, however, the emotions no longer seem to be rooted in a moral order nor can they be substantially linked up with identifiable norms. Goethe's novel emphasizes the undefined, resonant quality of the emotions rather than attributing them to a specific moral meaning. *Werther* thus contributes to the development of a subjective and psychological literature" (231–32).

While Luserke would generally agree with this conclusion, he is anxious to introduce a more differentiated periodization. Scholars have long argued, for example, about whether to call *Werther* a Sturm und Drang text or one that belongs to *Empfindsamkeit*. Luserke finds the question irrelevant, in that it assumes an inappropriately static dichotomy. Like the whole of the Enlightenment, *Werther* carries within itself attitudes that represent overlapping developmental phases and cannot be attached solely to one movement or another.

Stuart Atkins's study, by concentrating on Lavater, does not paint nearly so broad an eighteenth-century context, but it does analyze Werther's condition in terms of modern psychological theory as well. Here Atkins finds a discrepancy. Unlike Tellenbach (1977), he concludes that Werther does not suffer from endogenous melancholia, the disorder normally associated with suicide. Its symptoms are a "feeling of worthlessness, brooding, *taedium vitae*, ineffectiveness of attempts at distraction — a pattern distorted in Werther's case because he has successfully compensated his inferiority complex" (1948, 544). Atkins finds that Werther conforms better to patterns of paranoid schizophrenia: suspiciousness, a persecution complex, illusions of grandeur, and "sudden schizophrenic transitions from calm to excitement or to violence" (544). However tragic paranoid schizophrenia may be for its victims, it does not, according to Atkins, lead to suicide. Does this discrepancy cast a shadow on Goethe's understanding of human behavior? No, Atkins claims, it emphasizes the inappropriateness of trying to fit any fictional character, and especially this one, into a system defined by rigid categories: "It cannot be too often pointed out that the interest of *Werther* is deliberately centered in the problem of how its hero will behave, not that of why he so behaves or that of what psychic disorder may account for his behavior; [...] the story of Werther is an *action* in the literal sense" (572–73). Astute readers will empathize with Werther in that they will take him as he is, accept the ambiguities of his portrayal, and not fix him in absolute categories. The danger to which too many critics succumb is to see "premises where there are only processes" (576).

Despite its influence, Atkins's essay did not end what he laments as the "ever-repeated pattern" that marks the history of *Werther* criticism: "the tendency to fill the vacuum of relativism with absolutes" (572). Thirty-seven years later, for example, Marvin Bragg still asserts that "Essentially, *Werther* is an exposition of Goethe's basic theories of psychology" (1976, 132). Nevertheless, we find most critics echoing Atkins's concerns. Hans Reiss, for example, states that "Werther is the prototype of the neurotic in the modern European novel," but he immediately cautions that "Goethe's main concern was not to describe a case of abnormal psychology" (1963, 45), adding that, "Inevitably, a psychological interpretation of the novel tends to overemphasize the diseased element of Werther's character. It can easily be seen as an attempt to attack Werther's view, to disparage it as a psychological aberration. But to do so — and to some extent, our interpretation has tended in that direction — is to do injustice to *Werther*. It produces a one-sided reading" (52–53).

The problem here, one we find in many interpretations, is an unclear concept of what is meant by "psychology." Reiss repeatedly refers to Werther's "disease," but his definition of that term remains vague. He says that the "signs and symptoms of the disease increase as the action proceeds," that an "important cause of [Werther's] disease is [...] his refusal to accept the world as it is, his inability to forget past sorrows," and that the "first outbreak of his disease" occurs after Werther has met Lotte, when "he says that he does not know whether it is day or night, and he is quite unconscious of the world around him" (42). At one point, Reiss hints at a Freudian model, telling us that "Werther's feeling springs from the dark caverns of his subconscious. His ego cannot resist it" (34). At another, he points to "images that suggest the progress of a neurosis: he is suddenly seized by a contraction of his senses, his mind becomes clouded; he feels as if someone were clutching him by the throat and he must free himself with one wild blow. Eventually the neurosis becomes all-powerful" (43). Here, as above, Reiss applies his terms loosely; while a neurosis does involve "symptoms such as insecurity, anxiety, depression, and irrational fears," it by definition does not include "psychotic symptoms such as delusions or hallucinations" (American Heritage Dictionary 2000). It is neither a "disease" nor "all-powerful" in the way Reiss claims. Nor does Reiss give any evidence for his assertion that Goethe's "portrayal is so convincing that it has stood the test of time in the light of modern psychological findings" (45).

Helmut Schmiedt is somewhat more careful in identifying Werther's pathology. With just a passing nod or two to psychoanalytic theory, he describes Werther's "extreme narcissism" in lay terms, grounding his analysis in a careful reading of the text that also takes the narrator's subjectivity into account. The etiology of Werther's condition remains vague, however. Schmiedt implies that his identification with children signals an arrested development, possibly resulting from his earliest relationship with his mother. Whatever the first cause, Schmiedt is more interested in the mother's later utilitarian, careerist ambitions for her son that fail to help him to develop a healthy interaction with the world. Instead Werther aspires to a childlike condition, in which he is at one with the natural world and protected by a maternal presence. When the circumstances do not allow Lotte to serve this function, he retreats further into fantasies of an intact family presided over by Lotte's mother and God the Father. His suicide represents the last phase of his regression (1979, 150–60; on Werther's vision of family, see also Strack 1984, 70–72). In fairness it should be pointed out that Schmiedt is ultimately concerned with distinguishing the novel's psychological determinants from societal ones (see chapter 4); his discussion of the former does not offer a rigorous psychological analysis as such, even though he includes it in his own anthology of such studies (Schmiedt 1989b). It represents more of a thematic approach, describing the novel, as did Eric Blackall, as "a man's attempt to construct an artificial world as a surrogate for reality" (Blackall 1976, 21). Each of these approaches is justified, but the two should not be confused. As Wolfgang Kaempfer reminds us, the terms "subjectivism" and "narcissistic crisis" may appear to point to the same phenomenon, but they imply very different explanations (1979, 266; for a clear elucidation of narcissism, see Kowalik 1999, 126–27).

Among the psychological approaches to Werther, psychoanalysis plays a particularly large role. Thomas Mann echoes *Werther's* early admirers when he describes the book as "a masterpiece of inevitability, an unbroken, intelligently, tenderly, and consciously constructed mosaic of emotional details, psychological moments and characteristics that together offer a picture of charm and of death" (Mann 1939, 96). For all its complexity, Mann's image of a mosaic implies a surface structure, a causal nexus made up of visible elements. Psychoanalytically oriented critics, in contrast, look beneath these elements to find an underlying, unconscious deep structure to explain the novel and/or its author.

Beginning with Freud, psychoanalysts have seen a strong connection between their discipline and imaginative works of art (see, among others, Schmiedt 1989b: 10–24), although they often disagree with one another about how to define this relationship. Mostly conscious of their own and others' methodologies, these critics tend to contrast the explanatory power of their particular theoretical frameworks with those of their colleagues, articulating the implications of their various approaches. In fact, the psychoanalytical interpretations of *Werther,* taken together, provide a history of the major developments within this field. In undertaking a survey of these studies, however, we need to bracket out those that merely avail themselves of psychoanalytic terms. When Paul Mog calls Werther's ecstatic union with nature an "oceanic feeling" (1976, 123–25), his allusion to Freud's *Das Unbehagen in der Kultur* (Civilization and Its Discontents, 1930) is not an application of psychoanalytic method; it is part of a discussion of Rousseau's cultural pessimism and of the contradiction between individual identity — here, in society — and mystical dissolution of the self. Similarly, Ignace Feuerlicht explains little by attributing Werther's suicide to the death instinct without determining how this Freudian concept applies to *Werther* in particular (1978, 479–80). Gerhard Schmidt's 1968 study of Werther's "*Krankheit zum Tode*" (sickness unto death) also concludes that *Werther* reflects an acute phase in its author's life-long "death-neurosis," as well as the general pathology of its time, but it has the virtue of drawing evidence from the work itself before comparing the results with details from Goethe's life and with analyses of other works; only then does it differentiate between the work and its author.

Any psychoanalytic approach implies certain fundamental questions: Can we reduce the creative process to unconscious conflicts? Is it appropriate to analyze fictional characters, who clearly have neither an unconscious nor the opportunity to interact with their analysts? Does a novel have its own artistic integrity, or can it be read like a rebus, as a reflection of its author's unconscious workings? Freud himself stressed that psychoanalysis does not explain poetic genius but can reveal motives that have awakened it. He justifies the analysis of artists by observing that it is particularly appealing to study the laws governing human behavior as they are realized in outstanding individuals (Freud 1933, 276). In considering such questions, Peter Fischer maintains that a great author's inner life may indeed interest the psychoanalyst, but that it is of no concern to the literary critic (1986, 206). Fictional characters, on the other hand, are fair game for analysis; a novel's hero may lack an unconscious, but its readers do not, and they will respond to its fictional representation. Similarly, whatever the ostensible subject of a novel — love, family, society, etc. — the problems that are depicted necessarily result from underlying psychological conflicts that are susceptible to analysis (207).

As noted earlier, the biggest controversy among psychologically oriented critics, whatever their persuasion, is the extent to which authors' biographies and their fictional works illuminate one another or even intersect. At the one pole are the critics who claim to find biographical associations problematic and who stress the need to interpret a text first in terms of itself and only after that — if at all — to consider the author's life. It must be said, however, that these interpreters all too often honor that principle only in the breach. In practice they treat the two realms as if they formed one seamless entity. At the other pole stands a mostly older psychoanalytical tradition, associated with early theorists like Otto Rank, Theodor Reik, and Erik Erikson, that actively treats literary works as reflections of their creator's inner conflicts. One of the most elaborate of these biographical investigations is Kurt Robert Eissler's monumental *Goethe: A Psychoanalytic Study, 1775–1786*. This detailed look at Goethe's early life draws on previous theoretical work by Rank (1912) and Brunold Springer (1926) to assert that Goethe's real subject in *Werther* "is the traumata he suffered in relation to [his sister] Cornelia" (Eissler 1963, 98): Goethe's unacknowledged incestuous feelings for his sister particularly troubled him when she married in 1773 and soon afterwards became pregnant. This situation, according to Eissler, informs the novel and explains its psychological structure. While most subsequent critics admire the enormous amount of material that Eissler assembles to support his thesis, they are troubled by the methodological problem of treating *Werther* so readily as an autobiographical document (for example, Reinhart Meyer-Kalkus 1977, 97). His study commands respect but, with some notable exceptions, exerts little influence.[5]

Surprisingly, given his fascination with Goethe, Freud's own analyses of literary works did not include *Werther*. Various of his successors did treat the novel, however, often using it self-consciously to illustrate their own schools' theories. The first such study expressly devoted to *Werther* was published in 1926 by Ernst Feise.[6] Its title, "Goethes Werther als nervöser Charakter" (Goethe's Werther as a Neurotic Figure), announces the influence of Alfred Adler, who, after breaking with Freud, published *Über den nervösen Charakter* in 1912 (translated in 1917 as *The Neurotic Constitution*). Feise attributes Werther's condition to Adler's most famous concept, the inferiority complex. Driven by feelings of his own insufficiency, and undermining himself with impossible *heteronom* (other-directed) goals, rather than *autonom* (self-directed) ones, Werther dismisses all of his own efforts toward self-actualization as either meaningless or doomed to failure. Then, faced with the effects of his self-fulfilling prophecy, he takes solace in saying "I told you so" (Feise 1926, 187–88; 193–94). He compensates for his feelings of inferiority in other ways, as well: he identifies with peasants and children, who, he imagines, lead a harmonious existence free of the self-consciousness that plagues him; he loses himself in fictional worlds or in feelings of mystical union with nature; he wallows in a fatalistic acceptance of outer forces that destroy his free will and responsibility; and he frequently imagines himself to be superior in all things, including in the extent of his suffering.

Feise shows that Werther's earliest letters already document how his sense of insufficiency and fatalistic despair alternate with manic feelings of megalomania and joy. One origin of Werther's neurosis is his difficult relationship with his mother, although here, Feise concedes, the novel does not offer the reader much direct evidence (196–97). What is certain is that Werther finds in Lotte a mother figure in whose presence he can become a protected child (211). In this sense, Lotte feeds his narcissism, just as the older, deceased "friend of his youth" once mirrored his heightened sense of self-worth (198–202). When Lotte's heart, rather than his own, becomes the object of his desire, however, Werther becomes disturbingly vulnerable (200). This kind of ambivalence defines and, in the extreme, also destroys the neurotic person. While a healthy individual exists within a rhythm of tension and release, and feels pleasure in the release phase, the neurotic lives for tension alone, not just relishing, but actually requiring the conflict between arrogant self-assertion and the anxiety of low esteem (200–201). Lotte is thus perceptive when she accuses Werther of desiring her precisely because he cannot have her. This ambivalence finally plays itself out in Werther's suicide, where he can simultaneously declare the enormity of his suffering — see what you have done to me? — and punish himself (220).

While Feise is not the first to consider the problem of analyzing a fictional character as if it were a real person, he does explicitly raise the question of whether treating poetic figures in this way does violence to a work of art. (221). By "poetic figures" (*dichterische Gestalten*) he actually means not just Werther, but also Goethe himself, for Feise maintains that any psychoanalytical approach necessarily implicates the novel's author as well as its characters. He finds a kind of solution by dividing his study: the first half "more or less" looks at Werther as if he were a living being, while the second examines the relationship between author and work (186). In the latter discussion (221–53), Feise treads lightly, however. Despite tracing the story of *Werther's* genesis in some detail, he only tentatively suggests connections between the neurotic constitution and Goethe himself. Above all he stresses two points: that Goethe did not begin his novel with the intention of presenting a case study or an abstract concept, and that proper psychoanalysis is the opposite of reductive; it enriches our understanding of the creative process. Both points rest on the assumption that the basis of all art is its deeply human quality, not its conformity to theory.

Heidi Rockwood's essay of 1980, "Jung's Psychological Types and Goethe's *Die Leiden des jungen Werthers*," represents another attempt to apply a particular school of psychoanalysis to *Werther*. In this case, Rockwood considers the "attitudes" of the conscious psyche that Carl Jung formulated and applies this matrix to the novel's main characters. These figures, she posits, are complementary and together make up a single psyche. Werther is an "introverted feeler," Albert an "extroverted thinker." "Both are so predominantly examples of their personality type and its negative aspects that they seem almost like allegorical figures" (1980, 121). Lotte, somewhat less distinctly drawn, is a "sensing type" with both introverted and extroverted characteristics, who serves as the anima for both men. At this point, Rockwood's argument takes on a circular quality. She posits a Jungian structure and then uses its assumed existence as evidence for her analysis: "Unless, however, Goethe has left us with an oddly truncated psyche, we still have to identify the representative of the dominant function, intuition" (122). Acknowledging the tenuousness of her choice, she decides that Wilhelm represents the type she requires to fill out her scheme and includes him in the structure:

> We can now say that Werther constitutes a psyche trying to realize itself as a whole, a Self, with the Ego (dominantly intuitive) mainly looking on as an outside observer, the two auxiliary functions (thinking and feeling) fighting for dominance and possession of the fourth function (sensing). Werther, the feeling component, is the loser in the struggle. Unable to obtain compatibility with the others, he, probably the only introvert in the group, abandons the struggle, seeing his sole recourse in suicide. He might have been saved if he had moved in the direction Wilhelm tried to steer him, but his one-sidedness would not permit it and therefore proved to be destructive to individuation. While the collective psyche is momentarily badly shaken by his death [. . .] there is no doubt that life will go on and in a more tranquil manner than before. (122)

This interpretation has the appeal of tidiness, as well as the virtue of viewing Werther within a relational context, rather than of seeing him as just a solitary, sick figure. But the elegance of this "surprisingly accurate image of a complete and complex human psyche" (118) has been achieved by some sleight of hand and relies on an *a priori* assumption of Jung's validity. It moves back and forth as needed between the inductive and the deductive and presents other methodological difficulties, as well. Rockwood does not, for example, explain why her interpretation is limited to just these four characters, other than to say that she needs a "quaternity" (122) to construct Jung's schema. And she herself acknowledges that the information that she uses to analyze these characters derives exclusively from Werther, a questionable source (119).

Gustav Hans Graber, a Swiss therapist best known for his work in prenatal psychology, also approaches *Werther* under Jung's influence (1958, 69–84), but with only passing reference to types. He describes Werther as a pathological case whose defense mechanisms are too weak to defend his ego from becoming lost in the unconscious self. In the maternal figures of Lotte and "Mother Nature," Werther unsuccessfully tries to regain the primal union of self with the mother that he had experienced *in utero*. His father's early death has thrust him into the oedipal situation of replacing this dead father in the relationship with the mother, a guilt-inducing development marked by ambivalence toward her: he is torn between a maternal image of nourishment and an opposing one of devouring possessiveness. While he several times responds to this conflict by fleeing, he is also compelled to reenact the oedipal triad with the mother substitute Lotte, whom he desires to possess, and the father substitute Albert, whom he wishes dead. These feelings, says Graber, fill him on the one hand with a remorse that calls for self-inflicted punishment, and on the other with an aggressive desire for revenge on Lotte and his mother. Each side of this ambivalence pushes him toward suicide.

According to Jung's concept of the mother complex, this kind of arrested development can also lead a young man to substitute a homosexual attachment in the place of a "healthier" bond with a woman. Graber finds just such a relationship between Werther and Wilhelm, whose connection, he claims, is closer, longer-lasting, and less marked by ambivalence than that between Werther and Lotte (75; for a much more sophisticated discussion of the Werther-Wilhelm-Lotte triad, see Gustafson 2003, 92–99). Here again Jungian theory trumps the evidence. As Elisabeth Auer (1999, 166) points out, Graber can reach his conclusions only by first assuming that Werther is a real human being and then speculating on a relationship that is not defined in the book. What impels him to do so is clearly a desire to fit Werther to a hypothesis. That is not to say, however, that only a Jungian approach would identify homoeroticism in the novel. Harry Slochower, whose analytic method is close to Eissler's, also concludes that "Werther's passion for Charlotte hides homoerotic and incest drives. He never becomes aware that he chooses death because he cannot free himself from his attachment to Albert nor renounce his wish for union with Charlotte, a mother-sister figure" (1975, 404).

Mel D. Faber's study determines to be rigorous in its application of psychoanalytical insights to *Werther* and carefully articulates its own theoretical framework. Without knowing Graber's work, Faber, too, concludes that the problem lies in the mother-bond:

> What the hero of this novel is faced with achieving [...] is the basic psychosexual maturity which enables the emerging individual to sever maternal, primarily oral, ties and to attain his own masculine (in this case) identity so that he may proceed in life as a separate, autonomous person able to develop relatively normal object relations with members of the opposite sex who become to him something in addition to maternal substitutes and with whom he can enjoy a union that is not unconsciously incestuous. In his subsequent attachment to Charlotte [Werther] is trying to escape the difficult task of separation [from the mother] by merging utterly with one who, as we shall see, fulfills the most exacting requirements of the Oedipal drive. In fact, *The Sorrows of Young Werther* presents us with a hero who is tragically unable to achieve psychosexual maturity, so pronounced is his fixation at the oral and Oedipal levels. (1973, 244)

Faber traces a chain of surrogates that Werther adopts in order to compensate for the original loss of the mother: "*Werther has substituted Charlotte for nature,* just as he has substituted nature for his deceased female friend, who served, in her own turn, as a substitute for the original 'heavenly' creature (here is the deepest significance of the hero's 'heavenly' imagery), the Mother" (256). A psychoanalytic understanding of the dynamics at work, Faber claims, makes these linkages apparent, letting us see how maternal, oedipal, and oral constellations of imagery are transferred from one context to another. Faber is more careful than Graber in establishing the connections among these signifiers. He uses Werther's own choice of images to demonstrate nature's maternal aspects, for example, instead of merely assuming the existence of a Mother Nature. But he works under the handicap of not reading German, which forces him to rely on Victor Lange's — admittedly excellent — translation (Lange 1949). He is usually on solid ground in his argument, but some problems arise when he approaches his "text" closely. He finds, as in the quotation above, significance in Werther's use of the word "heavenly" to refer to his friend's patience (letter of May 17) as well as to Lotte. But the original German says *göttlich* (divine), a word that Werther employs just one other time, on September 5, to describe the benefits of the imagination. "Heavenly" (*himmlisch*) is indeed frequently applied to describe Lotte, but never the friend. One could of course argue that "divine" and "heavenly" are sufficiently similar to suggest an association, but with less assurance than a direct repetition would provide. The verbal linkage breaks down completely, however, when Faber draws similar conclusions from Werther's employment of the verb "to bury." In his letter of February 20, Werther reports that he intends to "bury" Lotte's silhouette among his papers; on May 5, he tells how his mother moved from her old, idyllic town and "buried herself" in a new one. The repetition of this word leads Faber to equate the two acts, as well as the two women, symbolically and to connect them with death (262–63). But this associative leap fails when we turn to the German original. The letter of February 20 does indeed use *begraben* (to bury), but on May 5 Werther describes his mother as locking herself up (*einsperren*). Here, in other words, the burial image is Lange's, not Goethe's. In another case, Faber claims that the letter of September 5 borrows "a line from *Macbeth,* another imaginative work in which a protagonist cannot break free of destructive influences" (265). Lange's version, "My leaves are sear [*sic*] and yellow" does indeed seem redolent of Macbeth, who complains that his "way of life is fall'n into the sere, the yellow leaf" (act 5, scene 3). But the allusion, if indeed it is one, is a gratuitous addition in the translation. Werther's German says merely, "Meine Blätter werden gelb" (my leaves are turning yellow). Unless Faber is prepared to argue that a translation has as much legitimacy as the original, his associative method is clearly marred by such linguistic difficulties.

Reinhart Meyer-Kalkus's analysis, which draws on Jacques Lacan's work, concludes that Werther's pathological suffering stems from the structure of his erotic desire, which in turn springs from "eine spezifisch matriarchale 'Hominisation' unter den Bedingungen der patriarchalen Familie"

(1977, 87; a specifically matriarchal 'hominization' within the conditions of the eighteenth-century patriarchal family). Like most other psychoanalytically oriented critics, Meyer-Kalkus sees Lotte as a maternal substitute, an attempt to fill the gap created by Werther's insufficient relationship with his own mother. Unable to overcome the "mirror-phase" defined by Lacan, Werther reenacts a series of narcissistic relationships — for example, with nature, the "friend of his youth," or the Homeric world — that intend to satisfy his desire for the imagined fusion with the mother. His fixation on Lotte is a unique link in this chain of substitutions, not only because it combines the irreconcilable roles of lover, son, and brother, but also because it requires the impossible, that he become the object of Lotte's desire. The only remaining substitution at this point is death, which will symbolically overcome all of the displacements that make Werther's situation untenable (127).

Early in the second part of the novel, after unsuccessfully reenacting the desires of his "first childhood," Werther compulsively returns to the origin of this structure, his birthplace. Here, says Meyer-Kalkus, he originally lost his father not so much through death as through the mother's "foreclusion" (*Verwerfung,* or, in Lacan's terminology, *forclusion*) of the symbolic order of "the name of the father." Lacan describes a process in which the child expands the mother-son dyad to include the father, who, as an ego-ideal, comes to symbolize the larger order ("law") in which the child will participate. Part of a normal development, this dissolution of the original bond with the mother, and of a hopeless oedipal rivalry with the father, represents a "symbolic castration" that emancipates the child from its incestuous desires and its narcissistic fantasies of omnipotence — both its own and its mother's. In Werther's case, says Meyer-Kalkus, his mother occludes this maturation process by usurping the father's symbolic function; he can seek to duplicate his original fusion with her only through the increasingly psychotic construction of fantasies that serve as mother surrogates and even symbolically replace the phallus in the act of procreation. Lotte replicates this one-sidedness. Part of a matrilineal succession, she receives her maternal function at her mother's death, while her father plays a negligible role in the family. In a more abstract but parallel one-sidedness, Werther's heart by itself creates all power, joy, and misery. When Georg Christoph Lichtenberg defines the subject of sentimental fiction as a heart with testicles, he aptly describes Werther (126–31).

According to Meyer-Kalkus, the gap created by the missing father explains Werther's enthusiasm for Ossian, who seeks his forefathers' footsteps and finds instead their graves (letter of October 12). It accounts as well for his fantasy of uniting with Lotte, her mother, and God the Father in an "absolute family" (140) after death. This fragmented familial structure is not confined to *Werther,* says Meyer-Kalkus, who extends his analysis from the personal to the political, asserting that the novel achieved its popularity in part because it mirrors eighteenth century historical changes that are also reflected in bourgeois tragedy. As the nuclear family increasingly supplants the "household economy" of earlier times, the symbolic function of the father loses its transcendental authority and is forced to rely on the much shakier bond of filial affection.

Alice Kuzniar also draws on Lacan to demonstrate that Werther's "mirror-stage narcissism" is at work throughout the novel as "an iterative pattern, tracing the oscillations of the destabilized subject." Her interpretation goes beyond the notion that Werther suffers from a frustrated self-development. It asserts instead that, "From the first epistle to the end, there is no self for Werther to speak of — it is 'gone'" (1989, 23–24). Proceeding from a sense of void, he compulsively seeks to find a mirror image of his self; he briefly imagines his own coherence in a total fusion with his representations of the Other, such as Lotte or nature, but "the narcissistic sign marks only redundancy and reflects back the vacuousness and dependency out of which it arose" (18; see also Davis 1994, 108–15).

Kathryn Edmunds, too, finds a Lacanian chain of substitutions at work in *Werther*, but she sees it as leading to a positive conclusion. Though a narcissist throughout most of the novel, Werther undergoes a transformation in the act of writing his last letter to Lotte, beneficently substituting a text for his own person so that she will have an object, instead of a mere absence, for her mourning process: "He places all his hope in a mediation when he finally pulls the trigger: he wants his story to stand in his place, and as a narrative, or even as text, to provide union where he, as a person, caused strife" (1996, 49). This interpretation recalls that of Clark Muenzer (see above), in which Werther "sets the stage for his own transformation from a person to a book" (1984, 35). Whereas most critics see Werther's literary identifications as evidence of his delusional state, Edmunds regards them as "a process through which he, like Ossian, would be recorded and passed down as text" (1996, 51). His suicide becomes the final step in this altruistic transition: "His textual remains, the letters to Wilhelm and to Lotte, will represent him as he was prior to the death of his body, but they will also *be* him as he is, now that he has become 'Werther,' a literary figure, like Ossian and Christ" (60). Unlike Reinhard Assling (1981; see chapter 5), Edmunds finds this intention to be at cross-purposes with the fictional editor's role. Her argument is weakened from having to rely on speculations about Werther's motives — speculations much less convincing than Thomas Saine's contention that Werther intended his final letter to be as traumatic for Lotte as possible (1980, 342). Jill Anne Kowalik levels the more serious charge that Edmund's study is "psychoanalytically uninformed" and "beholden to pop psychological notions of 'sudden insight' or 'breakthrough'" (1999, 125). Kowalik objects to the "(Lacanianesque) belief in the omnipotence of language to accomplish a psychological task that simply could not be carried out in a single act of verbalization" (125–26).

In her published dissertation, written at the University of Stockholm, Elisabeth Auer represents yet another school of psychoanalysis, Object Relations Theory. This form of therapy was developed by Melanie Klein and continued by, among others, Auer's immediate inspiration, Donald Woods Winnicott. It emphasizes transitions in interpersonal relationships, especially the mother-child dyad, and the patient's attraction to objects that symbolize aspects of these relationships and compensate for disturbances within them. Another key concept in this theory is "splitting" (*Spaltung*), by which an imago (the subjective experience of another) is fragmented in order to eliminate an unacceptable ambiguity. Werther, for example, is unable to reconcile his early negative and positive experiences of his mother and so splits her imago into "bad" and "good" images. The most dramatic example of the former is his experience of a meaningless, all-devouring nature in the letter of August 18. But his "real" mother, from whom he is distanced, is also part of this imago. Werther fears her dominance and holds her and Wilhelm responsible for all his problems with the ambassador (1999, 179–86). The most obvious "good mother" is Lotte, who is in turn split into two parts: a narcissistic fantasy of wholeness, nurture, and intimacy, and an oedipal fantasy of a lover won from a rivalry with Albert. Because of this split, Werther can draw only brief satisfaction from his attachment to Lotte as an object (176–78).

Auer disputes the usual diagnosis of Werther's condition as narcissism. A narcissist, she points out, not only fails to display intense emotions but is also likely to hide behind success in a career. Clearly, neither condition applies in Werther's case. Instead she diagnoses a borderline personality disorder, the symptoms of which include intense but unstable relationships, dramatic mood swings, an inability to sustain work, feelings of deprivation, a loss of contact with reality, and, sometimes, suicide (95–112). The cause of this affliction lies in a disturbance in the early mother-child dyad. Object Relations Theory stresses that all infants must come to terms with the frustration and anxiety of separation from the nurturing mother. This crucial early phase is difficult to negotiate under the best of circumstances, but Werther carries the symptoms of a traumatic experience that has completely interrupted it. This disturbance is particularly evident in the many transitional objects that he adopts: things, people, or even fantasies that become fetishes meant to serve as at least temporary surrogates for a lost object, ultimately the mother. Such transitional objects can include Lotte herself, her gaze, her favorite song, articles of clothing associated with her — Werther's blue coat or Lotte's pink bow — her silhouette, or a servant who has recently been in her presence. They extend to other mother-figures he meets, as well as to the "friend of his youth." They can also include objects less obviously tied to a mother fixation: Homer, Ossian, children, the two walnut trees at the vicarage, and so on.

Auer identifies a number of passages that suggest that Werther has regressed to an anal stage. One describes his pained reaction when Lotte distributes to others the oranges that he has given to her as a gift, something that Auer associates with the sense of rejection that, according to Freud, a child in the anal phase feels when the mother disposes of its feces (190; for an alternative interpretation of this scene, see Roland Barthes 1977, 110–11). Anal-retentive compulsions are also suggested by the book's many reported fears of losing money, its preoccupation with settling debts, and its concerns with collecting an inheritance (151). Not just Werther, but also other figures exhibit these pecuniary concerns, including the schoolmaster's son-in-law, the widow's brother in the farmhand episode, and Albert. Surprisingly, Auer does not cite the novel's various images of digestion and blockage that would contribute to her argument (compare Kurz 1982, 106; Renner 1985; Duncan 1987).

Throughout her study, Auer repeatedly stresses that Werther is a fictional construct with no existence outside the text and continually refers to him as the *Werther-Gestalt* (Werther-figure). As such, he cannot be said to have had a childhood separate from what is described in the book, nor can he be diagnosed as an actual borderline personality — we can state only that the characteristics attributed to him in the novel are consistent with that disorder. Even then, Auer notes, we need to be reminded that such maladies are themselves theoretical abstractions, that modern psychoanalysis prefers descriptions of dynamic, interpersonal processes to static classifications (1999, 102).

Auer is further careful to acknowledge that we cannot extend a diagnosis of the book's figures to include their author; *Werther* is an artistic achievement with its own aesthetic integrity. At the same time, however, the ultimate source of these characteristics, indeed, of all of the novel's themes, are Goethe's unconscious desires, and it can, says Auer, be instructive to proceed in the other direction, to use elements from the author's biography to illuminate the text (122). Actually, she makes such comparisons only rarely, but she does go readily from book to author, despite her own cautions and her stated goal of simply pointing to "unbewusste und implizierte Phantasien, Abwehrmechanismen, Objektbeziehungen und Beziehungskonflikte *im Text*" (101; unconscious and implied fantasies, defense mechanisms, object relations and relational conflicts *within the text*). Even this assurance contains a contradiction, for the unconscious and the act of implication obviously reside in the author, not the text. Auer hopes to navigate around this inconsistency with the concept of an "implied author" (for example, 147), but in effect she also uses the novel to try to understand Goethe himself: "Goethes Übergangsobjekt ist natürlich der Werther-Roman, den er m.E. *unter anderem* aus dem Grund schreiben musste, um die Tatsache (in der äußerlichen Wirklichkeit) zu bewältigen, dass sowohl die Wetlarer Lotte als auch seine Schwester Cornelia mit ihrem ersten Kind schanger waren" (123; Goethe's transitional object is of course the Werther-novel, which, in my opinion, he had to write, *among other reasons,* to come to terms with the fact (in external reality) that the Wetzlar Lotte and his sister Cornelia were both pregnant with their first child).

Christel Zahlmann offers a variation within Object Relations Theory, drawing on the concept of "primary love" that was developed by the Hungarian psychoanalyst Michael Balint. This term describes an egoistic object relation, a passive, one-sided love that "does not recognize any difference between one's own interests and the interests of the object, it assumes as a matter of fact that the partner's desires are identical with one's own. Claims of the object which go beyond this harmony are intolerable, they call forth anxiety or aggressiveness" (Balint 1950, 270). Such a relationship is appropriate to the early child-mother dyad, but it also, according to Zahlmann, characterizes Werther's love for the "friend of his youth." The traumatic loss of this relationship through death fills Werther with unconscious guilt and rage, and his attempts to replicate it with Lotte are marked by all of the attendant conflicts. Only at the moment in which she furnishes the pistols that end his life — that is, combines the functions of "good" and "bad" object — does he again achieve an absolute and eternal union in a primary love (Zahlmann 1987, 62–63).

Wolfgang Kaempfer, finally, represents one other school of psychoanalysis, Self-psychology. He employs the terminology of Heinz Kohut to stress that it is Werther's narcissism, present in the very first letter, and not his frustrated love, that serves as his death's root cause. Lotte is merely a self-object who gives shape to his motivation for suicide (1979, 285–94).

In these various psychoanalytical interpretations we find a certain unity. Almost everyone agrees that Werther's capacity for interaction with the world has been compromised at an early stage of his development, and that unconscious motivations compel him to revert to that point. His love for Lotte is an unconscious attempt to realize an ideal version of his first relationship with his mother, and it is necessarily frustrated by the ambiguities of the actual relationship. The critics' interpretations differ about the nature and timing of his primary dysfunction, as well as about the terminology best used to describe it. But whether his problem began in the prenatal, oral, anal, or oedipal stages; whether he is a narcissist or borderline personality; and whether Lotte is a mother-substitute, surrogate sister, transitional object, self-object, or a reenactment of a primary union or primary love — all psychoanalytic interpreters conclude, as does Werther himself, that his condition and suicide are determined by forces beyond his conscious control.

At the same time, all of the studies explicitly or implicitly address the question that first arose immediately after *Werther's* publication, and which we will examine further in chapter 5: what is the relationship between the book and its author?

Notes

[1] The abbreviation *HA* (Hamburger Ausgabe) refers to Goethe's *Werke,* ed. Erich Trunz, published in Hamburg by Wegner, 1961–64.

[2] See Fuchs and Milar 2003, 1–6. Psychiatry became an academic specialty somewhat earlier; the University of Leipzig began offering lectures on psychiatry and neurology in the 1780s and established Europe's first chair of psychiatry in 1811 (Steinberg and Angermeyer 2002).

[3] Victor Lange (1970, 141) describes Carus as an important neurologist and psychotherapist, but his specialty was in fact gynecology. He did lecture and write on psychological topics, however, including the subconscious and phrenology (see Hans Krey's afterword in Carus 1843, 211–45).

[4] Klaus Oettinger advances this same very same argument again 107 years later, when he takes issue with Klaus Scherpe's contention (1970, 76) that *Werther* is not a *Krankengeschichte* (history of an illness). At the same time, Oettinger accepts Scherpe's political approach, described in chapter 4, by ascribing Werther's "abnormality" to society's frustration of his legitimate need for a liberated existence (1976, 69–70).

[5] Two such exceptions are Rüdiger Scholz and Peter Fischer, who together translated Eissler's book into German in 1983–85. Their own *Werther* studies (1988 and 1986), though psychoanalytically based, will be considered primarily in chapter 4, which discusses political interpretations.

[6] Feise was born in 1884. His earlier writings (e.g. 1914a, 1914b, 1917) do not reflect this interest in psychoanalysis, which seems to have begun later — the edition of Adler that he cites is from 1922. His own career experienced a hiatus around this time: in the anti-German hysteria of 1917 he lost his assistant professorship at the University of Wisconsin and worked as a plumber and electrician until the end of the war. He briefly taught at Aleman College in Mexico City and, in 1924, returned to the United States and the Ohio State University for three years before moving to Johns Hopkins for the rest of his career. He died in 1966.

Works Cited

Abbott, Scott. 1992. "The Semiotics of 'Young Werther.'" *Goethe Yearbook* 6 (1992): 41–65.

Assling, Reinhard. 1981. *"Werthers Leiden": Die ästhetische Rebellion der Innerlichkeit.* Frankfurt am Main, Bern: Lang.

Atkins, Stuart P. 1948. "J. C. Lavater and Goethe: Problems of Psychology and Theology in *Die Leiden des jungen Werther.*" *PMLA* 63 (1948): 520–76.

Auer, Elisabeth. 1999. *"Selbstmord begehen zu wollen ist wie ein Gedicht zu schreiben": Eine psychoanalytische Studie zu Goethes Briefroman "Die Leiden des jungen Werther."* Stockholm: Almqvist & Wiksell.

Balint, Michael. 1950. "Early Developmental States of the Ego: Primary Object Love." *International Journal of Psycho-Analysis* 30 (1950): 265–73.

Barthes, Roland. 1977. *A Lover's Discourse: Fragments.* Trans. Richard Howard. New York: Hill & Wang, 1978.

Bickelmann, Ingeborg. 1937. *Goethes "Werther" im Urteil des 19. Jahrhunderts. (Romantik bis Naturalismus 1830–1880).* Diss., Frankfurt am Main.

Blackall, Eric A. 1976. *Goethe and the Novel.* Ithaca: Cornell UP.

Bragg, Marvin. 1976. "The Psychological Elements of 'Werther.'" *South Central Bulletin* 36 (1976): 132–37.

Carus, Carl Gustav. 1843. *Goethe, zu dessen näherem Verständnis.* Leipzig: Weichardt. Repr., ed. Hans Krey, Dresden: Jess, 1949.

Clark, Robert T. 1947. "The Psychological Framework of Goethe's 'Werther.'" *JEGP* 46 (1947): 273–78.

Davis, William Stephen. 1994. "The Intensification of the Body in Goethe's *Die Leiden des jungen Werther.*" *The Germanic Review* 69 (1994): 106–17.

Diez, Max. 1936. "The Principle of the Dominant Metaphor in Goethe's *Werther.*" *PMLA* 51 (1936): 824–41, 985–1006.

Dilthey, Wilhelm. 1867. "Die dichterische und philosophische Bewegung in Deutschland, 1770–1800." In *Gesammelte Schriften* 5:12–27. Leipzig: Teubner, 1924.

———. 1887. *Die Einbildungskraft des Dichters.* In *Gesammelte Schriften* 6:103–241. Leipzig: Teubner, 1924.

Duncan, Bruce. 1987. "Werther's Reflections on the Tenth of May." In *Exile and Enlightenment. Studies in Honor of Guy Stern,* 1–10. Detroit: Wayne State UP.

———. 2003. "Sturm und Drang Passions and Eighteenth-Century Psychology." In *Literature of the Sturm und Drang,* ed. David Hill, 46–68. Rochester, NY: Camden House.

Düntzer, Heinrich. 1849. *Zu Goethes Jubelfeier.* In *Studien zu Goethes Werken,* 89–257. Elberfeld und Iserlohn: Baedeker.

Eckermann, Johann Peter. 1824. *Gespräche mit Goethe in den letzten Jahren seines Lebens.* Ed. Gustav Moldenhauer. Vol. 3. Leipzig: Reclam, 1884.

Edmunds, Kathryn. 1996. "'Der Gesang soll deinen Namen erhalten': Ossian, Werther, and Texts of/for Mourning." *Goethe Yearbook* 8 (1996): 45–65.

Eichendorff, Joseph, Freiherr von. 1851. *Der deutsche Roman des achtzehnten Jahrhunderts in seinem Verhältniß zum Christenthum.* Vol. 8, part 2 of *Sämtliche Werke: Historisch-kritische Ausgabe,* ed. Wolfram Mauser. Regensburg: Habbel, 1965.

Eissler, Kurt Robert. 1963. *Goethe: A Psychoanalytic Study, 1775–1786.* Detroit: Wayne State UP.

Faber, M. D. 1973. "The Suicide of Young Werther." *Psychoanalytical Review* 60 (1973): 239–76.

Feise, Ernst, ed. 1914a. *"Die Leiden des jungen Werthers," von Johann Wolfgang Goethe*. With a Critical Essay. New York: Oxford UP.

———. 1914b. "Zu Entstehung, Problem und Technik von Goethes 'Werther.'" *JEGP* 13 (1914): 1–36.

———. 1917. "Lessings 'Emilia Galotti' und Goethes 'Werther.'" *Modern Philology* 15 (1917): 321–38.

———. 1926. "Goethes Werther als nervöser Charakter." *Germanic Review* 1 (1926): 185–253.

Feuerlicht, Ignace. 1978. "Werther's Suicide: Instinct, Reasons and Defense." *The German Quarterly* 51 (1978): 476–92.

Fischer, Peter. 1986. "Familienauftritte: Goethes Phantasiewelt und die Konstruktion des 'Werther'-Romans." In Schmiedt 1989a, 189–220.

Flaschka, Horst. 1987. *Goethes "Werther": Werkkontextuelle Deskription und Analyse*. Munich: Fink.

Freud, Sigmund. 1933. "Vorwort" to *Edgar Poe, étude psychoanalytique*, by Marie Bonaparte. In *Gesammelte Werke: Chronologisch geordnet*, ed. Anna Freud et al., 16:276. Frankfurt am Main: Fischer, 1968–87.

Fuchs, Alfred H., and Milar, Katherine S. 2003. "Psychology as a Science." In *History of Psychology*, vol. 1 of *Handbook of Psychology*, ed. Donald K. Freedheim, 1–26. Hoboken: Wiley.

Goethe, Johann Wolfgang von. 1813. Ed. Erich Trunz. Vol. 9 of *Werke*. Hamburg: Wegner, 1961–64. (This Hamburg edition of Goethe's works is cited in the text as *HA*).

Gose, Hans. 1921. *Goethes "Werther."* Halle an der Saale: Niemeyer. Reprint Walluf bei Wiesbaden: Sändig, 1973.

Graber, Gustav Hans. 1958. "Goethes Werther: Versuch einer tiefenpsychologischen Pathographie." In Schmiedt 1989a, 69–84.

Gundolf, Friedrich. 1916. *Goethe*. Berlin: Bondi, 1920.

Gustafson, Susan E. 2003. *Men Desiring Men: The Poetry of Same-Sex Identity and Desire in German Classicism*. Detroit: Wayne State UP.

Herder, Johann Gottfried. 1774. *Übers Erkennen und Empfinden in der menschlichen Seele*. Vol. 8. of *Sämmtliche Werke*, ed. Bernhard Suphan. Berlin: Weidmann, 1902.

Herrmann, Hans Peter, ed. 1994. *Goethes "Werther": Kritik und Forschung*. Darmstadt: Wissenschaftliche Buchgesellschaft.

Herrmann, Helene. 1904. *Die psychologischen Anschauungen des jungen Goethe und seiner Zeit*. Diss., Berlin.

Herrmann, Max. 1904. Introduction to *Goethes Sämtliche Werke: Jubiläums-Ausgabe*, 16:v–xli. Stuttgart and Berlin: Cotta.

Hettner, Hermann. 1869. *Literaturgeschichte des achtzehnten Jahrhunderts*. Pt. 3, book 3, 1. Braunschweig: Vieweg, 1894.

Hillebrand, Karl. 1885. "Die Werther-Krankheit in Europa." In *Völker und Menschen*, 283–320. Strassburg: Trübner, 1914.

Jenkins, Sylvia P. 1992. "The Depiction of Mental Disorder in 'Die Leiden des jungen Werthers' and 'Torquato Tasso' and Its Place in the Thematic Structure of the Works." *Publications of the English Goethe Society* 62 (1991/92): 96–118.

Kaempfer, Wolfgang. 1979. "Das Ich und der Tod in Goethes 'Werther.'" In Hans Peter Herrmann, 1994, 266–94.

Kittler, Friedrich. 1980. "Autorschaft und Liebe." In Hans Peter Herrmann, 1994, 295–316.

Kowalik, Jill Anne. 1999. "Pietist Grief, Empfindsamkeit, and Werther." *Goethe Yearbook* 9 (1999): 77–130.

Kurz, Gerhard. 1982. "Werther als Künstler." In *Invaliden des Apoll: Motive und Mythen des Dichterleids,* ed. Herbert Anton, 95–112. Munich: Fink.

Kuzniar, Alice. 1989. "The Misrepresentations of Self: Werther versus Goethe." *Mosaic* 22 (1989): 15–28.

Lange, Victor, ed. and trans. 1949. *Johann Wolfgang von Goethe, "The Sorrows of Young Werther," "The New Melusina," "Novelle."* New York: Holt, Rinehart & Winston.

———. 1970. "Goethe in psychologischer und ästhetischer Sicht." In *Psychologie in der Literaturwissenschaft: Amherster Kolloquium zur Modernen Deutschen Literatur (4th: 1970),* ed. Wolfgang Paulsen, 140–56. Heidelberg: Stiehm, 1971.

Lukács, Georg. 1936. "'Die Leiden des jungen Werther.'" In Hans Peter Herrmann, 1994, 39–57.

Luserke, Matthias. 1995. *Die Bändigung der wilden Seele: Literatur und Leidenschaft in der Aufklärung.* Stuttgart: Metzler.

Mann, Thomas. 1939. "Goethes 'Werther.'" In *Goethes "Werther": Kritik und Forschung,* ed. Hans Peter Herrmann, 1994, 85–97.

Menzel, Wolfgang. 1828. *Die deutsche Literatur.* Stuttgart: Gebrüder Franckh, 1828. In English, *German Literature,* trans. C. C. Felton, vol. 3. Boston: Hilliard, Gray, 1840.

Meyer, Richard Moritz. 1901. "Goethe als Psycholog." *Goethe-Jahrbuch* 22 (1901): 3*–26*.

Meyer-Kalkus, Reinhart. 1977. "Werthers Krankheit zum Tode: Pathologie und Familie in der Empfindsamkeit." In Schmiedt 1989a, 85–146.

Michels, Josef. 1936. *Goethes "Werther": Beiträge zum Formproblem des jungen Goethe.* Diss., Kiel.

Möbius, Paul Julius. 1898. *Über das Pathologische bei Goethe.* Leipzig: Barth. Repr. Munich: Matthes & Seitz, 1983.

Mog, Paul. 1976. *Ratio und Gefühlskultur: Studien zur Psychogenese und Literatur im 18. Jahrhundert.* Tübingen: Niemeyer, 1976.

Muenzer, Clark. 1984. *Figures of Identity: Goethe's Novels and the Enigmatic Self.* University Park: Penn State UP.

Oettinger, Klaus. 1976. "'Eine Krankheit zum Tode': Zum Skandal um Werthers Selbstmord." *Deutschunterricht* 28 (1976): 55–74.

Pongs, Hermann. 1927. *Das Bild in der Dichtung.* Vol. 1: *Versuch einer Morphologie der metaphorischen Formen.* Marburg: Elwert.

Prutz, Robert Eduard. 1856. *Goethe, eine biographische Schilderung.* Leipzig: Brockhaus.

Rank, Otto. 1912. *Das Inzest-Motiv in Dichtung und Sage: Grundzüge einer Psychologie des dichterischen Schaffens.* Leipzig: Deuticke, 1926.

Reiss, Hans S. 1963. *Goethe's Novels.* New York: St. Martin, 1969.

Renner, Karl N. 1985. "'Laß das Büchlein dein Freund seyn.' Goethes Roman 'Die Leiden des jungen Werther' und die Diätetik der Aufklärung." In *Zur Sozialgeschichte der deutschen Literatur von der Aufklärung bis zur Jahrhundertwende,* ed. Günter Häntzschel et al., 1–20. Tübingen: Niemeyer.

Rockwood, Heidi. 1980. "Jung's Psychological Types and Goethe's 'Die Leiden des jungen Werthers.'" *The Germanic Review* 55 (1980): 118–23.

Saine, Thomas P. 1980. "Passion and Aggression: The Meaning of Werther's Last Letter." *Orbis litterarum* 35 (1980): 327–56.

Sauder, Gerhard. 1974. *Voraussetzungen und Elemente.* Vol. 1 of *Empfindsamkeit.* Stuttgart: Metzler.

Scherpe, Klaus R. 1970. *Vier Wertherschriften aus dem Jahre 1775 in Faksimile.* Appendix to *"Werther" und Wertherwirkung: Zum Syndrom bürgerlicher Gesellschaftsordnung im 18. Jahrhundert.* Bad Homburg: Gehlen.

Schmidt, Gerhard. 1968. *Die Krankheit zum Tode: Goethes Todesneurose.* Stuttgart: Enke.

Schmiedt, Helmut. 1979. "Woran scheitert Werther?" In Schmiedt 1989a, 147–72.

Schmiedt, Helmut, ed. 1989a. *"Wie froh bin ich, dass ich weg bin!": Goethes Roman "Die Leiden des jungen Werther" in literaturpsychologischer Sicht.* Würzburg: Königshausen & Neumann.

———. 1989b. "Einleitung: Werther und die Geschichte der Literaturpsychologie." Introd. to Schmiedt 1989.

Scholz, Rüdiger. 1988. "Frühe Zerfallserscheinungen des bürgerlichen Selbst." *Jahrbuch der Psychoanalyse* 23 (1988): 213–41.

Schubart, Christian Friedrich Daniel. 1774. Review of *Werther. Deutsche Chronik* (December 5, 1774). Repr. in *Der junge Goethe im zeitgenössischen Urteil,* ed. Peter Müller, 205–6. Berlin: Akademie Verlag, 1969.

Siebers, Tobin. 1993. "The Werther Effect: The Esthetics of Suicide." *Mosaic* 26 (1993): 15–34.

Slochower, Harry. 1975. "Suicides in Literature: Their Ego Function." *American Imago* 32 (1975): 389–416.

Springer, Brunold. 1926. *Der Schlüssel zu Goethes Liebesleben: Ein Versuch.* Berlin: Verlag der Neuen Generation.

Steinberg, Holger, and M. C. Angermeyer. 2002. "Two Hundred Years of Psychiatry at Leipzig University: An Overview." *History of Psychiatry* 13 (2002): 267–83.

Strack, Friedrich. 1984. "Vater, Söhne und die Krise der Familie in Goethes Werk." *Jahrbuch des freien deutschen Hochstifts* (1984): 57–87.

Tellenbach, Hubertus. 1960. "Gestalten der Melancholie." *Jahrbuch für Psychologie, Psychotherapie und medizinische Anthropologie* 7 (1960): 9–26.

———. 1977. "The Suicide of the 'Young Werther' and the Consequences for the Circumstances of Suicide of Endogenic Melancholics." *Israel Annals of Psych. & Related Disciplines* 15 (1977): 16–21.

Viëtor, Karl. 1949. "La maladie du siècle." In *Goethe: A Collection of Essays*, ed. Victor Lange, 26–32. Englewood Cliffs, NJ: Prentice-Hall, 1968.

Wellbery, Caroline. 1986. "From Mirrors to Images: The Transformation of Sentimental Paradigms in Goethe's *The Sorrows of Young Werther*." *Studies in Romanticism* 25 (1986): 231–49.

Wellbery, David E. 1994. "Morphisms of the Phantasmatic Body: Goethe's *The Sorrows of Young Werther*." In *Body and Text in the Eighteenth Century*, ed. Veronica Kelly and Dorothea von Mücke, 181–208. Stanford: Stanford UP.

Wellek, René. 1965. *The Later Nineteenth Century*. Vol. 4 of *A History of Modern Criticism: 1750–1950*. New Haven: Yale UP.

Wille, Ludwig. 1877. *Goethe's Werther und seine Zeit: Eine psychiatrisch-litterarische Studie*. Basel: Schweighauser.

Zahlmann, Christel. 1987. "Werther als Tantalus: Zu seiner Angst vor der Liebe." *Text & Kontext* 15 (1987): 43–69.

Zimmermann, Georg. 1869. "Werther's Leiden und der literarische Kampf um sie." *Herrigs Archiv* 45 (1869): 241–98.

4: Political Interpretations

*W*ERTHER INVITES A POLITICAL APPROACH, in addition to a psychological one. Not only does it portray a wide spectrum of society, from farmhands to nobility, but several of Werther's letters contain reflections on the prevailing class system. These societal implications, we have already seen, caused the novel's earliest critics to consider the book a threat — welcome or not — to the established order. This response continued over the next two centuries, assuming various forms that reflect historical developments, from the rise of liberal nationalism through conservative nationalism to the Cold War clash between socialism and liberal democracy. Over time, the sometimes strident debate about the novel's politics has revolved primarily around two fundamental issues: the extent to which identifiable social forces impinge on Werther's behavior and the question of whether or not the novel reflects or even promotes historical change.

In reviewing these political interpretations, however, we must remind ourselves of Peter Hohendahl's warning to "treat with some reserve the notions that historical development proceeds either continuously or discontinuously and that there exist particular historical situations in which certain tendencies have dominated while others have withdrawn into subordinate roles" (1985b, 180). Literary criticism is in fact far more motley than historical surveys, including this one, would suggest, and the patterns that do emerge at least partly reflect scholarly convenience. In short, all generalizations should be taken with a grain of salt.

Werther's first critics consider the psychological and the political to be of a piece when they laud or fault its hero for embodying his generation's emotional concerns; they delight or despair in the thought that he represents a new phase in Germany, one defined by the assertion of subjective values. This conflation of the two perspectives, as we saw in chapter 3, can lead to ambivalence. As Martin Swales points out, "Whereas the psychological issue provides us essentially with a critique of Werther, the novel's social dimension gives us a sense that, however imperfectly focused Werther's disparagement of the outer world may be, there is yet a measure of justification for some of his responses" (1987, 48–49). A failure to distinguish the two explanations creates a conflict: we grow impatient with Werther for not getting a grip on life and simultaneously sympathize with him for being subject to overwhelming forces. One traditional response to this ambivalence, as the previous chapter shows, is to contrast Werther's weakness with Goethe's own strength in coping with *Werther-Krankheit* (Werther-disease).

No matter how they judge Werther, however, most nineteenth-century observers, including Goethe himself, begin to characterize "Wertherism" as "a kind of blind struggle against the evils that lay around it" (Carlyle 1838, 208–9). What these evils are depends of course on the commentators' own political inclinations. Some Germans, soon joined by British and American commentators, define it as a European-wide phenomenon, a kind of general malaise of the age. Even nineteenth-century critics who stress *Werther's* special place in German national literature often hold this view. Karl Hillebrand's *Völker und Menschen,* for example, equates "Wertherism" with "Byronism" and defines it as a moral disease that struck victims all over Europe (1885, 283; see also Vilmar 1845, 400–403 and Taylor 1879, 304–15). Certain twentieth-century comparatists (for example, Wilson 1975, Siebers 1993) still define *Werther-Krankheit* as part of European Romanticism, considering it to be a chapter in the intellectual history of the entire continent, rather than a product of the specific German *misère* that Friedrich Engels describes (1845).

Most reviewers, however, agree that Werther's malaise derived in some measure from Germany's political impotence and resulting lack of a national identity. This view predominated especially in the period before 1848, when critics on both the right and the left were apt to treat the history of literature as a medium for promoting national feeling (see Fohrmann 1991). Gustav Schlesier, writing in 1834, claims that the literary critic's proper role is helping to get the history of his people onto its feet (cited by Hohendahl 1985b, 203), and Georg Gottfried Gervinus, for all his disgust with Werther's passivity, values the novel's role in helping German national literature to break away from foreign influences (1835, 474–78). While the Young Germans Karl Gutzkow and Theodor Mundt regret *Werther's* lack of an overtly political component, they too find an implicit protest in the novel's aesthetic innovations (cited by Bickelmann 1937, 25–27).

Looking back from the perspective of 1859, the liberal Robert Prutz sees the restoration period of the 1820s as a kind of dark ages in which only literary history afforded some form of public life, keeping alive the patriotic hopes of the nation and supporting the notion of German unity (1859, 3). As a permitted public sphere, then, literary history of the time enabled critics to wage their own immediate political battles (see Batts 1993, 1–33). Though they explicitly ascribed Werther's frustrations to an eighteenth-century malady, they were able to suggest parallels to their own situation as well. For example, Friedrich Christoph Schlosser's history of the eighteenth century, published in 1843, describes *Werther* as part of an energetic youth movement that disturbed the encrusted structures of its time, but Schlosser simultaneously invites his readers to see that situation as analogous to their own: "Die aristokratischen Magistrate unserer sogenannten freien Reichsstädte, die steifen Höfe, die pedantischen

Universitäten, die despotischen Beamten und die im Dunkeln, im Style des siebenzehnten Jahrhunderts dekretirenden Kanzleien der Juristen erschracken nicht wenig, als ihrer Polizei und Gravität zum Trotz sich eine ultraliberale Generation von Schriftstellern zu erheben drohte, die alle Regel und alle Ordnung und Zucht als altmodisch verschmähte" (1843, 148; The aristocratic magistrates of our so-called Free Imperial Cities, the rigid courts, the pedantic universities, the despotic officials, and the juristic chancelleries that issued their decrees in darkness, in the style of the seventeenth century, were not a little terrified when, despite their police and seriousness of purpose, an ultraliberal generation of writers threatened to rise up, disparaging all rules and all order and decorum as old-fashioned). Schlosser extends the object of his interpretation to include *Werther's* earliest reception — anticipating a strategy employed later by Marxist interpreters. While the novel itself, he claims, is an artistic achievement independent of any moral or political message, few critics in a culturally retrograde Germany were able to recognize its aesthetic purpose. Most of Goethe's contemporaries comprehended only the text's tertiary aspects, such as its real-life models or its depiction of suicide (152). If we are to gain a true picture of the political forces at work, says Schlosser, we must scrutinize these critical responses, rather than the work itself. When he does just that and describes what he calls the ecclesiastical zealots, prosaic philistines, and insipid "weise Männer Berlins" (wise men of Berlin) who attacked the novel, Schlosser's tone changes dramatically. He presents a truly eccentric version of the controversy surrounding *Werther's* first reception, reporting that the crusading forces of reaction, with Pastor Melchior Goeze "mit der Fahne des bedrängten Zions an ihrer Spitze" (at their head, waving the banner of hard-pressed Zion), produced a popular counter-reaction. The people (*Volk*) began to see, if only dimly, the light that was then dawning in Germany; they were aroused, and ran wild (*tobte*). The cities and the princes' police joined together to fight the "Männer des Lichts" (men of light), but the latter were in the end victorious. Just in case his liberal readers might miss the point, Schlosser adds that he and they "verzagen daher auch nicht, wenn die Wächter Zions jetzt aufs neue schreien" (will thus also not quail when the guardians of Zion again raise their cry).[1] He then quotes a few passages from Goeze's review of *Werther* to remind his own readers of where, as he puts it, the pious rantings of zealots can still lead, and of how blind Lutheran orthodoxy subverts the nation's literature (154). And lest one think that Goeze was merely an isolated bible-thumper, Schlosser relates how the police and courts stood shoulder-to-shoulder with the conservative Lutherans, even in the Imperial Free City of Frankfurt (155). Schlosser's language makes it clear that he is describing not a past literary dispute so much as the coming liberal revolution. Nor is he alone in employing this tactic. Karl Grün, writing three years later, also credits *Werther* with revealing the essential rottenness of society by attacking its religious-philosophical foundation (1846, 95). In this way, Grün maintains, the novel prepared the ground for the French Revolution (84). Johannes Scherr, on the other hand, is even more direct, seeing *Werther* as an active protest against the social structures of its time and thus as a precursor to the upheavals of 1848 (quoted by Bickelmann 1937, 33).

In general, however, left-leaning critics before 1848 disparage Werther for being incapable of real political action (for example, Mundt 1834, 26). Friedrich Engels derisively mocks Grün's interpretation and accuses him of confusing genuine social criticism with Werther's lamentations about the discrepancy between bourgeois reality and his equally bourgeois illusions. Werther, says Engels, is a "schwärmerischer Tränensack" (dreamy lachrymal sack; Engels 1847, 235).

The Wilhelminian Era, in contrast, is by and large satisfied with the sense of national purpose that a united Germany has granted, and its critics look back with some degree of smugness on *Werther's* "protest against a condition of society which cannot make worthy use of the brilliant talents of an ardent youth" (Scherer 1886, 113; see also, among others, Koldewey 1881, 182; Hirsch 1885, 674). Werther, they imply, would obviously have fared better under the Kaiser. Within this general unanimity, however, come variations: Michael Bernays characterizes Werther as participating in the Sturm und Drang's general emancipation of inner forces (1875: xxxii); Wilhelm Dilthey sees him as entering unarmed into an unequal struggle between genius and society, with predictably tragic results (1867, 20); the liberal Wilhelm Scherer cites the novel's protest "against inequality of classes and the haughtiness of the nobility" (1886, 113) but also emphasizes that its influence was evolutionary in character, rather than revolutionary, especially after the appearance of the "toned-down" edition of 1787 (150); the more conservative Julian Schmidt couches his remarks on *Werther* in bellicose terms: it is the fanfare that called the youth of its time into battle against society's arbitrary rules (Schmidt 1861, 185). Though predominant in the Second Reich, this kind of diagnosis also persists long afterwards. In 1949, for example, Karl Viëtor still claims that the cause of Werther's disease "lies in the fatal conditions under which the intellectual young men of the age had to live. Since the age denied them the opportunity to act greatly, they were left with no other satisfaction than to dream and feel greatly" (32).

These nineteenth-century commentators, who locate the novel's social criticism in Werther's inability to realize his subjective values, represent the mainstream. But some critics on the left are more specific in their attacks against the social system. Another, more overtly political strain begins to emerge with time, as investigators devote more attention to the class distinctions of which Werther himself is conscious. One passage, from his letter of December 24, assumes particular significance: "Was mich am meisten neckt, sind die fatalen bürgerlichen Verhältnisse. Zwar weiß ich so gut wie einer, wie nötig der Unterschied der Stände ist, wie viel Vorteile er mir selbst verschafft: nur soll er mir nicht eben gerade im Wege stehen, wo ich noch ein wenig Freude, einen Schimmer von Glück auf dieser Erde genießen könnte" (What irritates me most are the wretched circumstances of bourgeois society. Of course I know as well as anybody how necessary differences in rank are, and how many advantages I gain from them. But they should not be an obstacle where I could enjoy a little happiness, a shimmer of joy; translation by Swales 1987, 53). Modern readers need to approach this passage warily, however. Hans Robert Jauss takes it to mean that "Werther cannot be thought of as a pioneer in the struggle against class society and absolutism because it is the incipient bourgeois society itself — the class of his own origin — whose 'disgraceful... conditions' he condemns" (1982, 186). But, as various other commentators note, Werther's use of *bürgerlich* is different in meaning from the post-Marxian "bourgeois"; the eighteenth-century definition actually corresponds more to the term "civil" (see, for example, Alewyn 1970, 756; Flaschka 1987, 63–66; Hohendahl 1972, 179–202; Kaiser 1971, 195).

The incident in which Werther is humiliatingly dismissed from the aristocrats' soirée has also received increased attention over time. In 1828, Heinrich Heine wrote that when *Werther* first appeared, all that almost anybody cared about was that the hero shot himself; his suicide was why people had read the book, and it was what had upset critics like Nicolai. Only a few readers, he says, noticed the scene in which Werther was expelled from the aristocratic gathering. Heine contrasts that period with his own age, which is much more attuned to political concerns: were the novel to appear now, at a time attuned to social equality, this passage would cause a far greater uproar than would a pistol shot (1828, 226). Actually, Heine is here a little ahead of his fellow critics. Few of his contemporaries mention the incident with any emphasis, either. Even forty-one years later, in 1869, the liberal literary historian Georg Zimmermann is still the exception when he finds particular significance in Werther's expulsion: "Die hier in einem Beispiele sich veranschaulichenden faulen Zustände des Staates und der bevorzugten Gesellschaft bieten uns allerdings den Schlüssel zu einem tieferen Verständnisse der Zeit und lassen die Schuld Werther's in einem bei Weitem milderen Lichte erscheinen. Wir können sagen: wo sich begabte, feurige Naturen in ein solches Gehäuse elender Verhältnisse eingesponnen sehen, sei es kaum zu verwundern, dass ihre Thatkraft verkrüppelt, verkommt und mit einer mörderischen Leidenschaftlichkeit die eigenen Lebenswurzeln angreift" (Zimmermann 1869, 253; The corroded conditions of the state and of the privileged society that are illustrated in this one example offer us the key to a profounder understanding of the time and allow Werther's guilt to appear in a much milder light. We can say: where gifted, fiery natures find themselves entangled in such a construction of miserable circumstances, it should hardly be surprising that their capacity for action is hamstrung, degenerates, and attacks its own life source with murderous passion). More representative is Julian Schmidt, who stresses that Goethe himself did not share Werther's negative attitude toward the aristocracy, but used such an attack only as a conventional element in the novel's structure (1861, 186–87). Not until the twentieth century does the Count's soirée assume a truly central role, becoming so important that Horst Flaschka can usefully limit his survey of political interpretations to how the various critics handle just this incident (1987, 79–84).

Surprisingly, National Socialism had little overt influence on *Werther* scholarship, even though Joseph Goebbels drew inspiration from the novel for his own *Michael* (1929), and even though the National Socialists celebrated the Sturm und Drang movement as their precursor (for example, Fricke 1937; Kindermann 1939, 1941; Kluckhohn 1934; W. Müller 1938). For whatever reason, studies published in Germany between 1933 and 1945 did not actively use *Werther* to promote the Nazi cause (see, for example, Beutler 1940, 1941; Blumenthal 1940; Kayser 1941; Schöffler 1938). Aside from its publication date, 1937, and its introduction's claim that literature is an outgrowth of the *Volk*, Walther Linden's history of literature fits easily into the scholarly mainstream that was the norm both before and after the Third Reich. It presents Werther as a sensitive being tragically at odds with an insensitive world: "Seine wogende, rauschende, ungefesselte Empfindung stößt überall an die harten Schranken der äußeren Welt, an Standesvorurteile, eherne Sitte, Beschränktheit. In diesem Kampfe reibt er sich innerlich auf. Seine verletzte Ehre, seine unerwiderte Liebe sind nur Anlässe, ihm den unlösbaren Zwiespalt von Seele und Welt vor Augen zu führen und ihn dem Freitod zuzutreiben" (1937, 285; His surging, rushing, unfettered feeling bumps everywhere against the outer world's restraints, against social prejudice, petrified custom, narrowness. He exhausts himself inwardly in this struggle. His wounded honor, his unrequited love are merely the occasions that make apparent to him the irresolvable duality of soul and world and drive him toward suicide). While Linden's sympathy with Werther's emotionality and his use of terms like "Kampf" (struggle) are consistent with National Socialism, they are hardly unusual in the longer history of *Werther* reception.

One study occupies a unique position within this context, however, at least implicitly engaging in Third Reich politics. In the foreword to his dissertation on Goethe's *Werther,* in which he applies the morphological method used by Hermann Pongs in 1927 (see chapter 3), Josef Michels stresses that his work was completed in the summer of 1933, but that "economic difficulties" caused its publication to be delayed until 1936. With the encouragement of his adviser, Benno von Wiese, Michels used this hiatus to incorporate the results of Paul Böckmann's research on

Hölderlin (1935) into the printed version (1936, 7–8). Although he does not say so explicitly, he also took the opportunity to ally himself with Pongs in the latter's quarrel with Gerhard Fricke about the subjective sources of creative art (11–13). This controversy played an important role in the academic power struggles among National Socialist literary critics in the 1930s (see Dainat 1994). Pongs's notion of a meta-personal reality and his concepts of a "Gemeinschaftsgrund" (communal basis) and an "umgreifende Ordnung des Daseins" (encompassing order of existence) seem mysterious today, but they found resonance under National Socialism (Demetz 1967, 172).

After 1945, the political interpretations of *Werther* predictably fall more or less neatly into the categories established by the Cold War. On the one side, we find Marxist critics in the German Democratic Republic, but also, especially in the 1970s, in the West. Opposed to them are a variety of Western critics representing various schools of interpretation.

Analysts who wish to see Werther as a progressive participant in the Marxist class struggle immediately encounter a stumbling block: he is not only a privileged member of the bourgeoisie, but also a mignon of the aristocracy. His mother's funds make possible a life of leisure, complete with a personal servant and, as Ulrich Plenzdorf's hero, Edgar Wibeau, enviously points out, a horse (Plenzdorf 1973, 57). And even if Werther cannot be included in all of their social occasions, the Prince, the Court Minister, and the Count support him generously. The aristocratic Fräulein von B. seems equally well-disposed toward his company. Admittedly, Werther repeatedly declares his solidarity with the uneducated poor, who strike him as being more in keeping with ideal human nature, but his stylized fantasies of sharing their lot hardly constitute a serious political stance, as even left-leaning commentators like Klaus Hübner point out (1982, 150; see also the earlier study by Bickelmann 1933, 12). In one of several study guides that appeared in the 1970s to help teachers present the novel politically, Arndt and Inge Stephan indicate that both Werther's own attraction to figures from the lower classes and his identification of their sufferings with his own never extend beyond his personal horizon to a recognition of the political forces at work (1975, 156).

Martin Swales points to another difficulty facing politically oriented interpreters: "the novel does not concern itself in any sustained or thorough-going way with social particulars" (1987, 49). Some critics, Swales complains, turn this absence to their advantage by arguing "that the lack of evidence also constitutes evidence. . . . Because Werther is only imperfectly aware of the social causes of so much of his malaise, he is the victim of that characteristically bourgeois thinking which transposes social issues into issues of metaphysics and psychology" (49). Indeed the Stephans extend this argument to *Werther's* readers, as well: "So wie Werther auf der Handlungsebene des Romans nicht in der Lage ist, seine durch die Gesellschaft vermittelten

'Leiden' gesellschaftlich, d.h. politisch zu lösen und stattdessen in eine privatistische, selbstzerstörerische Lösung verfällt, so ist das bürgerliche Lesepublikum nicht in der Lage, sich der Gesellschaftskritik des Romans direkt zu stellen; es versucht diese vielmehr in der Interpretation als privaten, durch individuelles Fehlverhalten hervorgerufenen Konfliktfall zu neutralisieren" (175, 158: Just as Werther, on the novel's story level, is incapable of finding a social, i.e. political, solution to his socially-mediated sufferings, but instead falls into a privatized, self-destructive solution, so too are his bourgeois readers incapable of directly coming to terms with the novel's social criticism; rather they attempt to neutralize the invoked conflict by interpreting it as the result of private, individual misconduct). Swales finds this kind of justification dangerous: "If both the presence of evidence and the absence of evidence are equally convincing 'proofs' of the case being advanced, then the differences between one literary work and another simple evaporate before an all-embracing doctrine in which everything is grist to the ideological mill" (1987, 49–50).

Georg Lukács set the parameters for Marxist elucidations of *Werther* in a treatise that was written in Moscow in 1936, published there in 1939, and then reissued in East Germany in 1947. This study, however, rarely leaves the realm of theory to look at the text itself. Lukács's first goal is to restore the novel to its rightful position within the revolutionary Enlightenment; he disparages those reactionary bourgeois critics who set up a false dichotomy between feeling and reason in order to link *Werther* with reactionary Romanticism (1936, 39–44). Today, especially after Gerhard Sauder (1974) and others have shed so much light on the complexity of eighteenth-century attitudes toward feeling and reason, Lukács's attack on older critics like Hermann Hettner (1850) seems oddly vitriolic, but in the 1930s he was also trying to "save Goethe from the Nazis" (Vazsonyi 1997, 95). The threat was real. At the University of Kiel's fourth anniversary celebration of Hitler's seizure of power, for example, Gerhard Fricke lauds the Third Reich as the triumph of German irrationalism, which begins with a rejection of Enlightenment reason and continues on a straight line through Romanticism to the Führer himself (1937, 17). Indeed, as post-war critics on the left point out, such attitudes did not end in 1945; the ostensibly apolitical West German interpretations are in some regards very similar to fascist approaches (see Lämmert 1967). These critics can point to the post-war career of someone like Fricke, whose continuing praise of the irrational no longer supports National Socialism by name, but whose approbation of Werther's "heart" makes room for it. In his article "Werther und Goethe," published in 1950, Fricke stresses how Werther's emotional world — indeed, that of every genius — is wholly removed from empirical existence (146). That displacement is in fact necessary to the novel's aesthetic value: If Werther were curable, he would not be Werther, and rather than an immortal work of literature, the novel would be a psychopathological study of mere cultural-historical interest (152).

Lukács, of course, begins with the opposite assumption: Werther's character is inconceivable without its historical context and requires a dialectical model to be properly understood. At that period of German development, he maintains, the bourgeoisie was erecting a challenge to the feudal structure, but it was simultaneously anticipating its next stage of development by splitting itself into reactionary and revolutionary elements. Goethe's criticism, says Lukács, assails not only the feudal absolutism of his time, but also the underlying contradictions within emerging capitalism, a perspective that helps to account for the novel's enormous popularity in all of the more advanced countries (1936, 44–45). It also explains the negative response of contemporaries like Goeze, who well understood the novel's revolutionary implications.

Werther, Lukács maintains, represents the humanistic ideal that belongs to the revolutionary stage of capitalism: he displays the freely developed, rounded personality that Herder defined in *Übers Erkennen und Empfinden in der menschlichen Seele* (On Perception and Sensation in the Human Soul, 1774). Seen in this light, Goethe's hero is engaged in a tragic struggle against the subsequent fragmentation of that personality, which is caused by the capitalist division of labor (45–46). His suicide testifies to his uncompromising resoluteness and lends his demise a "radiant beauty" that ultimately derives from his participation in the pre-revolutionary, heroic period of bourgeois development (56). The young Goethe, Lukács admits, was himself no political revolutionary, not even to the limited extent possible in Germany at the time, but he did evince a plebeianism, in non-political form, that asserted humanistic-revolutionary ideals both against the estate system of feudal absolutism and against bourgeois philistinism (49).

Lukács's heroic image of Werther sets the agenda for most subsequent discussions in the GDR (see Scharfschwerdt 1978, 238–57). The choice to follow Werther's example is not an obvious one. Engels, as we have seen, proposed exactly the opposite, and the nineteenth-century liberal Karl Hillebrand also expressly contrasted Werther and his contemporaries, who are "elegisch-passiv, weinerlich-sentimental, weiblich-empfindlich" (1885, 288: elegiac-passive, weepy-sentimental, effeminate-sensitive), with Goethe's other creation, the titanic Prometheus (283; 290). Lukács's essay, however, especially after it was republished in 1947, led Marxist critics in the GDR to consistently pair Werther with Promethean rebellion and approvingly cite Lenz's description of him as a "crucified Prometheus" (Lenz 1775, 685). Edith Braemer's *Goethes Prometheus und die Grundpositionen des Sturm und Drang* (Goethe's Prometheus and the Fundamental Position of the Sturm und Drang) further simplifies Lukács's description of the class system to make Werther a wholly unambiguous warrior against feudalism: "Die Art, die Werther der Natur gegenübersteht, ist bürgerlich, die Art, wie er zeichnet, welche Objekte er sich wählt, ist es auch; die Art, wie er liebt, ist ebenso weit von höfischer Galanterie entfernt, wie sein Verlangen, in einer beruflichen Tätigkeit seine Kräfte entfalten zu können. (. . .) Alles das sind verschiedene Weisen, sich bürgerlich mit der Gesellschaft des Feudalabsolutismus auseinanderzusetzen, und sie alle kulminieren in dem Protest, den Werther gegen den Adelszirkel erhebt, der ihn hinausweist" (1963, 106; The way in which Werther approaches Nature is bourgeois; the way in which he draws, the subjects he chooses, are [bourgeois] as well; the way in which he loves is as far removed from court gallantries as is his desire to be able to develop his powers in an occupational activity. [. . .] All these are different ways in which to oppose the society of feudal absolutism, and they all culminate in the protest that Werther raises against the aristocratic circle that expels him). The ultimate form of this protest is his suicide, which she sees as a Sturm und Drang rebellion, a personal act of tearing off those chains from which the people as a whole cannot yet free themselves (108 — here Braemer alludes to Werther's own metaphor for suicide in his letter of August 12). Yet even Braemer stops short of considering Werther a consciously revolutionary hero. She points out, for example, that he fails to recognize that the order against which he struggles is in decline. In effect, however, he promotes revolutionary change through his tragic assertion of subjective values against repressive social forces and by his demand to be active beyond merely making a living, as well as to be able to love without regard to unnatural and restrictive societal conventions. His positive contribution to the progress of history is to embody a future reality: "Werther war bereit zum Leben, aber das Leben war nicht für ihn bereit" (106; Werther was ready to live, but life was not ready for him).

Hans-Heinrich Reuter later refines this notion of Promethean sacrifice: Werther's suicide is not, he claims, a conscious political protest, but a desperate response to a society that gives him no chance to realize his human potential. Nonetheless, his death represents a heroic resistance to reactionary forces. It raises the reader's gaze beyond the narrow horizon of Germany to an inspiring vision of a fulfilling humanistic future. By combining realistic depiction, penetrating criticism of social conditions, and a vision of hope, *Werther* exemplifies the best of socialist realism (1972, 104–5; for an altogether different comparison of Werther and Prometheus, see Bennett 2001, 57–61).

Reuter's interpretation leans heavily on the most influential, although also the most controversial, East German study of *Werther,* Peter Müller's dissertation of 1965. Excerpts of this work appeared in 1967 in *Sonntag,* the weekly publication of the official *Kulturbund* (Cultural Federation), and then the whole was published as a monograph in 1969. Müller's Werther, even more than Lukács's, is an extremely positive figure who achieves the ideal synthesis of perception and feeling that Herder had envisioned as the natural state of humankind: he is a complete, total being ("ein vollendetes ganzheitliches Sein") combining profound perception, intense feeling, consistency in action, a capacity for joy, and an insistence on truth uncompromised by convention (1965, 87). To Müller, Werther's debate with Albert about suicide reveals that his choice to kill himself is an individual one, based on his own perception of personal limits and unaffected by church or state or, as his example of the young plebeian girl indicates, by class (143). The novel's effect is nevertheless revolutionary because Werther presents a new human possibility, one in which individual integrity contrasts with the feudal world's fragmentation. Even though he fails in the end, his ascendance to self-realization marks the dawn of a new world and a renewed humanity (93). Müller assigns *Werther* a crucial position in Germany's national literature because it condenses a whole generation's experience of standing at the threshold between the feudal and bourgeois worlds (Müller 1965, 46; 7. For a discussion of what is meant here by "national literature," see Schiller 1970).

Müller's analysis, in contrast to Lukács's, has the virtue of paying close attention to the text. While Marxist assertions appear repeatedly throughout, this is because Müller tries to infer them from his detailed descriptions of Werther's development as a "whole man." The East German reviews of his study acknowledge this close reading of Werther's inner development, but they fault its deviation from socialist principles. Hans-Georg Werner, for example, takes Müller to task for accepting the assumption that a psychological state of nature antedates socialization, that human capacities can develop or even exist outside a social-historical context. Progress, Werner insists, cannot consist of returning to a previous, "natural" form of being; it is achieved only through "gigantic social upheavals" (Werner 1970, 195).

Hans Kortum and Reinhard Weisbach, in a review entitled "Unser Verhältnis zum literarischen Erbe" (Our Relationship to the Literary Heritage, 1970), likewise find Müller's grasp of Marxist principles to be wanting. His notion of self-realization, they say, all too often confuses historical illusion with genuine problems and thus fails to come to terms with Germany's peculiarly retarded development in the eighteenth century. While in England, for example, a well-defined middle class stood in a dialectical relationship with bourgeois individualism, the lack of a viable bourgeoisie in Germany distorted the problem of individual identity and gave it an illusory value (1970, 218). As the title of their review indicates, Kortum and Weisbach are less interested in the text of *Werther* than in how to appropriate older literature correctly for socialist purposes: *literarisches Erbe* was the official designation for this process. In one regard, their approach resembles Nicolai's two centuries earlier: it requires literature — and literary criticism — to promote proper social ends. Müller's contention that Werther pursues individual self-fulfillment outside society, they find, exerts an illusory appeal and thus requires a corrective. "Unsere Gesellschaft, die im Zusammenhang mit der sozialistischen und der wissenschaftlich-technischen Revolution auch diese Beziehung (zwischen Individuum und Gesellschaft) praktisch umgestaltet und sozialistisch ordnet, ist an einer solchen Lösung jedoch interessiert. Im Interesse dieser unserer gemeinsamen Sache haben wir darum unsere Einwände vorgetragen, zumal sich eine falsch verstandene 'Selbstverwirklichungstheorie' nicht nur in Peter Müllers Buch, sondern auch in anderen literaturwissenschaftlichen Veröffentlichungen zeigt" (219; Our society, which, in combination with the socialist and the scientific-technical revolution has reformulated this relationship (between individual and society) in practice and organized it according to socialist principles, is, however, profoundly interested in such a solution. In the interest of this, our common cause, we have introduced our objections, especially since a falsely understood 'theory of self-realization' is to be found not only in Peter Müller's book, but also in other publications of literary criticism).

In an act of self-criticism several years later, Müller accepts this reprimand: "Es gehört zu den selbstverständlichen Geflogenheiten der marxistisch-leninistischen Literaturwissenschaft, daß sie ständig ihre Ergebnisse überprüft und zu neuen Positionen gelangt. Ganz in diesem Sinne enthält die hier entwickelte Plazierung und genaue soziale Profilierung der bürgerlichen Individualitätsproblematik eine Korrektur an fehlerhaften Auffassungen meines Werther-Buches. Dies Korrektur zielt auf eine deutliche Abhebung des sozialistischen vom bürgerlichen Menschenbild, des bürgerlich-utopischen vom realen Humanismus" (Müller 1973: Heft 3, 109; It is of course part of the practice of Marxist-Leninist literary study to continually reexamine its results and adopt new positions. Entirely within this spirit, the classification and detailed social profile developed here for discussing issues of bourgeois individualism contain a correction of the flawed concepts in my *Werther* book. This correction aims at a clear contrast between the socialist and the bourgeois images of humankind, between bourgeois-utopian and real humanism). Müller's acquiescence should not automatically lead us to assume a crudely enforced consensus, however. As Daniel Farrelly points out, there is really "a *spectrum* of views rather than *the* GDR-Marxist view" of *Werther* (1997, 60). At the same time, however, unanimity does exist on key points, and we find no real departures from the 1956 characterization by the *Kollektiv für Literaturgeschichte* (Collective for Literary History): "Der ganze 'Werther' ist ein glühendes Bekenntnis zu jenem neuen Menschen, der im Laufe der Vorbereitung der bürgerlichen Revolution entsteht, zu jener Menschwerdung, zu jener Erweckung der allseitigen Tätigkeit des Menschen, die die Entwicklung der bürgerlichen Gesellschaft hervorbringt — und zugleich tragisch zum Untergang verurteilt. (. . .) Die volkstümlich-humanistische Revolte im 'Werther' ist eine der wichtigsten revolutionären Äußerungen der bürgerlichen Ideologie in der Vorbereitungszeit der Französischen Revolution" (1956, 117–18; All of *Werther* is a glowing testimony to that new man that arises in the course of preparation for the bourgeois revolution, to that process of becoming human, to that awakening of wholly rounded human activity that brings about the development of bourgeois society — and simultaneously condemns it to destruction. [. . .] The national-popular-revolutionary revolt in *Werther* is one of the most important revolutionary expressions of bourgeois ideology in the time of preparation of the French Revolution). Any published criticisms that challenge such assumptions directly (for example, Rothmann 1972) originate outside the GDR.

Farrelly raises a different kind of objection to the East German studies. What he misses in all of them is any attempt to discover a narrative strategy within the novel, "to get beyond the horizon of Werther's own consciousness." We find "no systematic attempt . . . to arrive at the *author's* point of view, no full discussion of the *narrator's* relationship to the text, no attempt to discuss Werther's *own* role as a narrator in the text" (1997, 60–61).

The political interpretations proposed in the West are more varied than those in the East, ranging from denials that Werther plays any historical role whatsoever to Marxist readings that may or may not be at odds with those proposed by colleagues in the GDR. Some *werkimmanente* (roughly: New Critical) interpreters find so little appeal in political approaches that they consider Werther's experiences of social phenomena to be no more than a narratological feature, a structural counterpoint to his inwardness (for example, Storz 1953; Hass 1957; Kluge 1971). Emil Staiger, one of the most prominent post-war advocates of *Werkimmanenz*, does take on the Marxists directly, however. Lukács, he says, has been moved, "das Buch als Phase des großen revolutionären Prozesses, als Wegbereiter des Klassenkampfes aufzufassen. Es eignet sich schlecht für diese Rolle. Denn Werther leidet wohl an vielem, was ihn in seinem Alltag umgibt; und er ist [. . .] überzeugt, daß manches sich vermeiden ließe, was Menschen einander gedankenlos antun. Aber er glaubt nicht, daß man das Übel beheben könne, indem man die Standesunterschiede beseitigt" (1952, 158; to understand the book as a phase in the great revolutionary process, as a precursor of the class struggle. It does not fit well into this role. Werther does admittedly suffer from much that surrounds him in his daily existence; and he is [. . .] convinced that much that people mindlessly do to each other could be avoided. But he does not believe that one could eliminate this evil by abolishing class distinctions).

Throughout the post-war period we repeatedly encounter the same phrase among Western critics: "Werther is no revolutionary." Hans Reiss expands on this claim, making the point that Werther's protests "are not rooted in concrete political or social situations, only in himself and in his emotional needs and desires. The further his disease advances, the more he is estranged from society" (1963, 44–45). Or, as Ludwig Fertig puts it, the novel does not attack aristocratic *rule,* just the social behavior and prejudices of the nobles. The feudal structure itself is never called into question (1965, 29–30). Hans Vaget does ascribe a class awareness to Werther, "that of an enlightened young burgher" — "But," he adds, "young Werther is no revolutionary. He even defends the existing order since he sees quite clearly that he too stands to benefit from it. Although he protests against social prejudices and privileges, he counts some aristocrats among the people he admires most" (1982, 18; see also Saine 1980, 332–34). Carol Ames goes even further, arguing that Werther's primary motivation throughout the book is to establish his own superiority by moving up within the class structure. His work at court and his attentions toward the aristocratic Fräulein von B. are aimed at "winning the competition" with Albert by becoming an even greater success (1977, 142). Being snubbed by the nobility has at first no effect, since he is convinced that he and the Count agree that his personal attributes raise him above such pettiness. It is only when he later hears that he has become the object of derision, rather than of the envy he so enjoys, that he sinks into an emotional crisis (146). In other words, according to Ames, Werther is the opposite of a tragic revolutionary; he is a failed social climber.

Martin Swales makes a similar point but draws more positive conclusions from it. The humiliation caused by the incident at the Count's party "suggests that Werther has in some measure become part of the pecking order of life in the diplomatic service — in the sense that he cannot answer the wagging tongues with any values that derive from his sense of his own professional worth. . . . With part of his self, [he] acknowledges the mechanisms against which he has offended" (1987, 54). In other words, Werther is both at odds with his time and a creature of it. He is not, Swales says "a budding revolutionary: Werther does not offer a social or political programme" (50). But "both the character and the linguistic mode of Werther's inwardness belong to . . . broader cultural currents" (56), and he embodies a whole generation's sense of being in conflict with a society that does not have room for its youth's aspirations and sensibility.

W. Daniel Wilson provides the perhaps most nuanced study of Werther's relationship to questions of class, work, and the public and private spheres, and he concludes that, for the fiasco at court, "Werther shares the blame with society. He has himself triggered the machinations of his rivals by deliberately choosing aristocratic friends and failing to envision — or putting to the test — their participation in [the] social and political dynamic. . . . Werther can thus be faulted for his idealism, his lack of insight into the nature of society. But it would be difficult to fault him for those social ills themselves" (1989, 39–40).

Most Western critics admonish their counterparts in the GDR for imposing a predefined ideology without first examining the novel itself.

Peter Fischer accuses Lukács and his "Gefolgsleute" (acolytes) of entertaining the pious hope that Werther can be seen as a bourgeois-humanistic rebel, but this interpretation "ist nicht durch den Text zu belegen, den Goethe geschrieben hat. Dieser hat die Geschichte eines emotional lebhaften Masochisten geschrieben, der in einer abhängigen Liebe befangen ist, aus dieser Perspektive heraus Gott und die Welt betrachtet und Gott und die Welt für sein Unglück verantwortlich macht. Kann dieser weinerliche Masochist, wie schön seine Gefühle auch sein mögen, einen 'fortschrittlichen' Standpunkt einnehmen? (...) Werther ist das genaue Gegenteil eines Kämpfers. Er kämpft weder um Lotte noch gegen Albert — noch gar gegen den Adel. Bekommt er nicht, was er haben will, läuft er schmollend davon, auch in den Tod" (Fischer 1986, 216; [This interpretation] cannot be substantiated by the text that Goethe wrote. He wrote the story of an emotionally animated masochist who is caught in a dependent love, looks at God and the world from this perspective, and makes God and the world responsible for his unhappiness. Can this whiny masochist, however beautiful his feelings may be, assume a 'progressive' standpoint? . . . Werther is the exact opposite of a fighter. He doesn't fight for Lotte or against Albert — much less against the aristocracy. When he doesn't get what he wants, he runs away in a sulk, even to his death).

This is not to say that even mainstream Western critics deny that *Werther* has a political import. John R. J. Eyck and Katherine Arens, in a recent study of *Werther*, see the novel as representing the deterioration of court society, in which individual desires take precedence over the larger good. Focusing on the open copy of Lessing's *Emilia Galotti* that lay on Werther's table when he shot himself, Eyck and Arens conclude that "Both the Prince [in Lessing's play] and Werther have fallen prey to the fallacy of the private and sentimental, driven to extreme acts by their recourse to emotion over reason: each acts only in his or her own interests, rather in those of the state" (2004, 56). The book, then, marks the beginning of a period of crisis in which the misuse of privilege is destabilizing the old order, but a new system has not yet been formulated that will replace it. Werther is not so much a harbinger of the bourgeoisie as a symptom of the dissolving feudal society.

On the whole, however, Western commentators assume a model more consistent with Marxist notions of class. Norbert Elias, for example, says that Werther was part of "the whole literary movement of the second half of the eighteenth century [which] was the product of a social class," and that "everywhere among middle-class youth one finds vague dreams of a new united Germany. . . . " The literature of the time, however, including *Werther*, contained "nothing that was in any sense to lead to concrete political action" (1976, 17). When Werther complains about "the wretched circumstances of bourgeois society," he can hardly be said to be differentiating himself from his class: "Nothing better characterizes middle-class consciousness than this statement" (18). On the other hand, this literary movement, while "not a political one, . . . was the expression of a social movement, a transformation of society. The bourgeoisie as a whole did not yet find expression in it. It was first the expression of a sort of bourgeois vanguard, . . . the middle-class intelligentsia" (17).

Peter Hohendahl extends this argument in a way not wholly at odds with Lukács: *Werther's* critique, he points out, is more modern than the social system it addresses. Its admittedly vague protest, couched in terms of spontaneous feeling, aims in effect at what is still a future component of liberal-bourgeois society: "die Emanzipation des bürgerlichen Individuums durch eine strenge Arbeitsmoral und den Erwerb von Privateigentum" (1972, 202; the emancipation of the bourgeois individual through a strict work ethic and the acquisition of private property). Werther is thus in conflict with the very same group of which he is a member. His situation is less representative of the bourgeoisie in a feudal society, "als für die progressive Intelligenz, die sich von der affirmativen Moralphilosophie der deutschen Aufklärung gelöst hat, ohne doch bei irgendeiner breiteren gesellschaftlichen Gruppe einen Halt zu finden" (203–4; than of the progressive intelligentsia that has unbound itself from the affirmative moral philosophy of the German Enlightenment, without yet having found a purchase in some other larger social group; see also Fertig 1965, 31).

In 1958, Arnold Hirsch published one of the earliest West German studies of *Werther* to stress class conflict. It bears the subtitle: "Ein bürgerliches Schicksal im absolutistischen Staat" (A Bourgeois Fate in the Absolutist State). Goethe's novel, according to Hirsch, establishes a new context for a return to nature; it develops what began as a Rousseauian critique of society into one that reflects the increasing economic and social importance of the middle class. Werther and his generation no longer tolerate the discrepancy between their ambitions and the possibilities available to them in an absolutist state. A career is open to him, but only an aristocratically defined one that does not acknowledge his bourgeois personality. He refuses to work within this social structure and returns to nature. His humiliation at the Count's soirée simply affirms his original rejection of a secretarial position (Hirsch 1958, 350–59). Werther's rebellion necessarily ends in tragedy, says Hirsch, for his inner feelings of freedom and human dignity cannot be expressed either within or outside the social order. Even the sympathies and largesse of the Prince, the Count, and Fräulein von B. cannot overcome the objective forces arrayed against him (359–67).

Undermining Hirsch's argument is his ready acceptance of Werther's version of his employment. Despite the highly questionable letter of December 24, which describes the ambassador's pedantic exactitude, Hirsch judges Werther to be a capable worker who performs well but does not wish to continue in an endeavor that he finds unsatisfying. Hirsch also accepts Werther's petulant letter of March 15 as an accurate analysis of the situation: "ihr seid doch allein schuld daran, die mich sporntet und triebt und quältet, mich in einen Posten zu begeben, der nich nach meinem Sinne war" (it's all your fault, all of you [meaning his mother and Wilhelm] who spurred and drove and tormented me into taking a post that wasn't suited to me).

When the rebellious generation of 1968 joined the discussion of *Werther,* the orientation became even more political and the tone more strident. In 1970 Klaus Scherpe's *Werther und Wertherwirkung: Zum Syndrom bürgerlicher Gesellschaftsordnung im 18. Jahrhundert* (Werther and Werther Effect: On the Syndrome of the Bourgeois Social Order in the Eighteenth Century) caused a remarkable stir, not only because of its conclusions, but also because of its Manichean separation of Werther's self-realization from the societal forces that are united in opposition to it, forces that Scherpe bundles under the rubric of "bourgeoisie." What makes Werther so threatening to this monolithic structure is his absolute assertion of what bourgeois society claims to support: his subjective, individual freedom (31). According to Scherpe, the social order was sufficiently self-assured to deal with Werther's rebellion against holding governmental office and engaging in commercial affairs, against the rules governing art and science, and against inappropriate personal interactions; far more menacing is his example of total self-realization, which might encourage imitative rebellion in the reader (72). "Man kann Werthers Versuch der Selbstverwirklichung als Akt der Antizipation interpretieren: mit dem Bewußtsein individueller Freiheit wächst die Notwendigkeit zur Veränderung der gesellschaftlichen Verhältnisse" (91; One can interpret Werther's attempt at self-realization as an anticipatory act: with the consciousness of individual freedom there arises the growing need to change social conditions).

To characterize the forces arrayed against Werther's individualism, Scherpe goes outside the text and cites the novel's early critics. These "Sachverwalter bürgerlicher Lebensordnung" (76; guardians of bourgeois virtue) close ranks against the peril that Werther represents. Their opposition takes various forms, but it always serves the same purpose: "Die von Philosophen, Theologen und Pädagogen verkündete Wertschätzung von Arbeit und Strebsamkeit entsprach den Interessen von Kirche, Staat und unternehmerisch tätigem Bürgertum. (...) Die Stilisierung von Arbeit zur religiösen und gesellschaftlichen Tugend glorifiziert Eigennutz und Gewinnstreben und verdeckt die tatsächlich bestehenden Abhängigkeitsverhältnisse." (38; The values of work and industriousness that the philosophers, theologians, and pedagogues proclaimed corresponded to the interests of church, state, and the entrepreneurial middle class. [. . .] The stylization of work into a religious and social virtue glorified self-interest and pecuniary rewards and obscures the actual existing dependency relationships.) Even the novel's apparent supporters defuse Werther's threat by seeing it as a disease to be treated with pity (77). The extreme dichotomy that Scherpe posits allows no compromise: "die Kluft zwischen der trägen Durchschnittsmoral des Bürgertums und der bürgerlich-progressiven Intelligenz, für die Werther spricht [ist] unüberbrückbar" (51–52; the chasm between the inert moral mediocrity of the bourgeoisie and the bourgeois-progressive intelligentsia that Werther represents is unbridgeable). Nor does does Werther attempt any such reconciliation. His threat to the bourgeoisie "besteht nun nicht etwa darin, daß er imstande wäre, den strengen Dualismus von innerer und äußerer Freiheit aufzuheben, vielmehr darin, daß er diesen Antagonismus durch seine bedingungslose Entscheidung für die innere Freiheit verschärft. Indem er sein Denken, Wollen und Handeln in den autonomen Bereich unbedingter Subjektivität zurücknimmt, durchbricht er den falschen Legitimationszusammenhang zwischen innerer und äußerer Freiheit" (54: does not have to do with a capacity to overcome the strict duality between inner and outer freedom; rather it lies in the fact that his unconditional choice of inner freedom aggravates this antagonism. By pulling his thought, volition, and actions back into the autonomous region of absolute subjectivity, he breaks through the false legitimization of a fictitious connection between inner and outer freedom).

Scherpe's book caused an uproar. Alluding to its provocative subtitle, Gerhard Kaiser calls his own response "Zum Syndrom modischer Germanistik" (On the Voguish German Studies Syndrome, 1971). He accuses Scherpe of circular thinking, oversimplification, sloppy reading, historical naïveté, and just plain bad will. It is a classic generational confrontation: Kaiser, born in 1927, began his studies in East Berlin before, as he puts it on his personal web page, fleeing to the West in 1950. Scherpe, born in 1939, studied and then later taught at the Free University of West Berlin in the 1960s. He later described his book as arising from a seminar taught there in 1968, at the height of the student movement (Scherpe 1974, 208).

Kaiser's most substantial quarrel is with "Scherpes ideologisch präformiertem Urteil über die bürgerliche Gesellschaft" (Scherpe's ideologically preformed judgment of bourgeois society). Scherpe, says Kaiser, mistakenly assumes that Werther's "Absolutismus des Herzens" (absolutism of the heart) originates in a reaction against that society, instead of causing his alienation from it. Consulting the text, however, shows this interpretation to be false; the only social *misère* that we see is filtered through the lens of that same "absolutism of the heart." The reader never has the opportunity to remove Werther's glasses to judge how miserable this society in fact is (197). Nor, says Kaiser, is Scherpe's approach historically valid. The middle class he describes had not yet established itself at the time of *Werther's* publication, and, in any case, Scherpe's analysis could account neither for the genesis of *Werther* in such a society nor for the novel's popularity in other, more advanced countries. Indeed, "sein Begriff von Bürgertum ist nicht historisch, er ist moralisch wertend" (his concept of the bourgeoisie is not historical; it is moralistically judgmental). Rather than present a rigorously defined concept of society, he simply lashes out in resentment against whatever features strike his fancy (196). He is, Kaiser says, equally cavalier with the critical tradition: "Problemlagen der bisherigen Forschung werden nicht aufgegriffen, sondern mit einem Gewaltstreich beiseitegeschoben, zugedeckt durch vermeintlich überlegene Ansätze, deren Überlegenheit vorwiegend darin besteht, daß sie nicht kritisch überprüft worden sind" (194; Problems raised by previous researchers are not taken up, but are forcefully pushed aside by ostensibly superior approaches, whose superiority mostly consists in their never having been critically examined). Even Scherpe's writing style leads Kaiser at one point to cry out in anguish, "welch ein Deutsch!" (what awful German!).

Richard Alewyn, born in 1902, represents an even older generation. His review of Scherpe's book is somewhat less blunt, but he similarly dismisses its method, which is "not sociological, but rather ideological" (1970, 756). Scherpe, he says, ignores or downplays those aspects of the novel and its reception that would contradict his thesis; he also blithely contradicts himself. He misuses the term "bourgeois," applying it to almost every eighteenth-century value or virtue, unconcerned on the one hand that the bourgeoisie was already a couple of centuries older, on the other that not just the bourgeoisie populated the eighteenth century (756). Still another suspect concept is the "bourgeois intelligentsia," to which Scherpe, without explanation, assigns Werther's adherents. But, Alewyn asks rhetorically, do not most of the *Werther*-opponents that Scherpe mentions — or fails to mention — figures such as Goeze, Nicolai, Lessing, also belong to the bourgeois intelligentsia? (756).

Another elder statesman of the profession, Stuart Atkins, who was born in 1914, also skewers Scherpe. "The author's reading of *Werther*," Atkins suggests, "is more *werkimmanent* than he realizes" — because he lacks "*literary*-historical knowledge" about the epistolary novel or the rhetorical traditions from which *Werther's* detractors draw their formulations (1972, 299). Scherpe's indignation at the societal constraints placed on Werther reflects "(ideological?) blindness to the fact that *any* society limits individualism" (298). Equally egregious is Scherpe's characterization of contemporary reactions to *Werther,* in which he "emphasizes moral, religious, economic, and social condemnations of Goethe's novel or of its protagonist and lets positive responses be represented almost exclusively by polemical answers to these condemnations" (298). It is also "methodologically dubious" to lump together all of these critics simply as representative of the middle class when we in fact know much more about them than that — "there are surely other possible antitheses than that with which he operates" (298). In the end, however, Atkins's greatest disagreement is with "the author's overt hostility to appreciations of *Werther* as a work of universal private-human significance" (300).

Stefan Blessin is more inclined to sympathize with Scherpe's roots in the student protest movement of the 1960s, seeing an underlying compatibility between Werther's frustrations and those of present-day youth (1979, 276–77). Nevertheless, he too criticizes Scherpe's method of grouping the critical responses to Werther in a way that makes them represent a bourgeois power structure that simply did not yet exist at that time (273; 277–79). He expresses reservations about an interpretation that imputes too much political significance to Werther's refusal to participate in societal structures and thus categorizes him as some kind of rebel. At the same time, however, Blessin sees *Werther* itself as having a revolutionary, or at least emancipatory, effect on readers, who necessarily experience an internal dialogue between their spontaneous empathy with Werther and their rejection of his choice of suicide (271).

Karl Robert Mandelkow also takes strong issue with Scherpe's form of historical analysis, while agreeing that the eighteenth-century controversy surrounding Werther was political, rather than literary (1980, 41). To claim that the middle class expected literature to combine pleasure and instruction in comfortable ways, he argues, is to create an anachronism. That description is invalid by the 1760s, if not before. Scherpe, says Mandelkow, has it backwards: *Werther* was in fact not shocking in this regard; both the book's enthusiastic reception and its vehement opposition derive from the general reading public's acceptance of — and hunger for — such an emotionally charged work (1980, 37).

Scherpe fares no better in East German responses. Peter Müller, in a detailed review, labels him a "pseudolinken 'Avantgardisten'" (1973: Heft 1, 110: pseudo-leftist "avant-guardist"), unwittingly in league with the reactionary imperialists, misrepresenting progressive humanistic literature by arbitrarily severing its relationship with the processes of social upheaval. Scherpe, says Müller, admittedly acknowledges and even emphasizes this relationship, but he negates *Werther's* social import "weil er die vorrevolutionäre bürgerlich-humanistische Literatur Deutschlands vorrangig als Produkt einer sterilen unrevolutionären gesellschaftsentwicklung begreift: Die Misere der deutschen Gesellschaft (seinem Argument nach) gebiert eine miserable Literatur" (110; because he understands Germany's pre-revolutionary bourgeois-humanistic literature primarily as the product of a sterile, unrevolutionary social development: The *misère* of German society gives birth [according to his argument] to a miserable literature). Like critics from the West, Müller accuses Scherpe of failing to differentiate adequately among the social forces at work in eighteenth-century Germany, as well as to recognize the larger European context within which these forces were developing. Whereas Stuart Atkins took Scherpe to task for not seeing "*Werther* as a work of universal private-human significance," Müller accuses him of the opposite, of approaching the notion of individuality unhistorically. He "verkennt den Ursprung der bürgerlichen Individualität in diesen weltgeschichtlichen Prozessen, weil er auf Grund seiner idealistischen Ausgangsbasis die Dialektik zwischen der langfristigen, seit dem 16. Jahrhundert einsetzenden Umwälzung der ökonomischen Basis und den Überbauprozessen nicht richtig zu erfassen vermag" (1973: Heft 3, 94; fails to recognize the origin of bourgeois individualism in these world-historical processes, because, as a result of his idealistic starting point, he is incapable of correctly understanding the dialectic at work between the economic upheavals that began in the sixteenth century and the processes at work within the superstructure). Not only does Scherpe rely on just one isolated, undeveloped aspect of eighteenth-century German culture to construct his concept of the individual; he also, says Müller, treats the problem of individuality as a moral and intellectual question, rather than one that has its roots in economic causes (96). The Werther that emerges from this interpretation is merely a victim who does no more than invite others to share his passivity. Scherpe's reading is not merely wrong, says Müller, but even malefic, in that it separates a key work of the national literature from its social-emancipatory function 104).

    Scherpe did not take these attacks lying down. In 1974 he published another study of *Werther* as part of his and Gert Mattenklott's "Grundkurs" (basic course) called "Die Funktion der Literatur bei der Formierung der bürgerlichen Klasse Deutschlands im 18. Jahrhundert" (The Function of Literature in the Formation of Germany's Bourgeois Class in the Eighteenth Century). This essay largely restates Scherpe's original thesis, although it does take subsequent studies into account. Unapologetic, but acknowledging that his first book was conceived in the heat of the student revolts (1974, 208), he generally refines his concept of the bourgeoisie and shores up the validity of his approach with references to other scholarship. He does not mention Atkins's review, but he does criticize Atkins's own listing of works inspired by *Werther* (1949) for one-sidedly disqualifying all such works as less artistic than Goethe's novel (211). He then turns to Alewyn and Kaiser, whose "Polemik" (polemics) against his book, he says, represent the kind of rearguard action that antiquated bourgeois critics fight against historically based interpretations. It is *they* who are ideological, as especially Kaiser's virulence reveals. They remind us, says Scherpe, of how easily such a critical approach lends itself to Hitler-fascism when it limits its awareness to just the basic existential orientation within the literary text. Such interpretations are especially dangerous when they are then naively applied to current political issues, without rigorous historical analysis (213). As a particularly egregious example Scherpe cites Hans Egon Holthusen's lachrymose report of how the feelings that he experienced when reading *Werther* were transformed into compassion for Vietnamese peasants (1968).

Because he considers them to be formalists at heart, intent on separating literature from its social-historical function, Scherpe can dismiss Alewyn and Kaiser out of hand. Peter Müller, in contrast, aspires to the same critical goals and thus requires more rigorous rebuttal — although Scherpe cannot resist pointing out that Müller's review from 1973 enjoys the support "ausgerechnet (. . .) des energischen Antimarxisten Gerhard Kaiser" (215; from, of all people [. . .] the aggressively anti-Marxist Gerhard Kaiser). He finds Müller's attack to be

> Ein Beispiel für ein derart verkürztes und enthistorisierendes Verfahren, das gleichwohl mit historisch-materialistischem Anspruch auftritt (. . .) Müller ist der Verfahrensweise einer orthodoxen bürgerlichen Literaturwissenschaft näher als er ahnt, wenn er Werthers Selbstverwirklichungsanspruch in anthropologischen Gemeinplätzen beschreibt, in der Werkinterpretation isoliert und vom so festgestellten revolutionären Impetus des Werkes auf ein der Tendenz nach revolutionäres Bürgertum schließt. (Scherpe 1974, 210)

> [An example of the kind of abbreviated and de-historicizing process that at the same time has historical-materialistic pretensions. (. . .) Müller is closer than he imagines to the methods of orthodox bourgeois literary criticism when he uses anthropological platitudes to describe Werther's claim to self-actualization, isolates it within the textual interpretation, and then, having thus established a revolutionary impulse in the work, concludes that a revolutionarily inclined bourgeoisie is present.]²

Even on a formalist level, says Scherpe, Müller gets caught in a contradiction: on the one hand he asserts that the unity of the novel is predetermined by its "Krankheit zum Tode" (sickness unto death); on the other he sees Werther as passing emotionally through positive as well as negative phases that suggest that his tragedy was in fact avoidable (212). But most regrettable, Scherpe finds, is Müller's misconception of the historical situation:

> Müller verkennt aufgrund seiner 'progressiven' Fehleinschätzung der ökonomischen und ideologischen Potenz der bürgerlichen Klasse in den 70er Jahren (vom Sturm und Drang führt eben kein direkter Weg zu den revolutionären Demokraten der 90er Jahre) die historisch erklärbare sezessionistische Grundtendenz des 'Werther.' Die Werther-Figur läßt sich nicht in einen positiven Helden als Vorbild der bürgerlichen Nation und einen melancholisch gedrückten Einzelgänger, an dem die dann doch festzustellende mangelnde 'Reife' des Bürgertums ihr trauriges Ebenbild hat, auseinanderdividieren. (212)

> [Because of his "progressive" misunderstanding of the economic and ideological potential of the middle class in the 1770s (there is simply no

direct path leading from the Sturm und Drang to the revolutionary democrats of the 1790s), Müller misapprehends *Werther's* historically explicable, fundamentally secessionist tendency. The figure of Werther cannot be divided into a positive hero who serves as a model for the bourgeois nation and a melancholy, oppressed loner who then becomes the doleful parallel of the palpably missing "maturity" of the bourgeoisie.]

It is worth noting how insignificant a role Goethe's text plays in this feud. Scherpe does briefly treat the implications of *Werther's* epistolary form and refers to certain scenes in the novel, and he invites readers interested in a linguistic analysis to consult Victor Lange's "helpful" essay of 1964 (212). But the overwhelming bulk of both his study and the reactions to it address ideological questions. Their primary goal is the correct assessment of the bourgeoisie's historical development.

For all the opposition that it aroused, Scherpe's approach achieved considerable currency in the 1970s. Arndt and Inge Stephan, for example, proposed a curricular model for presenting *Werther* that corresponds almost entirely to his ideas. Their aim is to provide young students with an appealing approach to a valuable work of older literature. Werther, as they define him, is an intellectual and artist caught between two classes: the aristocracy to which he feels equal, but which rejects him, and the bourgeoisie to which he technically belongs, but whose commercially defined norms impinge on his personal development. This contradiction leads to his disorientation and isolation, which in turn result in an emotional disturbance so severe that even his contacts with the lower classes cannot alleviate it (1975, 155–56).

The injection of Marxist analysis into *Werther* studies has had lasting effects, in that all subsequent commentators have been forced to come to terms with it, but even among those later critics who are sympathetic to such an approach there is also a retreat from militancy, or at least a return to considering other interpretive elements. Klaus Oettinger, for example, takes issue with Scherpe's rejection of *Werther* as a "Krankengeschichte" (history of an illness), but at the same time, he accepts a political approach, finding that this illness is based on Werther's unfulfillable but also justifiable need for an existence that is free from restrictions. Only thus, says Oettinger, can we explain the work's ambivalent reception, why Werther's sufferings were understood by some of his younger contemporaries as a positive symbol, as a representative fate (1976, 69–70). Hans Robert Jauss agrees with Lukács and Hohendahl (1972) that Goethe's condemnation "goes beyond Rousseau's critique of civilization, and — in a surprisingly anticipatory manner — beyond his contemporaries' horizon of expectations as well, when he recognizes the division of labor to be the fundamental principle upon which the emerging bourgeois economy was to be built. He condemns it as the actual and malevolent source of alienated existence in bourgeois society." But the novel's central theme, Jauss maintains, is that "Werther's fate reveals that the solitary individual's effort to slip behind society's back so to speak, to rediscover his lost wholeness through nature, and to find fulfillment in an autonomy based on self-esteem was doomed to failure" (1982, 188–89). Klaus Hübner's 1982 dissertation also gives Werther a narrower role, asserting that his social criticism never extends beyond the perspective of an educated bourgeois of his time (1982, 184–86). Here, too, Werther's political effect is derived negatively. His utopian fantasies are reactionary in character, and their insufficiency suggests the need to develop a more humane concept of existence (187).

Rüdiger Scholz offers an extreme example of a Marxist-like etiology that is transformed into a psychological approach: Werther suffers because narcissistically schizophrenic personality disturbances are inherent to capitalism (1988, 228). In the English summary to his article, Scholz asks rhetorically "whether the threat to the self by dissolution and fragmentation has not been a central theme of bourgeois world literature right from the beginning" and sees Werther as part of a tradition that stretches back to Hamlet. "The enormous influence over many generations of such leading figures in bourgeois identity leads one to suppose that also in reality bourgeois-like common citizens are threatened by narcissistic personality disorders, the cause of which is to be found in the position of the individuals within capitalism. The findings of research into narcissism and schizophrenia will change the existing image of the history of literature and social psychology, which was based hitherto on a sequence of oedipal and narcissistic phenomena" (238). In some regards, Scholz's analysis brings things full circle, combining, as Werther's first commentators did, the political with the psychological, subsuming each within the other.

Thomas J. Scheff and Ursula Mahlendorf also consider Werther's emotions from a Marxist perspective. His response to his expulsion from the soirée reveals the shame and rage with which the ruling classes enforce false consciousness. Instead of identifying the class system as the cause of his humiliation, he succumbs to poorly defined emotions. "With the shame completely denied, and no target for his rage, he cannot define what he is feeling. Since both emotions are undischarged, they haunt him to the point that he feels that he can be free only through death" (1988, 75). Scheff and Mahlendorf base their analysis on Helen Lewis's concept of "shame dynamics," as well as on Marx's concept of false consciousness, but the rigor of these notions is lost when the authors extend their attention beyond *Werther* to include speculations about almost every conceivable form of classism, racism, and sexism, including ethnic jokes. Their original assertion that the episode with the Count is paradigmatic for the phenomenon of false consciousness rapidly loses force.

Reinhard Assling's book on Werther's "ästhetische Rebellion" (aesthetic rebellion; 1981) is perhaps the most nuanced such study. While Marxist in perspective, he begins by refuting Lukács (1936), Scherpe (1974), and Müller (1965), accusing their analyses of being unrelated to the text and based on tautological reasoning. Assling's tone is polemical — he calls Müller's work "eine Katastrophe" (a catastrophe) and "ein schlechter Scherz" (a bad joke), for example (5), while Lukács's unsubstantiated assertions are "merkwürdig" (strange; 78) — but his own arguments are well fashioned and remain close to the text. At the same time, he takes on Scherpe's other opponents, disagreeing with Gerhard Kaiser's contention that Werther's subjectivity compromises any depictions of social misery (Kaiser 1971, 197): this, says Assling, is a novel in which the real misery of society jumps off almost every page (3). One of the examples that he offers is particularly crucial to his argument: early in the novel, nature becomes an idealized space into which one flees from society. This glorification of nature as a positive alternative to civilization, Assling argues, is uniquely a product of bourgeois society, which on the one hand promotes the ideal of the consciously autonomous subject and, on the other, crushes personal development with its constraints (112). Denied an authentic existence within society, the individual escapes into a subjectively defined nature that has no independent existence, but is merely an illusory, fictional space constructed in reaction to bourgeois alienation. In contrast to society, nature represents a world in which work and individual fulfillment stand in harmony, and in which self-consciousness plays no role. Werther defines this space variously: as the natural world in which he can lose himself, as the company of peasants and children, or as earlier, literarily defined historical periods (the times of Homer, Ossian, and the biblical patriarchs). What these ideal constructs share is their apparent offer of freedom from societal constraints. Their most radical manifestation is to be found in Werther's love for Lotte, which by its very nature implies a condemnation of capitalism: "Nur in einer Gesellschaft, in der die Menschen ihre Interessen im Regelfall nur auf Kosten ihrer Mitmenschen durchsetzen können — in einer Gesellschaft der Konkurrenz und der wechselseitigen Instrumentalisierung — kann die Liebe so zum Ideal erhoben werden, wie es bei Werther geschieht" (196; Only in a society in which human beings can as a rule achieve their interests exclusively at the cost of others — in a society of competition and reciprocal instrumentalization — can love be promoted to such an ideal as in the case of Werther). As with the novel's other utopias, this love's fictionality is foregrounded: the great love scenes do not depict the passionate encounters of two lovers; they represent the letter writer's fantasies of what might be (193; for a different interpretation of societal constraints and the different spaces within *Werther*, see Renner 1985, 9–13).

Two actual events intrude on Werther's imaginary worlds, says Assling. His failure at court, however, is not one of them, since he in fact provoked that disaster himself in order to confirm his unsuitability for work in the practical world (176). The first is the felling of the two walnut trees, as described in the letter of September 15. This action, claims Assling, represents institutional power's enforcement of modern utilitarianism; it was undertaken for economic reasons by the mayor and the parson's wife, over the objections of the older inhabitants. Under these circumstances, Werther's suffering becomes redefined as a general affliction, a powerlessness in the face of exploitative reason (181). His other setback occurs when his own sexual urges sully his idealized love for Lotte. Here his fancies prove to be incapable of suppressing natural human drives, as bourgeois society requires (196). This development, says Assling, explains the presence of *Emilia Galotti* on Werther's bedside table. Its heroine too chooses to die rather than fall victim to her sensuality (203). Werther's imaginary worlds are not just flights from societal contradictions, however. Through them he constructs a fictional self that lends him a kind of heroic status. His suffering and eventual suicide legitimize and thus, paradoxically, negate his alienation by placing him among or even at the head of other victims of human exploitation. He in fact becomes the author and the tragic hero of his own literary creation. (We will consider Assling's interpretation further in chapter 5. At this point it is sufficient to point out that he, like some of the other later Marxists, sees Werther as an unconscious victim of capitalism's indirect consequences.)

More representative of post-1970s political treatments is Horst Flaschka's comprehensive study. Flaschka includes a number of approaches and is aware of the history of each. After an extensive review of the political and sociological interpretations of *Werther* (1987, 57–84), he offers his own. Like Scherpe, he goes outside the text, but rather than focus on the contemporary responses to the novel, he seeks significance in its origins, in the circumstances that Goethe and Karl Wilhelm Jerusalem experienced in Wetzlar (again, see chapter 5). According to Flaschka, Goethe's account of Werther's employment with the Ambassador intends to castigate those exaggerated aspects of the aristocracy that the two young men found at the Imperial Court: arrogance, pomposity, snobbery, cynical ambition, and antiquated ceremony. Despite this critique, and despite his consistent assertions of bourgeois autonomy and individual emancipation, "verficht der junge Goethe nicht als blindwütiger Umstürtzler gegen das herrschende Feudalsystem, sondern als ziviler Rebell, den die Enge und Muffigkeit des schmarotzenden Bürgertums ebenso zur Opposition herausforderte wie der blasierte Führungsanspruch eines dekadenten Teils des Adels. So gesehen eintspringt seine Gesellschaftskritik im 'Werther' weder einem politischen Kalkül noch einem klassenkämpferischen Ideal" (98–99; the young Goethe was no raging revolutionary warring against the prevailing feudal system, but rather a civil rebel, as moved to opposition by an obsequious bourgeoisie's narrowness and fustiness as by a decadent part of the aristocracy's smug claim to leadership. Seen in this light, *Werther's* social criticism springs neither from political calculation nor from an ideal of class struggle).

Flaschka's interpretation points up a methodological problem that plagues many of the political approaches to *Werther,* as well as the psychological ones: a conflation of hero and author. When we say that *Werther* is revolutionary, or even socially critical, do we mean Goethe, Werther, or the text itself? Do we use the novel's categorical features to locate it somewhere on the continuum of historical change? Do we measure effect or intention — and, if so, whose? Scherpe's approach, for all its questionable features, at least tries to establish some sort of rigor by examining reactions to the book. Unfortunately, much gets lost in that process, including the text, which is reduced to a kind of black box. Especially in the 1970s, when political approaches to *Werther* seemed to carry such high stakes, the general rancor of the times often pushed aside these questions. Methodologically thoughtful studies, such as Hohendahl's (1972) are all too rare.

Notes

[1] 1843, 153–54. In referring to Zion, Schlosser seems to imply that Goeze was fighting for a fictional utopian community rather than participating in a reactionary Jewish conspiracy — which would be a strange accusation indeed. I am grateful to Susannah Heschel and Jonathan L. Sheehan for their opinions on this question.

[2] Scherpe's repetitious, nominal style and strong affinity for the passive voice and extended adjectival modifiers make him difficult to read and even more difficult to translate. Here, for German-speakers, is another typical sentence: "In der literarischen Widerspiegelung wird die in Wetzlar erlebte gesellschaftliche Konfliktsituation in ihrer Widersprüchlichkeit konkretisiert und verallgemeinert zum Konfliktfall des durch reiche Anlagen und umfassende Produktivität ausgezeichneten bürgerlichen Individuums in dem in Unproduktivität erstarrten feudalabsolutistischen System" (196).

Works Cited

Alewyn, Richard. 1970. Review of Scherpe 1970. *Germanistik* 11 (1970): 756–57.

Ames, Carol. 1977. "Competition, Class, and Structure in 'Die Leiden des jungen Werther.'" *The German Quarterly* 50 (1977): 138–49.

Assling, Reinhard. 1981. *Werthers Leiden: Die ästhetische Rebellion der Innerlichkeit*. Frankfurt am Main, Bern: Lang.

Atkins, Stuart. 1972. Review of Scherpe 1970. *Germanic Review* 47 (1972): 297–300.

Batts, Michael S. 1993. *A History of Histories of German Literature, 1835–1914*. Montreal and Kingston: McGill-Queen's UP.

Bennett, Benjamin. 2001. *Goethe as Woman: The Undoing of Literature*. Detroit: Wayne State UP.

Bernays, Michael. 1875. Introd. to *Der junge Goethe: Seine Briefe und Dichtungen von 1764–1776*, ed. Salomon Hirzel, 1:iii–xcvii. Leipzig: Hirzel, 1887.

Beutler, Ernst. 1940. "Wertherfragen." *Viermonatsschrift der Goethe-Gesellschaft* 5 (1940): 138–60.

———. 1941. "Das ertrunkene Mädchen." In *Essays um Goethe*, 111–20. Wiesbaden: Dieterich, 1947.

Bickelmann, Ingeborg. 1937. *Goethes "Werther" im Urteil des 19. Jahrhunderts. (Romantik bis Naturalismus 1830–1880)*. Diss., Frankfurt am Main.

Blessin, Stefan. 1979. *Die Romane Goethes.* Königstein/Ts.: Athenäum.

Blumenthal, Herrmann. 1940. "Ein neues Wertherbild?" *Viermonatsschrift der Goethe-Gesellschaft* 5 (1940): 315–20.

Böckmann, Paul. 1935. *Hölderlin und seine Götter.* Munich: Beck.

Braemer, Edith (Abel). 1963. *Goethes Prometheus und die Grundpositionen des Sturm und Drang.* Weimar: Arion.

Carlyle, Thomas. 1838. *Lectures on the History of Literature, Delivered by Thomas Carlyle, April to July 1838.* New York: Scribners, 1892.

Dainat, Holger. 1994. "Voraussetzungsreiche Wissenschaft: Anatomie eines Konflikts zweier NS-Literaturwissenschaftler im Jahre 1934." *Euphorion* 88 (1994): 103–22.

Demetz, Peter. 1967. "Zur Situation der Germanistik: Tradition und aktuelle Probleme." In *Methodenfragen der deutschen Literaturwissenschaft*, ed. Reinhold Grimm and Jost Hermand, 162–84. Darmstadt: Wissenschaftliche Buchgesellschaft, 1973.

Dilthey, Wilhelm. 1867. "Die dichterische und philosophische Bewegung in Deutschland, 1770–1800." In *Gesammelte Schriften*, 5:12–27. Leipzig: Teubner, 1924.

Elias, Norbert. 1976. *The Civilizing Process: Sociogenetic and Psychogenetic Investigations.* Trans. Edmund Jephcott. Oxford: Blackwell, 2000.

Engels, Friedrich. 1845. Letter to the editor. *The Northern Star* (Oct. 25, 1845).

———. 1847. "Karl Grün, *Über Goethe vom menschlichen Standpunkte.* Darmstadt, 1846." In *Karl Marx, Friedrich Engels: Werke.* 4:222–47. Berlin: Dietz, 1969.

Eyck, John R. J., and Katherine Arens. 2004. "The Court of Public Opinion: Lessing, Goethe, and Werther's *Emilia Galotti.*" *Monatshefte* 96 (2004): 40–61.

Farrelly, Daniel. 1997. "Marxist 'Werther' Interpretations Reviewed." In *Schein und Widerschein: Festschrift für T. J. Casey*, ed. Eoin Bourke et al., 54–65. Galway: Galway UP.

Fertig, Ludwig. 1965. *Der Adel im deutschen Roman des 18. und 19. Jahrhunderts.* Diss., Heidelberg.

Fischer, Peter. 1986. "Familienauftritte: Goethes Phantasiewelt und die Konstruktion des 'Werther'-Romans." In Schmiedt 1989a, 189–220.

Flaschka, Horst. 1987. *Goethes "Werther": Werkkontextuelle Deskription und Analyse.* Munich: Fink.

Fohrmann, Jürgen. 1991. "Deutsche Literaturgeschichte und historisches Projekt in der ersten Hälfte des 19. Jahrhunderts." In *Wissenschaft und Nation: Zur Entstehungsgeschichte der deutschen Literaturwissenschaft,* ed. Jürgen Fohrmann and Wilhelm Voßkamp, 205–15. Munich: Fink.

Fricke, Gerhard. 1937. *Die Entdeckung des Volkes in der deutschen Geistesgeschichte vom Sturm und Drang bis zur Romantik: Rede, gehalten bei der Universitätsfeier am 30. Januar, 1937, dem 4. Jahrestag der Begründung des Dritten Reichs.* Hamburg: Hanseatische Verlagsanstalt.

———. 1950. "Goethe und Werther." In *Goethe on Human Creativeness and Other Essays,* ed. Rolf King, C. Brown and E. Funke, 29–75. Athens: U of Georgia P.

Gervinus, Georg Gottfried. 1835. *Geschichte der deutschen Dichtung.* Vol. 4. Leipzig: Engelmann, 1850.

Goebbels, Joseph. 1929. *Michael: ein deutsches Schicksal in Tagebuchblättern.* Munich: Eher.

Grün, Karl. 1846. *Über Göthe, vom menschlichen Standpunkte.* Darmstadt: Leske.

Hass, Hans Egon. 1957. "Werther-Studie." In *Gestaltprobleme der Dichtung: Günther Müller zu seinem 65. Geburtstag,* ed. Richard Alewyn et al., 83–125. Bonn: Bouvier.

Heine, Heinrich. 1828. "Beers 'Struensee.'" In *Heines Werke,* ed. Ernst Elster, 7:224–38. Leipzig, Wien: Bibliographisches Institut, 1890.

Herder, Johann Gottfried. 1774. *Übers Erkennen und Empfinden in der menschlichen Seele.* Vol. 8 of *Sämmtliche Werke,* ed. Bernhard Suphan, 236–62. Berlin: Weidmann, 1902.

Herrmann, Hans Peter, ed. 1994a. *Goethes "Werther": Kritik und Forschung.* Darmstadt: Wissenschaftliche Buchgesellschaft.

Hettner, Hermann. 1850. *Die romantische Schule in ihrem inneren Zusammenhange mit Göthe und Schiller.* Braunschweig: Vieweg.

Hillebrand, Karl. 1885. "Die Werther-Krankheit in Europa." In *Völker und Menschen,* 283–320. Strasbourg: Trübner, 1914.

Hirsch, Arnold. 1958. "'Die Leiden des jungen Werthers': Ein bürgerliches Schicksal im absolutistischen Staat." In *Sturm und Drang,* ed. Manfred Wacker, 341–67. Darmstadt: Wissenschaftliche Buchgesellschaft, 1985.

Hirsch, Franz. 1885. *Geschichte der deutschen Litteratur von ihren Anfängen bis auf die neueste Zeit.* Vol. 2. Leipzig: Friedrich.

Hohendahl, Peter Uwe. 1972. "Empfindsamkeit und gesellschaftliches Bewusstsein: Zur Soziologie des empfindsamen Romans am Beispiel von *La vie de Marianne, Clarissa, Fräulein von Sternheim,* und *Werther.*" *Jahrbuch der deutschen Schillergesellschaft* 16 (1972): 176–207.

———. 1985b. "Literary Criticism in the Epoch of Liberalism, 1820–70." In *Geschichte der deutschen Literaturkritik (1730–1980),* ed. Hohendahl, 179–276. Stuttgart: Metzler.

Holthusen, Hans Egon. 1968. "Vietnam und die Pistolen aus Lottes Hand . . . oder: Die Aktualität eines klassischen deutschen Romans — Anläßlich einer Lektüre von Goethes 'Werther.'" *Die Welt* 77 (30 March 1968): iii.

Hübner, Klaus. 1982. *Alltag im literarischen Werk: Eine literatursoziologische Studie zu Goethes "Werther."* Heidelberg: Groos, 1982, 1987.

Jauss, Hans Robert. 1982. *Question and Answer: Forms of Dialogic Understanding.* Trans. Michael Hays. Minneapolis: U of Minnesota P, 1989.

Kaiser, Gerhard. 1971. "Zum Syndrom modischer Germanistik: Bemerkungen über Klaus Scherpe, *Werther und Wertherwirkung; Zum Syndrom bürgerlicher Gesellschaftsordnung im 18. Jahrhundert;* Bad Homburg v.d.H. 1970." *Euphorion* 65 (1971): 194–99.

Kayser, Wolfgang. 1941. "Die Entstehung von Goethes 'Werther.'" In Herrmann 1994a, 128–57.

Kindermann, Heinz. 1939. *Kampf um das soziale Ordnungsgefüge.* Vol. 1. Leipzig: Reclam.

———. 1941 "Die Sturm-und-Drang-Bewegung im Kampf um die deutsche Lebensform." In *Von deutscher Art in Sprache und Dichtung,* ed. Gerhard Fricke, et al., 4:3–52. Stuttgart, Berlin: Kohlhammer.

Kluckhohn, Paul, ed. 1934. *Die Idee des Volkes im Schrifttum der deutschen Bewegung.* Berlin: Junker & Dünnhaupt.

Kluge, Gerhard. 1971. "Die Leiden des jungen Werthers in der Residenz: Vorschlag zur Interpretation einiger Werther-Briefe." *Euphorion* 65 (1971): 115–31.

Koldewey, Friedrich. 1881. "Werther's Urbild." In *Lebens- und Charakterbilder,* 167–202. Wolfenbüttel.

Kollektiv für Literaturgeschichte. 1956. *Erläuterungen zur deutschen Literatur.* Vol. 4. Berlin: Volk und Wissen.

Kortum, Hans, and Reinhard Weisbach. 1970. "Unser Verhältnis zum literarischen Erbe: Bemerkungen zu Peter Müllers 'Zeitkritik und Utopie in Goethes *Werther.*'" *Weimarer Beiträge* 16, Heft 5 (1970): 214–19.

Lämmert, Eberhard. 1967. "Germanistik — eine deutsche Wissenschaft." In *Germanistik — eine deutsche Wissenschaft: Beiträge von E. Lämmert, W. Killy, O. Conrady, P. v. Polenz,* 9–41. Frankfurt am Main: Suhrkamp.

Lange, Victor. 1964. "Die Sprache als Erzählform in Goethes 'Werther.'" In *Formenwandel: Festschrift zum 65. Geburtstag von Paul Böckmann,* ed. Walter Müller-Seidel and Wolfgang Preisendanz, 261–72. Hamburg: Hoffmann & Campe.

Lenz, Jakob Michael Reinhold. 1775. "Briefe über die Moralität der 'Leiden des jungen Werthers.'" In *Werke und Briefe,* ed. Sigrid Damm, 2:673–90. Leipzig: Insel, 1987.

Linden, Walther. 1937. *Geschichte der deutschen Literatur von den Anfängen bis zur Gegenwart.* Leipzig: Reclam.

Lukács, Georg. 1936. "'Die Leiden des jungen Werther.'" In Herrmann 1994a, 39–57.

Mandelkow, Karl Robert. 1980. *Goethe in Deutschland: Rezeptionsgeschichte eines Klassikers.* Vol. 1. Munich: Beck.

Michels, Josef. 1936. *Goethes "Werther": Beiträge zum Formproblem des jungen Goethe.* Diss., Kiel.

Müller, Peter. 1965. *Zeitkritik und Utopie in Goethes Roman "Die Leiden des jungen Werther": Analyse zum Menschenbild der Sturm- und Drang-Dichtung Goethes.* Diss., HU, Berlin, 1965; Berlin: Rütten & Loening, 1969.

———. 1973. "Angriff auf die humanistische Tradition." *Weimarer Beiträge* 19 (1973): Heft 1, 109–27; Heft 3, 92–109.

Müller, Wilhelm. 1938. *Studien über die rassischen Grundlagen des "Sturm und Drang."* Berlin: Junker & Dünnhaupt.

Mundt, Theodor. 1834. *Moderne Lebenswirren: Briefe und Zeitabenteuer eines Salzschreibers.* Leipzig: Reichenbach.

Oettinger, Klaus. 1976. "'Eine Krankheit zum Tode.' Zum Skandal um Werthers Selbstmord." *Deutschunterricht* 28 (1976): 55–74.

Plenzdorf, Ulrich. 1973. *Die neuen Leiden des jungen W.*, ed. Richard A. Zipser. New York: Wiley, 1978.

Pongs, Hermann. 1927. *Versuch einer Morphologie der metaphorischen Formen.* Vol. 1 of *Das Bild in der Dichtung.* Marburg: Elwert.

Prutz, Robert. 1859. *Die deutsche Literatur der Gegenwart: 1848 bis 1858.* Vol. 1. Leipzig: Voigt & Günther.

Reiss, Hans S. 1963. *Goethe's Novels.* New York: St. Martin, 1969.

Renner, Karl N. 1985. "'Laß das Büchlein dein Freund seyn': Goethes Roman 'Die Leiden des jungen Werther' und die Diätetik der Aufklärung." In *Zur Sozialgeschichte der deutschen Literatur von der Aufklärung bis zur Jahrhundertwende*, ed. Günter Häntzschel et al., 1–20. Tübingen: Niemeyer.

Reuter, Hans-Heinrich. 1972. "Der gekreuzigte Prometheus: Goethes Roman 'Die Leiden des jungen Werthers.'" *Goethe-Jahrbuch* 89 (Weimar, 1972): 86–115.

Rothmann, Kurt. 1972. "War Goethes Werther ein Revolutionär? Auseinandersetzung mit Georg Lukács." *University of Dayton Review* 9, no. 1 (1972): 77–90.

Saine, Thomas. 1980. "Passion and Aggression: The Meaning of Werther's Last Letter." *Orbis Litterarum* 35 (1980): 327–56.

Sauder, Gerhard. 1974. *Voraussetzungen und Elemente.* Vol. 1 of *Empfindsamkeit.* Stuttgart: Metzler.

Scharfschwerdt, Jürgen. 1978. "'Werther' in der DDR: Bürgerliches Erbe zwischen sozialistischer Kulturpolitik und gesellschaftlicher Realität." *Jahrbuch der Deutschen Schillergesellschaft* 22 (1978): 235–76.

Scheff, Thomas J., and Ursula Mahlendorf. 1988. "Emotion and False Consciousness: The Analysis of an Incident from 'Werther.'" *Theory, Culture, and Society* 5 (Cleveland 1988): 57–80.

Scherer, Wilhelm. 1886. *A History of German Literature*. Trans. F. C. Conybeare. ed. F. Max Müller. Vol. 2. New York: Scribners.

Scherpe, Klaus R. 1970. *Vier Wertherschriften aus dem Jahre 1775 in Faksimile*. Appendix to *Werther und Wertherwirkung; Zum Syndrom bürgerlicher Gesellschaftsordnung im 18. Jahrhundert*. Bad Homburg: Gehlen.

———. 1974. "Natürlichkeit und Produktivität im Gegensatz zur 'bürgerlichen Gesellschaft': Die literarische Opposition des Sturm und Drang; Johann Wolfgang Goethes 'Werther.'" In *Grundkurs 18. Jahrhundert: Die Funktion der Literatur bei der Formierung der bürgerlichen Klasse Deutschlands im 18. Jahrhundert,* ed. Gert Mattenklott and Klaus Scherpe, 2:189–215; supporting materials, 2: 113–35. Kronberg/Taunus: Scriptor.

Scherr, Johannes. 1861. *Allgemeine Geschichte der Literatur: Ein Handbuch*. Stuttgart: Franckh.

Schiller, Dieter. 1970. "Sozialistisches Erbe und Nationalliteratur." *Weimarer Beiträge* 16, Heft 5 (1970): 117–38.

Schlosser, Friedrich Christoph. 1843. *Geschichte des achtzehnten Jahrhunderts und des neunzehnten bis zum Sturz des französischen Kaiserreichs mit besonderer Rücksicht auf geistige Bildung*. Vol. 4. Heidelberg: Mohr, 1864.

Schmidt, Julian. 1861. *Geschichte der deutschen Litteratur von Leibniz bis auf unsere Zeit*. Vol. 2. Berlin: Hertz, 1886–96.

Schöffler, Herbert. 1938. "Die Leiden des jungen Werther. Ihr geistesgeschichtlicher Hintergrund." In Herrmann 1994a, 58–87.

Scholz, Rüdiger. 1988. "Frühe Zerfallserscheinungen des bürgerlichen Selbst." *Jahrbuch der Psychoanalyse* 23 (1988): 213–41.

Siebers, Tobin. 1993. "The Werther Effect: The Esthetics of Suicide." *Mosaic* 26 (1993): 15–34.

Staiger, Emil. 1952. *Goethe: 1749–1786*. Zürich: Atlantis.

Stephan, Arndt, and Inge Stephan. 1975. "'Werther' und 'Werther'-Rezeption — Ein Unterrichtsmodell zur Aufarbeitung bürgerlichen Selbstverständnisses." In *Projekt Deutschunterricht*, 9:146–76. Stuttgart: Metzler.

Storz, Gerhard. 1953. "Der Roman 'Die Leiden des jungen Werthers.'" In *Goethe Vigilien oder Versuche in der Kunst, Dichtung zu verstehen*, 19–41. Stuttgart: Klett.

Swales, Martin. 1987. *Goethe: "The Sorrows of Young Werther."* Cambridge: Cambridge UP.

Taylor, Bayard. 1879. *Studies in German Literature*. New York: Putnam.

Vaget, Hans. 1982. "Goethe the Novelist: On the Coherence of His Fiction." In *Goethe's Narrative Fiction: the Irvine Goethe Symposium*, ed. William J. Lillyman, 1–20. Berlin; New York: de Gruyter, 1983.

Vazsonyi, Nicholas. 1997. *Lukács Reads Goethe: From Aestheticism to Stalinism.* Columbia, SC: Camden House.

Viëtor, Karl. 1949. "La maladie du siècle." In *Goethe: A Collection of Essays,* ed. Victor Lange, 26–32. Englewood Cliffs, NJ: Prentice-Hall, 1968.

Vilmar, August Friedrich Christian. 1845. *Geschichte der deutschen National-Literatur.* Marburg, Leipzig: Elwert, 1877.

Werner, Hans-Georg. 1970. Review of Peter Müller's "Zeitkritik und Utopie in Goethes '*Werther.*'" *Weimarer Beiträge* 16, Heft 7 (1970): 193–99.

Wilson, James D. 1975. "Goethe's 'Werther': A Keatsian Quest for Self-Annihilation." *Mosaic* 9/1 (1975): 93–109.

Wilson, W. Daniel. 1989. "Patriarchy, Politics, Passion: Labor and Werther's Search for Nature." *Internationales Archiv für Sozialgeschichte der deutschen Literatur* 14 (1989): 15–44.

Zimmermann, Georg. 1869. "Werther's Leiden und der literarische Kampf um sie." *Herrigs Archiv* 45 (1869): 241–98.

Etching by Daniel Berger, copied from Nikolaus Daniel Chodowiecki and printed in Friedrich Himburg's pirated edition of Werther *(Berlin, 1775). Courtesy of Goethe-Museum, Düsseldorf, photograph by Walter Klein.*

5: Goethe, Werther, Reading, and Writing

WERTHER'S ORIGINAL APPEAL derived not only from its articulation of a new generation's sensibilities, but also from the titillating effect of its being a *roman à clef*. Everyone knew that Karl Wilhelm Jerusalem's shocking suicide in 1772 was the model for Werther's death. Indeed, most readers considered that prominent clergyman's son and Goethe's fictional hero to be interchangeable. When Friedrich Christian Laukhard, writing in 1792, recalled the *Werther*-inspired midnight ceremonies at Jerusalem's burial site 16 years earlier, he added that "young Werther's grave is still being visited" (1792, 219). That was still the case in 1839, when the *Rheinische Provinzialblätter* (Rhineland Provincial Journal) reported on continuing pilgrimages to "Werther's grave in Wetzlar" (quoted in Bickelmann 1937, 27). Equally interesting to contemporary readers was that Charlotte Buff and Johann Georg Christian Kestner had inspired, indeed *were*, Lotte and Albert. The thirst for information about such real-life models seemed unquenchable, and the very first monograph about *Werther*, published in 1775, provided a number of keys to their identity. Its author, Karl Wilhelm Freiherr von Breidenbach zu Breidenstein, had lived in Wetzlar from 1772 until 1776 and was thus able to identify Werther's "Wahlheim" as the nearby village of Garbenheim, to locate the well in Wetzlar that is described in the letter of May 12, and, most important, to name the models for the novel's characters, albeit in still slightly encoded form. The "Magistrate S . . . ," says Breidenbach, is actually "Magistrate B..f" (Heinrich Adam Buff), while "Lotte" is his daughter Charlotte — "schlank, blond, mit blauen Augen, naiv, und sonst liebenswürdig" (6: slim, blonde, with blue eyes, naive, and charming besides). Albert is the "Archival Secretary Ke..r" (Johann Christian Kestner), now married to her and living in Hannover (1775, 5–6). Abbreviating these names was only an affectation: it did not take long to establish that "Ke..r" was "Kestner" and "B..f" was "Buff," especially when Breidenbach added the address of the family's house. Fräulein von B. and Count von C. are similarly identified. Jerusalem's role was already so obvious that Breidenbach simply refers to him as "Werther" when recounting his story.

While Breidenbach also stresses that no one should expect a literary work like *Werther* to report real events accurately, he nevertheless assumes that readers would be interested in "the facts" (4). And indeed they were. Goethe grew so annoyed at questions about what was "true" in *Werther* that he took to traveling incognito (*HA* 9: 592–93[1]). The history of Breidenbach's book also testifies to the strength of this fascination. The first printing reported, as does the novel itself, that a magistrate had attended Jerusalem/Werther's burial. The implication that a suicide had received such official sanction precipitated a scandal, and a chastened Breidenbach bought up all of the remaining copies of his book and issued a "zweite, verbesserte Auflage" (second, improved printing) that pointedly leaves out "eine Anecdote" (an anecdote) that might prove injurious to the exequies' organizer (1775, 16). It was this version of the monograph that received wide circulation, especially when Nicolai appended it to the publication of his parody of *Werther* (Flaschka 1987, 17 and 300).

This enormous public interest in *Werther* as a *roman à clef* of course affected the principals involved. Reading the advance copy that Goethe sent him, Kestner recognized himself in Albert and was unhappy about the unflattering portrayal, even after acknowledging that artists may legitimately take liberties with their fictional characters. While he and his wife eventually accepted and even largely enjoyed the fame that *Werther* brought them (see Meyer-Krentler 1989, 241–48), they understandably wanted to appear in as positive a light as possible — he as an open and generous friend, she as the chaste and innocent object of a genius's passion. Certainly their concern was justified, for their celebrity lasted even well beyond their lifetimes. In the middle of the next century, their son August responded to the continuing public fascination by publishing documents pertaining to his parents' relationship with Goethe (Kestner 1854). In 1928, the hundredth anniversary of Lotte's death still generated considerable attention (Weber 1928, 83), while Thomas Mann's *Lotte in Weimar* traded on the same degree of interest in 1939. As recently as 1994, a biography of *Werthers Lotte*, by Ruth Rahmeyer, appeared for the popular market. This absorption with the real-life models for Goethe's fictional characters is not confined to the general public; it affects scholars as well. Karl Goedeke reflects the nineteenth century's particular interest in biographical approaches when he goes so far as to claim that *Werther's* most interesting literary feature is Goethe's own emotional attachment to his material; to view the novel only aesthetically, separate from its origins, is to miss not just its primary appeal, but its true artistic meaning. At the same time, says Goedeke, the book also suffers aesthetically from Goethe's failure to exercise control over the emotions and experiences that he presents directly, without artistic shaping (1859, 9–11). Goedeke's approach is no quaint remnant of a former time. Even today it is hard to find a study of *Werther*, no matter what methodology it employs, that does not begin with an account of the novel's origins in Wetzlar (see Wagenknecht 1973, 4).

Although contemporaries like Merck had already written privately about the real-life events and personalities that had inspired *Werther*, Breidenbach's monograph of 1775 touched off a kind of cottage industry that continues to the present day. Some of these biographically based studies seek to correct errors of perception, such as the popular notion that Jerusalem had been in love with Charlotte Buff (see Weber 1928, 90). August Kestner hopes to save his mother's reputation when he emphasizes that she and Goethe, unlike Lotte and Werther, never saw each other after her wedding, at least until she paid him her famous visit as a sixty-year-old widow (1854, 3). But most researchers simply assume that the biographical "keys" to the novel are significant in and of themselves. To list just a few: Lotte's piercing black eyes came not from Charlotte Buff, but from Maximiliane Brentano, née von La Roche, another young married woman with whom Goethe was infatuated; and in the 1787 version, *Werther's* heroine gained attributes from Charlotte von Stein (Schmidt 1879, 281–83; Vincent 1992); Albert, too, has multiple sources: some of his less-attractive qualities derived from Brentano's husband, Peter, as well as from Philipp Jakob Herd, whose wife, Elisabet, was the object of Jerusalem's passion (Feise 1914b, 2). And any number of scholars have mined Jerusalem's life for its many parallels with Werther's, including a hopeless love for a married woman, the court's favor, unhappy employment with an ambassador, a snub suffered at an aristocrat's soirée, and, of course, suicide (see, for example, Koldewey 1881). Goethe himself names some of these sources when he recounts the novel's genesis in his autobiography, *Dichtung und Wahrheit* (Poetry and Truth, *HA* 9:585–93), but his reliance on forty-year-old memories does not always make him a trustworthy informant. Ironically, our current "documentation of the poet's life and milieu exceeds even that of the poet himself; we have an overview that Goethe lacked" (Powers 1999, 48–49).

Over two centuries of *Quellenforschung* (research into sources) has included minor figures and locations, as well: Heinrich Düntzer identifies the innkeeper who serves Goethe/Werther milk in Garbenheim/Wahlheim as one Frau Koch (1849, 120). Erich Schmidt finds the model for Heinrich, the scribe who was driven insane by his love for Lotte, in Johann David Balthasar Clauer, who lived in Goethe's family's house (1879, 281–88; see also Möbius 1898, 115–17); Schmidt further suggests that the deceased "friend of Werther's youth" was inspired either by Susanna Katharina von Klettenberg, Goethe's tutor in things pietistic, or by Henriette Alexandrine von Roussillon, known as "Urania" in the *Darmstadter Kreis der Empfindsamen* (the Darmstadt Circle of Sentimentalists). Heinrich Gloël (1911) furnishes a biographical sketch of Count Johann Maria Rudolf Waltbott von und zu Bassenheim, the model for Count von C. Ernst Beutler points to Anna Elisabeth Stöber, the subject of a Frankfurt autopsy report, as the inspiration for the girl who drowns herself in Werther's story (1940, 138–44), and to the rectory of St. Peter's Church in Frankfurt as the model for the vicarage that Lotte and Werther visit (145–47). According to Robert Hering, Frankfurt's Gutleuthof is the basis for

Werther's hometown, described in the letter of May 9 (1935, 197–98; for a sampling of further portrayals of the novel's origins, see Goedeke 1859; Herbst 1881; Loewe 1901; Kaulitz-Niedeck 1908; Gloël 1922; Blumenthal 1940; Schrader 1952; Hass 1957; Migge 1967; Flaschka 1987; Schmidt 1988).

Though venerable, this positivistic biographical tradition has also always been dogged by questions about its efficacy. Johann Heinrich Merck's review of *Werther*, published in the same year as Breidenbach's book, 1775, chides present and future gossips for concentrating on what Goethe took from real life and ignoring the act of poetic composition (1775, 198). 174 years later, Stuart Atkins still complains that this "traditional biographical emphasis . . . is not only inadequate, as many critics have long realized, but actually misleading" (1948, 545). At their worst, investigations that draw on Goethe's life reduce the novel to misleadingly simplistic generalizations, such as the often expressed notion that the "first part of Werther is based on Goethe's relations with Lotte and Kestner. The second part is based on the unhappy experiences and fate of Jerusalem" (Rose 1931, 135; see also Kestner 1854, 16; Möbius 1898, 113; Kaulitz-Niedeck 1908, 8–9). In 1849, Heinrich Düntzer first assumes that Goethe slavishly stuck to his sources and then criticizes him for doing so: he claims that by insisting on portraying his own flight from Wetzlar in Werther's departure at the end of part one, Goethe adds an element that is incompatible with the rest of the book's structure, while his attempt to combine himself with the figure of Jerusalem fails utterly (Düntzer 1849, 134). This kind of critical approach, which Erich Trunz calls "petty philology" (1951, 558), easily descends into the sort of pedantry that Egon Friedell and Alfred Polgar so successfully satirize in their popular cabaret sketch, "Goethe" (1908). It was explicitly to counter such excesses that Michael Bernays and Salomon Hirzel produced their edition of Goethe's early works, so that readers could enjoy the texts in and of themselves (Bernays 1866, 1875).

At the same time, however, there are occasions when biographical details benefit even close readings. Frank Ryder, for example, contends that a knowledge of the text's sources can help to highlight those presumably significant places at which Goethe deviates from them. One example is a change in both the date and the time of Jerusalem's suicide: "In a novel the author of which is painfully willing to identify his protagonist chronologically (birthday, departure from Wetzlar), and in every other way, with himself, something of moment obviously transcended the temptation to autobiographical equations" (1964, 389). Ryder uses this particular insight to explicate the metaphor of cyclical time that pervades the book. Benjamin Bennett employs a similar, but far more tenuous argument when he ascribes significance to the month of Lotte's wedding date and asks rhetorically: "why does Goethe, in the fiction, push Lotte's marriage up to

February . . . from April (1773) when the Kestners were married, if not to give Lotte plenty of time to get pregnant, and indeed time to bear a child, by the story's end at Christmas?" (2001, 119). The discrepancy between Charlotte Kestner's pregnancy and the fictional Lotte's lack of a child is, according to Bennett, a structural element of the narrative that highlights Werther's attraction to her. "It might be maintained, in fact, that if Lotte had gotten pregnant in time, the whole text of *Werther* would not exist. Would Werther think of returning to her, in June or July, if Albert's proprietary right had been sealed by her pregnancy?" According to Bennett, the implied arbitrariness of this non-development thus serves a kind of deconstructive function: "The potentially fruitful body of the woman is a kind of explosive that bears within itself the possibility of the text's nonrealization, its reduction to nothing" (120).

Horst Flaschka, in discussing Werther's employment with the ambassador, argues only slightly more convincingly that knowing the novel's sources is necessary to its proper understanding. He claims that Goethe's reliance on Jerusalem's actual experiences with Ambassador Johann Jakob Höfler, together with the fact that August Siegfried von Goue, Jerusalem's predecessor in the position, had similar difficulties, lends greater weight to this particular episode in the novel. Instead of reading the figure of the ambassador merely as an unpleasant individual who makes difficulties for Werther, we see him, according to Flaschka's logic, as representing the arbitrary power of the state bureaucracy and are thus ready to give the novel's political dimension its due (1987, 84–93). Erich Schrader, however, argues just the opposite case. After investigating the history of Höfler and Goue (not, he insists, "Goué"), he finds significance in the fact that Goethe gave his fictional ambassador only some of Höfler's less-obnoxious qualities, leaving out, for example, his laziness and alcoholic rages; the point, says Schrader, was not to create an ogre, but to construct a character whose function in the narrative would be limited to preventing Werther from finding fulfillment in his work (1952, 153).

While most recent critics disparage the biographical approach in general — without ignoring it completely — there are exceptions. In 1972, Momme Mommsen presented an interpretation in which an idealized biography trumps the text. Looking at Goethe's own infatuations with Charlotte Buff-Kestner and Maximiliane von La Roche-Brentano, he concludes that the poet practiced Christian renunciation by resisting the strong erotic impulses that are evident in Goethe's farces from the same time, such as *Hanswursts Hochzeit* (Harlequin's Wedding, 1775). Given the remarkable seductive powers that Mommsen ascribes to him, Goethe could easily have bedded either of these women, but he withstands the temptation to do so. Mommsen attributes this same Christian sacrifice, as he defines it, to Werther, even though he finds little evidence for it in the novel itself. Goethe's biography, he finds, is sufficient not only to suggest the interpretation, but also to explain the absence of textual evidence. In fact, says Mommsen, Goethe deliberately set out to hide the basis for this reading, because he was too modest either to parade his own moral achievement before the public or even to give his hero the same degree of sexual appeal that he himself possessed. Goethe himself would have had no trouble pulling Lotte away from Albert; that Werther does not possess the same kind of power is, according to Mommsen, still further evidence of the author's renunciation. Only occasionally does the text provide glimpses of Werther's charisma, such as in the letter of May 17, in which the hero marvels at how popular he is (19–22).

In a different, ultimately psychoanalytical approach to biographical interpretation, Peter Fischer stresses that any legitimate interpretation of a literary work necessarily begins with a thorough analysis of the author's "persönlichen Mythos" (personal myth), the structure of his psychological conflicts. Only then can we ask larger social or historical questions (1986, 207). Deirdre Vincent, however, mounts a strong defense from another perspective: "Ill served as we may have been by Goethe's early biographers and by critics who used his biography as a primitive key to what he wrote, the fact remains that he asserted again and again that his literary works were an expression of his emotional life, and consciously so" (1992, 231). Indeed, says Vincent, we can view neither Goethe's writings nor his life in isolation, because the two were in dialogue with one another. His works became part of his life, not just vice versa (231–34). Finally, Benjamin Bennett takes perhaps the most extreme approach in relating Goethe's biography to *Werther,* asserting that "in real life, Goethe used the book to assert his possession of a real woman, Charlotte Kestner, to translate her frustrating reality into a form that would be irrevocably his property, under his authorial control." This act of appropriation, says Bennett, extends beyond the act of first capturing her in his text; Goethe's letter to Charlotte's husband on November 21, 1774, in which he promises to revise the novel to improve the couple's image, is, Bennett claims, in effect a reminder, even a boastful assertion, of his power over them (2001, 109).

Locating *Werther's* intellectual sources is a less controversial undertaking that brings more obvious benefits, especially in helping modern critics to understand the assumptions that the text's original readers brought to it. To this end, scholars have examined the novel's roots in a variety of cultural and historical phenomena, including: eighteenth-century medical theory (Renner 1985), the culture of sensibility (Biedermann 1867; Hohendahl 1972; Sauder 1974, 1987; Finsen 1977; Paulin 1980; Meyer-Krentler 1982; Luserke 1995), pietism (Beutler 1940; Seeger 1968; Kowalik 1999), Gottfried Arnold's *Kirchen- und Ketzerhistorie* (History of Church and Heretics, 1699; Brinkmann 1976), the hermetic tradition (Zimmermann 1979), Montaigne (Bennett 1986, 2001), the idyll as literary genre (Powers 1999), the Great Chain of Being (Duncan 1987), the concept of the sublime (Walker 1999), Petrarch (Fechner 1982), and the precedents of both form and content in Sophie von La Roche's *Fräulein von Sternheim,* Rousseau's *La nouvelle Héloïse,* and in various English works, especially Samuel Richardson's novels (see, for example, Schmidt 1875; Scherer 1886; Bickelmann 1933; Maurer 1963; Miller 1981; Jauss 1982; Wellbery 1986; Lange 1989; Furst 1990; Kennedy 2000; Barton 2001).

Throughout the history of *Werther* research, however, the correspondence that intrigues critics the most is the one between the book's author and its hero. Robert Ellis Dye claims that "The insight that Werther is not Goethe has been the most important achievement of subsequent Werther criticism over that of the eighteenth century" (1975, 327), but that statement should not suggest that all of the earliest critics failed to make this distinction, nor that all critics do make it now. The first admirers of the novel, we saw, felt that reading Werther's letters grants an access to Goethe's heart, and some of the earliest critics blurred the figures of author and hero as casually as did the enthusiastic readers who so annoyed Goethe — in Anthony Thorlby's description, the author objected that his "readers had not admired the artistry of the novel but rather its hero, and its hero as if he were a real person; worse still, they partly admired Goethe, the author, as though he were his own fictitious hero. That is to say, they did not content themselves with literary appreciation, but wanted to have similar experiences themselves" (1976, 150). But, as Thomas Saine points out, the older commentators of the period were actually less likely to identify the novel's hero with its author. In fact, the "orthodox Christian critics . . . condemned Werther soundly as a fictional character . . . but they seem not to have been quite willing to make the same moral charges against Goethe, the author, without further proof of his sinful ways" (1980, 328). As we have already seen in chapter 2, in the survey of religious interpretations, it has been the subsequent critics who have been more likely to equate the two.

This notion of Goethe's and Werther's overlapping identities supports what is perhaps the single most enduring notion about the novel: that the author wrote himself out of the very malaise that claimed his hero (among many examples, see Hausmann 1955). Possibly most critics, including recent ones, are prepared to argue that at the very least Goethe's act of composition exerted a therapeutic effect and "was to a large extent the reliving of the Lotte [Buff] affair to a different (but of course fictional) conclusion" (Saine 1980, 342).

The pairing of hero and author, however, necessarily implies a significance different from that implied by combining Kestner and Albert or Charlotte Buff and Lotte. It involves not just the relationship between a real-life model and a fictional character, but also the artistic process by which the former creates the latter. While nineteenth-century critics mostly claim that the novel was written as a kind of exorcism, by means of which the psychologically more robust Goethe separated himself from his weaker alter ego, later interpreters tend to stress the role of art, both in the novel's creation and as its subject matter. As Thomas Mann puts it, Werther "is the young Goethe himself, minus the creative gift that nature bestowed on the latter" (1939, 95).

Unique among critics who try to distinguish Werther from Goethe, Max Diez attempts a statistical analysis of their writing styles. He compares Goethe's personal letters from the period, presuming that they represent Goethe's "own style," with Werther's letters from the novel. Counting the "psycho-physical metaphors" in each group of letters, he discovers a strong quantitative discrepancy between the two. Werther's letters are more than twice as likely as Goethe's to introduce sickness, pain, or death as metaphors, and almost three times as likely to use "psycho-physical metonymies" or "figures based on the human body." Diez cites these and other quantifiable differences as evidence of Goethe's conscious shaping of the novel (1936, 1006).

Ernst Feise, on the other hand, compares Werther and Goethe by contrasting their approaches to artistic creation. Werther, he claims, is not a real artist, but merely someone who longs for creativity. His talent goes far enough to express emotion but not to give it aesthetic form, much as Goethe's own attempts at visual art fell short of his aspirations (1914b: 14; for a contrasting view, as well as an analysis of Werther's literary portraiture, see Siegbert Prawer 1984). Hans Vaget later describes this phenomenon in somewhat different terms: "Throughout the book Werther expresses his despair over his inability to cope with the world in the manner of a great artist. . . . He attempts to recreate as a writer what he has experienced as a reader, and he kills himself in frustration when the discrepancy between reality and his expectations becomes unbearable" (1982, 13). Vaget, drawing on the eighteenth-century concept of dilettantism, also sees in Werther traces of Goethe's own doubts about his artistry. Thus the novel becomes "a magnified projection of Goethe's own, as yet unacknowledged sufferings as a dilettante" (13).

When critics claim, as so many of them do, that Goethe wrote *Werther* in order to purge himself of the same affliction that destroyed his hero, they take as their starting point the author's own account of the novel's composition: writing in 1813, some forty years after the fact in *Dichtung und Wahrheit,* Goethe describes his own suicidal state at the time, including his attempt to drive a knife into his chest in imitation of the Roman Emperor Marcus Salvius Otho. When he abandoned that effort and chose instead to live, he sought to complete his transition by putting his emotional experiences into written form. While searching for an appropriate vehicle to do so, he "assembled the elements" that had been occupying him for several years and conjured up the circumstances that had been affecting him. Nothing took shape, however, until the news of Jerusalem's suicide suddenly arrived and caused everything to crystallize. To describe this process, Goethe invokes the metaphor of a bowl of supercooled water that suddenly turns to ice at the least shake (*HA* 9:583–85).

In 1941, Wolfgang Kayser published a seminal article that finds anomalies in Goethe's story of *Werther's* genesis and uses them to examine the creative process at work. An undifferentiated reliance on Goethe's own account of the novel's inception, Kayser argues, distorts our reading of it. Goethe's autobiographical narrative, he says, is itself a literary creation in the form of a novella. Close scrutiny calls its accuracy into question, since the reasons that Goethe has given for his own *tedium vitae* do not really accord with Jerusalem's situation. Instead, the sixty-three-year-old Goethe's recollection of *Werther's* gestation is colored by the recent news that his friend Karl Friedrich Zelter had just lost a son to suicide (1941, 130–32). As Atkins puts it in a similar argument, "The young Goethe of *Dichtung und Wahrheit* is in no small measure a literary creation" (1948, 547).

Kayser's point here is not so much to correct factual details as to examine the authorial role from a new perspective. Goethe's skewed memory may have caused him to recall a hectic gestation period of only four weeks, rather than the eighteen months that the novel's composition actually required, but more important is our recognition that the "elements" that he assembled are themselves poetic creations, not yet-to-be-processed memories. Kayser identifies one example of such artistic mediation in the rhapsodic coda of Goethe's 1772 review of the *Gedichte von einem polnischen Juden* (Poems by a Polish Jew). Contemporaries had already identified this paean to love as an homage to Charlotte Buff (see Hass 1957, 96), but Kayser now stresses not just its lyrical character, but its role as an intermediate step between raw experience and the finished artistic form that is *Werther* (1941, 136).

Modern German critics consider Kayser's study to be the beginning of a qualitatively different consideration of *Werther's* sources, but we can identify earlier attempts to explain Goethe's aesthetic, rather than his psychological, relationship to his experiences. About seventy years earlier, Friedrich Spielhagen had cited *Werther* as an example of the process by which novelists interact with their models to create a third, corollary entity (1871, 5), and Hermann Hettner had stressed that it was Goethe's artistic shaping of his innermost experiences that made *Werther* such a great work (1869, 140). This particular biographical approach also got an early start in England, where it still continues to characterize *Werther* studies. As early as 1856, George Henry Lewes's biography of Goethe points out the chronological discrepancies in the traditional account of *Werther's* genesis: neither the news of Jerusalem's death, nor a "growing despair at the loss of Charlotte," nor "tormenting thoughts of self-destruction" precipitated the novel. "It was not to free himself from suicide that he wrote this story of suicide. All these several threads were woven into its woof; but the rigor of dates forces us to the conviction that *Werther*, although taken from his experience, was not written while that experience was being lived" (Lewes 1856, 214). *Werther*, to use Wordsworth's formulation, originates in emotion that has been recollected in tranquility. Like Kayser eighty-five years later, Lewes is interested here in more than just establishing an accurate chronology of *Werther's* genesis. He intends nothing less than to articulate "the true philosophy of art," using Goethe as an example: "although he cleared his 'bosom of the perilous stuff' by moulding this perilous stuff into art, he must have essentially outlived the storm before he painted it, — conquered his passion, and subdued the rebellious thoughts, before he could make them plastic to his purpose" (214).

This interstice between emotional response and artistic creativity is more than temporal, however. Goethe's review of the *Gedichte von einem polnischen Juden* is, as Kayser shows, not just evidence of biographical developments or of a state of mind, but rather a source of *Werther* in its own right. Albrecht Schöne (1967) finds a similar significance in Goethe's even earlier letters to Ernst Wolfgang Behrisch, while Nicholas Boyle stresses the role played by the letters to Johann Heinrich Merck (1991, 169). Boyle insists that Goethe's novel does not just record "events in which he had been involved: he drew on his formulation of those events two years before in his letters to Merck, and he wrote a novel about the mind that wrote those letters, as well as about the man that met Lotte Buff" (178). In other words, the sources for *Werther* were not just Goethe's personal experiences nor merely received aesthetic traditions, such as the epistolary novel; just as important were Goethe's own, earlier artistic shapings of his experiences, including his own letters. Interestingly, Deirdre Vincent follows this exchange in the other direction, drawing significance from the similarities to be found between the original version of *Werther* and Goethe's letters to Charlotte von Stein between 1783 and 1786 (1992, 91).

The rich fictionality of *Werther*, says Boyle, derives from this reciprocity between feeling and composition: "In order to fuse Goethe's feelings — that is, his letters to Merck — with Jerusalem's story — that is, Kestner's report on his last days and death — it was necessary to create the figure of Werther, at once a character and a consciousness" (169). In fact, Boyle adds Goethe's ambition to this mix. The young author is not simply looking for creative expression, but also trying to make a mark upon the world of letters; "by having recourse to the events of his own life, Goethe has found the answer to the question: what can be the subject-matter of a new, contemporary secular literature?" (178). In this regard, he is also going beyond his earlier success with *Götz von Berlichingen*, this time creating "a human symbol who both represented a social and cultural phenomenon of his time, as Götz did, and spoke, with a voice that said 'I,' of internal longing and division, as did Weislingen" (169; see also Flaschka 1987, 54–55). Thomas Mann means something similar when he claims that "Goethe did not kill himself because he had *Werther* to write — and more besides. Werther had no mission on earth other than to suffer in life" (1939, 95).

Ilse Appelbaum Graham also examines Goethe's story of *Werther's* gestation with a particular interest in the creative process that it describes. Goethe's metaphor of the supercooled water that suddenly turns to ice is especially evocative for two reasons: "Firstly that, in the case of the artist, form is concealed in what seems sheer amorphous flux, to become manifest instantly and spontaneously. Secondly, that a process of stabilisation corresponding to that of the flux which spontaneously assumes form takes place in the artist himself, a stabilisation which precedes the material work of art and is indeed its presupposition" (1974, 21). Graham concludes that creativity is a process with two stages, claiming "that an artist cannot make use of a single element as it has offered itself to his experience in a non-artistic context, that he must assimilate it and create it anew in the body of his medium" (1973, 123).

Hans-Egon Hass, on the other hand, invokes Goethe's concept of "wiederholte Spiegelung" (repeated mirroring; 1957, 105) to characterize the creation of *Werther* as an even more complex progression of "imaginative Steigerung" (imaginative intensification), in which emotional experiences, reflective recollection, and other literary productions, both by other writers and Goethe himself, interact to form and reform a creative structure that finally tips over into an aesthetic configuration — a work of art — with its own form of existence, distinct from the material that went into it (99). Hass concludes his study with an exemplary close reading of Werther's first letter that demonstrates how its multiple sources combine to form a rich, aesthetically shaped structure (106–19).

When Ilse Graham describes Goethe's creative process, she stresses the need for a stage of "stabilisation," not only of the raw material, but also of the creator's self. That is the step that Goethe, but not Werther, can take. "The obstinacy with which Werther cleaves to the personal sphere *from the very outset* precludes the inception of such an aesthetic structure" (1974, 23). For different reasons, then, Graham agrees with Feise and Vaget that "the difference between Goethe and his hero . . . is that between the creative mode of experiencing and an essentially uncreative one" (1973, 130; see also Schaeder 1947, 73; Jolles 1957, 176–79; Pütz 1982, 57–59; Kurz 1982, 95–112). This is also what Anthony Thorlby means when he says, "In a sense Goethe had experienced all that Werther experiences, just as Werther seems to be the author of the book and a great stylist in his letters. Yet the crucial point of difference between them could scarcely be more obvious: the culmination and fulfillment of this experience for Goethe is the writing of a book . . . ; for Werther, that he blows his brains out" (1976, 152). Werther, says Thorlby, confuses or at least wishes to marry reality and art; Goethe, in contrast, transforms reality into art: "everything is changed once it is part of a work of art, a word and not a thing, a touch of beauty and not of pain" (153). Peter Pütz finds Werther's non-creativity to be even more insidious; he suffers less from life than from his literary projections, as an imagined participant in the fictions of Homer and Ossian (1982, 67–68).

William Stephan Davis reverses this process. Werther's attempts at artistic expression fail because he faces the impossible task of producing a mirror that would confirm the integrity of his being. The fault lies not in the means of expression, but in the lack of a self to be expressed: "He is unable to paint an image that would represent such a mirror, not simply because the intensity of his own vision supercedes the language of visual art (as he suggests in his letter), or because his artistic abilities are lacking, but ultimately because the construction of such a mirror implies the possible existence of a whole, autonomous, and integrated self for the mirror to produce through reflection, and this is something Werther can never bring about" (1994, 108).

While many critics who are interested in the artistic process discuss Werther as a writer of letters, surprisingly few of them pay attention to the question of his creative capacities in his own chosen medium. They note that he identifies himself as a painter and that several times he makes attempts at drawing, with varying success, but they normally describe his artistic frustrations only in general terms (for example, Hass 1957, 92). Achim Aurnhammer is unusual in considering Werther's creativity in the context of eighteenth-century discourse on painting. He turns, for example, to Johann Georg Sulzer's warnings about undisciplined genius in his *Theorie der schönen Künste* (Theory of the Fine Arts, 1771–74) for insight into the dangers inherent in Werther's approach to painting Lotte's portrait (1995, 100–104).

Scott Abbott consults a different set of eighteenth-century sources to approach the question of Werther's artistry, reading the novel semiotically in terms of Herder's theories of language and Lavater's physiognomics. Werther's dissatisfaction with his attempts to portray Lotte, and his reliance on her silhouette, are not indications of artistic failure, but "marks of Werther's progress toward natural expression." Abbott points out that "eighteenth-century silhouette theory supplies support for an interpretation that sees in silhouettes a negative perfection not present in more complicated works of art" (1992, 50; see also Fetzer 1971). The novel, Abbott argues, shows Werther struggling within a particular semiotic system, attempting to achieve a mode of natural expression that escapes the mediacy of symbolic representation. This system includes not only linguistic signification and artistic rendering, but also facial expression, gesture, and blood. The scene in which Werther reads Ossian is a momentary breakthrough into wholly natural communication, from which Lotte literally calls him back into the symbolic order, while his suicide becomes a final escape "from the limitations of language and life to the total openness and emptiness of death" (59–60).

In "The Blind Man and the Poet," one of the most evocative studies ever done on *Werther*, Elizabeth M. Wilkinson and L. A. Willoughby take a broad view of the question of Goethe's — and Werther's — search for artistic form. Beginning with Goethe's early responses to Herder's theories of visual perception, they show how a discord between intention and the means of expression can lead to tragedy. An example that Goethe — and Werther — had before him was Lessing's *Emilia Galotti* (1772), in which the painter Conti, struck by Emilia's beauty, wishes that he could paint her portrait directly with his eyes, instead of through the mediacy of his hand. Lessing's Prince also longs to possess her and, impatient with the means, gives his evil henchman a free hand, with tragic results. The play, which Goethe famously dismissed as "zu gedacht" (too carefully thought-out), makes its moral positions obvious; it presents "ambivalence of feeling without uncertainty of standpoint" (Wilkinson/Willoughby 1965, 51). *Werther* is the superior work because, while developing the same moral premise, its presentation of Werther's emotional subjectivity

> shows the glory of its impulse as well as the disaster of its consequences — so that the suicide comes not just as an awful warning but as a challenge to understand that, though absolute adherence to such values may result in the self-destruction of him who holds them, the values themselves may well be forces productive of new effort in the life of society, thought, art, and language, forces which prevent stability from becoming static, common sense deteriorating into complacency, reason settling for solutions this side of the furthermost confines to which the human mind can stretch. That is why Goethe's novel has the sting of passion (in the original sense of the word), Lessing's play only the lash of indictment. (51)

Klaus Müller-Salget's analysis of *Werther* (1981), while it does not concern itself much with sources, nevertheless supports the contention that aesthetic, rather than just emotional, impulses went into the novel's composition. He demonstrates in detail that *Werther* is a highly self-conscious construct, in which the themes of art and nature form the poles of an artful — and artificial — structure. Yet, Müller-Salget stresses, even though Werther is the purported author of these highly crafted letters, we need to retain the distinction between him and Goethe: it was the latter who was able, by writing the novel, to liberate himself from his experiences; Werther, on the other hand, is incapable of giving himself distance from these emotions by objectifying them; indeed, he intensifies their effect (1981, 324–25).

Karl Maurer's exploration of the story of *Werther's* gestation also stresses the formal aspect of Goethe's creativity and the intervening role played by received aesthetic forms. As he provocatively puts it, "Der Briefroman führt nicht nur aus der Wertherkrise heraus, er fährt auch zuvor in sie hinein" (1963, 429; The epistolary novel not only leads the way out of the Werther-crisis, it first leads the way into it). Hartmut Vollmer (2003) also traces Werther's tragedy to the novel's narrative structure, in which a solitary writing subject problematically addresses a reader who inhabits a real, socially ordered world. The discrepancy between the letters' introspective, poetic language, which expresses an individual interiority, and the more prosaic narrative expectations of the letters' recipients, be they Wilhelm or the novel's readers, proves irreconcilable. The problem lies less in the letters' content than in their form. We have also already seen a similar kind of interpretation proposed by Clark Muenzer (1984) and Kathryn Edmunds (1996) in a psychological context, but Reinhard Assling (1981) formulates the role of writing even more radically. Assling proposes that Werther, in order to flee the destructive contradictions of capitalist society, reconstructs himself as a fictional character in a kind of "aesthetic rebellion." When the imaginary worlds he has forged for himself prove to be insufficient buffers against the alienation inherent in modern utilitarianism, he writes himself a new fictional status. Rather than just escape a consciousness of societal constraints, he converts that consciousness into its artistic expression. He literally — and literarily — becomes the author of his inner suffering, giving his subjectivity a public legitimization:

> Werthers Leiden geben sich in seinen Briefen als exemplarische Manifestationen jenes allgemeinen Leidens, das Werther als "Bestimmung des Menschen" beklagt. Je größer sein Leiden, desto mehr beansprucht Werther in ihrer brieflichen Darstellung Allgemeingültigkeit und geradezu kosmische Geltung. Am Ende sieht er sich as Repräsentnant [!] der leidenden Menschengattung, der ihrem Schmerzensschrei vor Gott Gehör verschafft. (143)

> [Werther's sufferings present themselves in his letters as exemplary manifestations of that general suffering that Werther deplores as "human destiny." The greater his sufferings, the more Werther can, in their epistolary representation, lay claim to their general validity and even cosmic significance. In the end he sees himself as the representative of suffering humanity, bringing its cry of pain to God's ear.]

This process, says Assling, represents more than just an emotional compensation for political impotence, the phenomenon that most Marxist commentators posit, for Werther transforms himself into an aesthetic construct. Obviously he is already a fictional character in a novel, but he is a character that gives the illusion of authenticity; this fictional being appears to feel and act in ways that could be imagined in the empirical world, and in this sense Werther is "realistic" (Assling 1981, 1–2). In the course of the novel, however, his fictionality — and his authorship of that fictionality — step further into the foreground. He is denied an authentic self in bourgeois society, and so, says Assling, he manifests himself as an increasingly stylized image of suffering humanity. Where he once allied himself with others' narratives from a past time (for example, Homer's and Ossian's), he now turns his experiences into his own fictional narrative. His suicide, the last step in this process, is staged in every regard, from its physical arrangements to its justification in his final letters. The figure of the fictional editor also participates in this development. Eric Blackall has shown in detail how this gatherer and presenter of Werther's letters is more than just a standard literary device that emphasizes Werther's historicity; he is a fictional figure in his own right, and also one whose perspective eventually melds with Werther's (1976, 44–55). Assling takes this idea even further, maintaining that at the point at which the editor abandons his role as literary executor to become an omniscient and empathetic narrator — when he steps in to speak for, and through, Werther, both are revealed to be literary constructs, and the novel's overt fictionality becomes total (1981, 190). Assling even asserts that the two figures collaborate: the scrap of paper on which Werther formulated his last thoughts was intended for the editor to use in the literary artifact that is now in every sense his story. Werther is the creator of the novel that is himself (202–3).

A number of other critics speculate about *Werther's* editor. In a comprehensive study that traces the editor's role from the opening dedication to the final report of Werther's death, Jürgen Nelles (1996) comes to a different conclusion from Assling's, seeing the editor as a separate consciousness integrated into the work's structure as its organizer and even interpreter. In standing between the author and the reader, however, the editor interrupts the immediacy of Werther's outpourings and thus emphasizes the work's artistic constructedness (see also Siebers 1993, 32). The most recent study finds a simple solution to the editor's complexity of voice: he is, asserts Christoph Schweitzer, none other than Wilhelm, who sets out to create a memorial to his friend but does so with ambiguous feelings, including guilt for not having intervened in time to prevent the suicide. "Only if we understand Wilhelm's many different feelings toward the dead Werther and equate Wilhelm with the Editor, can we explain the variations of the Editor's voice that reach from complete emotional empathy to uninvolved detachment" (Schweitzer 2004, 39).

Fritz Gutbrodt, on the other hand, posits a collaboration between Werther and the editor in the erection of a monument. Drawing on the ideas of authorship presented by Barthes (1977), Foucault (1976) and Kittler (1980), he interprets the novel as Werther's twofold effort to inscribe his name on the text. Names, Gutbrodt shows, play a complex role as signifiers throughout the book, and some of them carry meaning of their own, most notably "Werther," which as a noun indicates "one who is worthy" and as an adjective means "more worthy or valuable." In his relationship with Lotte, where he seeks to have his name replace Albert's, he fails, "and he ends up in a unmarked grave" (1995, 620). But the book, as cultural artifact, opens up a more promising route: "The fiction of the book, as opposed to the letters it publishes, refigures the constellation of agents in the narrative in such a way that Lotte disappears from the structure as the mother she is not in order to make room for a trio of men that will capitalize on her image as the Mother. Let us not forget, at this point, that the ardent love letters Werther writes are addressed to Wilhelm and, for their publication as a book, carefully arranged by the editor" (590). In the end, says Gutbrodt, Werther's popular success served to make a real name — indeed, a brand name — for both its hero and its author.

Joel Black also interprets *Werther* as an "aesthetic" solution, but his reading serves largely as a theoretical update of the traditional idea that "By writing his novel, Goethe . . . saved himself from possible self-destruction" (1994, 241). The novel consists of either a fictional autobiography by Werther or a kind of parallel autobiography by Goethe that makes his own suicide "unnecessary and altogether superfluous" (241). Either way, the genre implies "the author's own imminent demise, which provides the authorial subject with perhaps the most powerful motive for creating a self in and as discourse, and which can be considered autobiography's final cause" (236). Werther's impending suicide, says Black, makes this motive all the more poignant. The novel "can be read both as an autobiography of sorts culminating in the narrator's suicide note and as an autobiographical narrative that is, in its entirety, a suicide note in its own right — the record of a subject's self-creation through its own annihilation" (238). Thus we can see either Goethe or Werther writing himself into existence. Like Graham and Thorlby, Black locates the difference between the author and his hero in Werther's lack of creativity. In discussing the *Bauerbursch* (farmhand) in the 1787 version, Black says, "While Goethe countered his dangerous identification with the suicide Jerusalem by writing *Werther*, his blocked hero can only react to his identification with the servant-murderer (. . .) by accepting the unhappy man's fate as his own" (1994, 252–53). In fact, Black extends this lack of creativity to "Werther and his imitators," calling them all "blocked artists who, unable to produce any fictions of their own, enacted a ready-made script provided by someone else; Goethe, in contrast, was the true artist, who, rather than succumb to Jerusalem's example, went on to write the script that the young suicide might have followed — and that *Werther's* suicidal readers did follow. But then Goethe had only to contend with the straightforward circumstances of Jerusalem's actual fate, while his readers had to face the far more seductive prospect offered by a fictional character's demise" (255).

Black's interpretation appealingly combines several established interpretations of *Werther* from a Foucaultian perspective, but it unfortunately relies on three untenable assumptions. First, he claims that *Werther* touched off a wave of "mass suicide" (252) and thus "became an actual, public suicide note for all the sentimental youths who took their lives in imitation of the work's protagonist" (245). Despite David Phillips's proposal of the term of "Werther effect" for imitative suicide (1974; see also Siebers 1993), the "wave of suicides" supposedly caused by *Werther's* publication is largely a myth that began in the imaginations of zealous social guardians. Laurence Rickels's characterization of *Werther*'s "Jonestown-style readership" (1996, 151) has no factual basis. If there are any actual deaths that can truly be attributed to reading the novel, their number is certainly small. Second, Black uncritically accepts Goethe's autobiographical account of *Werther's* genesis (1994, 240–41), whereas, as we have seen, Goethe mixes a good deal of poetry in with his truth. Finally, Black cites this same account to identify Jerusalem's death as the source of Goethe's own obsession with suicide; Goethe in fact writes that he had already abandoned the idea of killing himself before receiving Kestner's letter with the news of Jerusalem's death. This letter did not give rise to his suicidal impulse, but rather supplied him with the literary structure that he was looking for after already having conquered that impulse.

In considering the biographical background of the novel's 1787 version, Deirdre Vincent's *Werther's Goethe and the Game of Literary Creativity* (1992) revives an issue that has, she feels, received less attention than it deserves: the relationship between the original *Werther* of 1774 and Goethe's revision of it in the following decade. While her point holds, she somewhat overstates the case. Critics have indeed been conscious of both *Werthers;* a number have devoted whole studies to their differences. Heinrich Düntzer (1849, 89–210) consistently distinguishes the two versions' descriptions of Lotte; Martin Lauterbach (1910) compares them through a detailed morphological analysis; Gottfried Fittbogen (1910) examines how all of the principal characters change, while Thomas Saine concentrates on Lotte's portrayal in the two versions (1981); Melitta Gerhard (1916) evaluates the addition of the story of the farmhand (*Bauerbursch*); Gertrud Riess (1924) studies the editions' "stilpsychologische" (stylistic-psychological) differences, stressing Goethe's desire to modify the reader's response; Dieter Welz (1973), who sets out to explore the different "meaning structures," concludes that the older, less revolutionary Goethe takes pains to distance himself further from his hero; and Annika Lorenz and Helmut Schmiedt (1997) invite readers to make their own comparisons in a synoptic edition that places the two versions side by side. Yet Vincent is not wrong in complaining that few of the novel's interpreters distinguish the editions conscientiously. Klaus Müller-Salget is unusually consistent in citing them as A and B (1981). At the same time, there are critics who give considerable thought to the question of which edition to favor. Hans Reiss, for example, discusses all of the major differences in detail before selecting the second for his analysis, considering it "aesthetically more satisfying . . . although the earlier version is perhaps somewhat livelier." He also points out that Goethe chose the second for the standard edition of his works (1963, 18–23; see also Fischer 1986, 203; Swales 1987, 15–23). The first version also has its champions, however. Thomas Saine considers it "artistically more successful" (1980, 327), while Alexander Lernet-Holenia insists that it is the one "true Werther" (1959; see also Wilson 1989, 15, 31–32). Martin Lauterbach joins Bernays (1875: lxxviii) in taking a Solomonic stance, declaring that each version has its advantages: that of 1774 has a greater immediacy of expression, while that of 1787 is more carefully shaped. Each is a valid product of a particular stage in Goethe's development (Lauterbach 1910, 127–28). Despite these examples, Vincent is correct in claiming that most critics simply adopt the second version by default. Those who do give the issue specific consideration tend to accept Goethe's explanation that he undertook his revision in order "den Roman noch einige Stufen höher zu schrauben" (letter to Kestner, May 2, 1783; to ratchet the novel up a few notches).

Philippe Forget finesses this issue of editions with a radical answer to the question of narrative voice. Invoking the structuralist concept of *écriture*, he rejects the idea that Goethe, Werther, or indeed any conscious entity, fictional or real, forms *Werther*. The written text does not encode a personal utterance, but is itself an autonomous entity through which culture, the unconscious, and language itself speak. In the process of being read, the text emancipates itself from the voice of its reputedly self-conscious subject (1984, 133). Where other critics might identify narrative irony in *Werther*, Forget sees a discourse so shot through with contradictions that the reader is invited to abandon the notion of authorial intention altogether and instead to follow the traces of the text's own logic (155).

> Nicht der vermeintlich allwissende empirische Autor (und natürlich auch nicht der auf triviale Weise mit dieser Autorinstanz identifizierte Autor) legt einen Text zugrunde, sondern der Text und dessen Signifikanz mitproduzierende, aber nie genau vorauszusehende und nie voll einkalkulierbare Anteile des Unbewußten produzieren den Künstler in der Fiktion — und so auch den Interpreten, dessen Interpretation auch eine Fiktion ist, da sie sich auf keinen letzten Wahrheitsgrund gründen kann. (161)
>
> [Not the ostensibly omniscient, empirical author (nor of course the fictional author so trivially identified with this authorial entity) forms the basis for a text; rather, the text and its signification, co-produced with the never completely predictable nor wholly measurable participation of the unconscious, produce the artist in its fictionality — and thus also the interpreter, whose interpretation is also a fiction, since it can never ground itself in a final truth.]

In subverting the inherited expectations that it would draw significance from either its origins or its reception (130–33), the text asserts its own autonomy, an independence that logically applies to either version of

Werther. In other words, the traditional investigations into the text's authenticity, its biographical sources, its author's intention, or its effect on readers are red herrings. They divert attention from — indeed, they suppress — critical insight into the text's "Kraftlinien" (lines of force). Forget's own interpretive strategy does not seek to reconstruct an ostensible original horizon, but to deconstruct inherited assumptions that prevent us from reading the text as text (177).

Whereas Forget presents his thesis in a closely argued essay, Roland Barthes makes a related case in a set of fragmentary musings that simulate *Werther's* function as a lover's discourse, which "exists only in outbursts of language, which occur at the whim of trivial, of aleatory circumstances." Although he focuses on the figure of Werther and frequently draws on Freud, Lacan, and Winnicott, Barthes proposes "not a psychological portrait; instead a structural one which offers the reader a discursive site: the site of someone speaking within himself, *amorously,* confronting the other (the loved object), who does not speak" (1977, 4). Werther, who first falls in love even before he meets Lotte and then transfers that love to her (136), is writing out of the isolation of the amorous subject, addressing an other without means of reply. Barthes extends Werther's complaint of May 9 — that the prince values his knowledge, which anyone can share, but not his heart, which is his alone — to the lover's lament: "You wait for me where I do not want to go: you love me where I do not exist. Or again: the world and I are not interested in the same thing; and to my misfortune, this divided thing is myself; I am not interested (Werther says) in my mind; you are not interested in my heart" (52). This is not to say, however, that Werther's heart represents his essence. "The heart is what I imagine I give. Each time this gift is returned to me, then it is little enough to say, with Werther, that the heart is what remains of me, once all the wit attributed to me and undesired by me is taken away: the heart is what remains to me, and this heart that lies heavy on my heart is heavy with the ebb which has filled it with itself" (52–53). The "I" that speaks here is indeterminate; it is not (only) Werther nor any other lover nor Goethe nor any other author. It is the site at which a particular discourse writes itself (compare Corbineau-Hoffmann 1992).

In radical fashion, Forget and Barthes touch on a central question that already occupied the novel's very first critics, and to which modern commentators continually return. Forming the theme of this chapter, it addresses the moral, psychological, and aesthetic ambiguities that the novel seems to present. To what extent should Werther be viewed as a figure of identification, either for Goethe or for the reader? Michael Bell articulates one pragmatic answer that many critics would find generally congenial:

> A convenient way of approaching this ambivalence . . . of *Werther* is to consider in turns the two possible, but opposed, ways of reading the

novel. First, we may consider the critical perception of Werther by which we can see him as a case, however, poignant, of neurotic hypersensitivity. Then we may posit the reading of which he is the tragic focus for a romantic conception of life in which the ultimate values of feeling and individuality are inevitably to be overcome by the other compelling but inferior values of social practicality. My contention is that these two possibilities are not merely there at different times, but pass through each within the same episodes without touching. There is no clear hierarchy by which the one has an unambiguous grip upon the other. (1983, 94–95)

Note

[1] The abbreviation *HA* (*Hamburger Ausgabe*) refers to Goethe's *Werke*, ed. Erich Trunz, published in Hamburg by Wegner, 1961–64.

Works Cited

Abbott, Scott. 1992. "The Semiotics of 'Young Werther.'" *Goethe Yearbook* 6 (1992): 41–65.

Assling, Reinhard. 1981. *Werthers Leiden: Die ästhetische Rebellion der Innerlichkeit*. Frankfurt am Main, Bern: Lang.

Atkins, Stuart P. 1948. "J. C. Lavater and Goethe: Problems of Psychology and Theology in *Die Leiden des jungen Werther*." *PMLA* 63 (1948): 520–76.

Aurnhammer, Achim. 1995. "Maler Werther: Zur Bedeutung der bildenden Kunst in Goethes Roman." *Literaturwissenschaftliches Jahrbuch im Auftrage der Görres-Gesellschaft* 36 (1995): 83–104.

Barthes, Roland. 1977. *A Lover's Discourse: Fragments*. Trans. Richard Howard. New York: Hill & Wang, 1978.

Barton, Karin. 2001. *Viel Licht, Viel Schatten: Rousseau, Goethe und die Unordnung der Geschlechter; Eine neue Interpretation der "Leiden des jungen Werther."* Diss., U of Toronto, 2001.

Bell, Michael. 1983. *The Sentiment of Reality: Truth of Feeling in the European Novel*. London; Boston: Allen & Unwin.

Bennett, Benjamin. 1986. "Werther and Montaigne: The Romantic Renaissance." *Goethe Yearbook* 3 (1986): 1–20.

———. 2001. *Goethe as Woman: The Undoing of Literature*. Detroit: Wayne State UP.

Bernays, Michael. 1866. *Über Kritik und Geschichte des goetheschen Textes*. Berlin: Dümmler.

———. 1875. Introd. to *Der junge Goethe: Seine Briefe und Dichtungen von 1764–1776*, vol. 1, ed. Salomon Hirzel, iii–xcvii. Leipzig: Hirzel, 1887.

Beutler, Ernst. 1940. "Wertherfragen." *Viermonatsschrift der Goethe-Gesellschaft* 5 (1940): 138–60.

———. 1941. "Das ertrunkene Mädchen." In *Essays um Goethe,* 111–20. Wiesbaden: Dieterich, 1947.

Bickelmann, Ingeborg. 1937. *Goethes "Werther" im Urteil des 19. Jahrhunderts (Romantik bis Naturalismus 1830–1880).* Diss., Frankfurt am Main.

Biedermann, Karl. 1867. *Deutschland im achtzehnten Jahrhundert.* Vol. 2, part 2. Leipzig: Weber.

Black, Joel. 1994. "Writing after Murder (and Before Suicide): The Confessions of Werther and Rivière." In *Reading After Foucault: Institutions, Disciplines, and Technologies of the Self in Germany, 1750–1830,* ed. Robert S. Leventhal, 233–59. Detroit: Wayne State UP.

Blackall, Eric A. 1976. *Goethe and the Novel.* Ithaca: Cornell UP.

Blumenthal, Herrmann. 1940. "Ein neues Wertherbild?" *Viermonatsschrift der Goethe-Gesellschaft* 5 (1940): 315–20.

Boyle, Nicholas. 1991. *The Poetry of Desire (1749–1790).* Vol. 1 of *Goethe: The Poet and the Age.* Oxford: Oxford UP.

Breidenbach zu Breidenstein, Karl Wilhelm, Freiherr von. 1775. *Berichtigung der Geschichte des jungen Werthers.* Freystadt, 1775; 2nd ed., Frankfurt and Leipzig, 1775.

Brinkmann, Richard. 1976. "Goethes 'Werther' and Arnolds 'Kirchen- und Ketzerhistorie': Zur Aporie des modernen Individualitätenbegriffs." In *Versuche zu Goethe: Festschrift für Erich Heller zum 65. Geburtstag am 27.3.1976,* ed. Volker Dürr und Géza v. Molnár, 167–89. Heidelberg: Stiehm.

Corbineau-Hoffmann, Angelika. 1992. "'Discours de la passion' als Selbstaussage: Goethe, *Die Leiden des jungen Werther,* Rousseau, *Julie ou la nouvelle Héloïse,* Richardson, *Pamela.*" *Colloquium Helveticum* 15 (1992): 27–52.

Davis, William Stephen. 1994. "The Intensification of the Body in Goethe's *Die Leiden des jungen Werther.*" *The Germanic Review* 69 (1994): 106–17.

Diez, Max. 1936. "The Principle of the Dominant Metaphor in Goethe's 'Werther.'" *PMLA* 51 (1936): 824–41, 985–1006.

Duncan, Bruce. 1987. "Werther's Reflections on the Tenth of May." In *Exile and Enlightenment. Studies in Honor of Guy Stern,* 1–10. Detroit: Wayne State UP.

Düntzer, Heinrich. 1849. *Zu Goethe's Jubelfeier.* In *Studien zu Goethe's Werken,* 89–257. Elberfeld & Iserlohn: Baedeker.

Dye, Robert Ellis. 1975. "Man and God in Goethe's 'Werther.'" *Symposium* 29 (1975): 314–29.

Edmunds, Kathryn. 1996. "'Der Gesang soll deinen Namen erhalten': Ossian, 'Werther,' and Texts of/for Mourning." *Goethe Yearbook* 8 (1996): 45–65.

Fechner, Jörg-Ulrich. 1982. "Die alten Leiden des jungen Werthers: Goethes Roman aus petrarkistischer Sicht." In Herrmann 1994a, 338–59.

Feise, Ernst. 1914b. "Zu Entstehung, Problem und Technik von Goethes 'Werther.'" *JEGP* 13 (1914): 1–36.

Fetzer, John. 1971. "Schatten ohne Frau: Marginalia on a Werther Motif." *Germanic Review* 46 (1971): 87–94.

Finsen, H. Carl. 1977. "Empfindsamkeit als Raum der Alternative: Untersucht am Beispiel von Goethes 'Die Leiden des jungen Werthers.'" *Der Deutschunterricht* 29 (1977): 27–38.

Fischer, Peter. 1986. "Familienauftritte: Goethes Phantasiewelt und die Konstruktion des 'Werther'-Romans." In *"Wie froh bin ich, dass ich weg bin!": Goethes Roman "Die Leiden des jungen Werther" in literaturpsychologischer Sicht,* ed. Helmut Schmiedt, 189–220. Würzburg: Königshausen & Neumann, 1989.

Fittbogen, Gottfried. 1910. "Die Charaktere in beiden Fassungen von 'Werthers Leiden.'" *Euphorion* 17 (1910): 556–82.

Flaschka, Horst. 1987. *Goethes "Werther": Werkkontextuelle Deskription und Analyse.* Munich: Fink.

Forget, Philippe. 1984. "Aus der Seele geschrie(b)en?: Zur Problematik des Schreibens (écriture) in Goethes 'Werther.'" In *Text und Interpretation: Deutsch-französische Debatte,* ed. P. Forget, 130–80. Munich: Fink.

Foucault, Michel. 1976. *The History of Sexuality.* Trans. Robert Hurley. Vol. 1. New York: Vintage, 1980.

Friedell, Egon, and Alfred Polgar. 1908. "Goethe: Groteske in 2 Bildern." In *Wozu das Theater? Essays, Satiren, Humoresken,* ed. Peter Haage, 197–210. Munich: Beck, 1966.

Furst, Lilian R. 1990. "The 'Imprisoning Self': Goethe's Werther and Rousseau's Solitary Walker." In *European Romanticism: Literary Cross-Currents, Modes, and Models,* ed. Gerhardt Hoffmeister, 163–79. Detroit: Wayne State UP.

Gerhard, Melitta: 1916. "Die Bauerburschenepisode im 'Werther.'" In Herrmann 1994a, 23–38.

Gloël, Heinrich. 1911. *Goethes Wetzlarer Zeit: Bilder aus der Reichskammergerichts- und Wertherstadt.* Berlin: Mittler, 1911. Repr. Wetzlar: Will, 1999.

———. 1922. *Goethe und Lotte.* Berlin: Mittler.

Goedeke, Karl. 1859. *Grundriß zur Geschichte der deutschen Dichtung aus den Quellen.* Vol. 4, section 2. Dresden: Ehlermann, 1910.

Goethe, Johann Wolfgang von. 1813. *Dichtung und Wahrheit.* Ed. Erich Trunz. Vol. 9 of *Werke.* Hamburg: Wegner, 1961–64. (This Hamburg edition of Goethe's works is cited in the text as *HA*).

Graham, Ilse Appelbaum. 1973. "'Die Leiden des jungen Werther': A Requiem for Inwardness." In *Goethe and Lessing: the Wellsprings of Creation,* 115–36. New York: Barnes & Noble.

———. 1974. "Goethe's Own Werther: An Artist's Truth about His Fiction." In *Goethe: Portrait of the Artist,* 7–33. Berlin, New York: de Gruyter.

Gutbrodt, Fritz. 1995. "The Worth of 'Werther': Goethe's Literary Marketing." MLN 110 (1995): 579–630.

Hass, Hans Egon. 1957. "Werther-Studie." In *Gestaltprobleme der Dichtung: Günther Müller zu seinem 65. Geburtstag,* ed. Richard Alewyn et al., 83–125. Bonn: Bouvier.

Hausmann, Manfred. 1955. *Die Entscheidung: Die Rolle des "Werther" in Goethes Leben und Werk.* Kassel: Goethe-Gesellschaft.

Herbst, Wilhelm. 1881. *Goethe in Wetzlar, 1772: vier Monate aus des Dichters Jugendleben.* Gotha: Perthes.

Hering, Robert. 1935. "Heimatliche Spuren in Goethes Jugenddichtung." *Goethe-Kalender* 28 (1935): 191–202.

Herrmann, Hans Peter, ed. 1994a. *Goethes "Werther": Kritik und Forschung.* Darmstadt: Wissenschaftliche Buchgesellschaft.

Hettner, Hermann. 1869. *Literaturgeschichte des achtzehnten Jahrhunderts.* Part 3, book 3, 1. Braunschweig: Vieweg, 1894.

Hohendahl, Peter U. 1972. "Empfindsamkeit und gesellschaftliches Bewusstsein: Zur Soziologie des empfindsamen Romans am Beispiel von *La vie de Marianne, Clarissa, Fräulein von Sternheim,* und *Werther." Jahrbuch der Deutschen Schillergesellschaft* 16 (1972): 176–207.

Jauss, Hans Robert. 1982. *Question and Answer: Forms of Dialogic Understanding.* Trans Michael Hays. Minneapolis: University of Minnesota Press, 1989.

Jolles, Matthijs. 1957. *Goethes Kunstanschauung.* Bern: Francke.

Kaulitz-Niedeck, Rosa. 1908. *Goethe und Jerusalem.* Giessen: Münchow.

Kayser, Wolfgang. 1941. "Die Entstehung von Goethes 'Werther.'" In Herrmann 1994a, 124–57.

Kennedy, Ellie. 2000. "Rousseau and Werther: In Search of a Sympathetic Soul." In *Material Productions and Cultural Construction/Culture materielle et constructions discursives,* ed. Robert Merrett et al., 109–19. Edmonton: Academic.

Kestner, Georg August. 1854. *Goethe und Werther: Briefe Goethes, meistens aus seiner Jugendzeit, mit erläuternden Dokumenten.* Stuttgart, Tübingen: Cotta.

Kittler, Friedrich. 1980. *"Autorschaft und Liebe."* In Herrmann 1994a, 295–316.

Koldewey, Friedrich. 1881. "Werthers Urbild." In *Lebens- und Charakterbilder,* 167–202. Wolfenbüttel.

Kowalik, Jill Anne. 1999. "Pietist Grief, Empfindsamkeit, and Werther." *Goethe Yearbook* 9 (1999): 77–130.

Kurz, Gerhard. 1982. "Werther als Künstler." In *Invaliden des Apoll: Motive und Mythen des Dichterleids,* ed. Herbert Anton, 95–112. Munich: Fink.

Lange, Victor. 1989. "Erzählformen im Roman des 18. Jahrhunderts." In *Illyrische Betrachtungen: Essays und Aufsätze aus 30 Jahren,* ed. Walter Hinderer and Volkmar Sander, 106–23. Bern; New York: Lang.

Laukhard, Friedrich Christian. 1792. "Werther-Cultus 1776." Excerpt from *Leben und Schicksale*. Halle, 1792. Repr. in *Weimarisches Jahrbuch fur deutsche Sprache, Litteratur und Kunst* 6 (1857): 218–19.

Lauterbach, Martin. 1910. *Das Verhältnis der zweiten zur ersten Ausgabe von "Werthers Leiden."* Strasbourg: Trübner.

Lernet-Holenia, Alexander, 1959. *Der wahre Werther.* Hamburg: Zsolnay.

Lewes, George Henry. 1856. *The Life and Works of Goethe: With Sketches of His Age and Contemporaries, from Published and Unpublished Sources.* Boston: Ticknor & Fields.

Loewe, Victor. 1901. "Neue Beiträge zur Charakteristik des jungen Jerusalem." *Euphorion* 8 (1901): 72–77.

Lorenz, Annika, and Helmut Schmiedt, eds. 1997. *Johann Wolfgang von Goethe: "Die Leiden des jungen Werthers"; Synoptischer Druck der beiden Fassungen 1774 und 1787.* Paderborn: Igel.

Luserke, Matthias. 1995. *Die Bändigung der wilden Seele: Literatur und Leidenschaft in der Aufklärung.* Stuttgart: Metzler.

Mann, Thomas. 1939. "Goethes 'Werther.'" In Herrmann 1994a, 85–97.

Maurer, Karl. 1963. "Die verschleierten Konfessionen: Zur Entstehungsgeschichte von Goethes 'Werther' (Dichtung und Wahrheit, 12. und 13. Buch)." In *Die Wissenschaft von deutscher Sprache und Dichtung: Methoden, Probleme, Aufgaben; Festschrift für Friedrich Maurer zum 65. Geburtstag,* ed. Siegfried Gutenbrunner et al. Stuttgart: Klett.

Merck, Johann Heinrich. 1775. Review of *Werther.* In *Der junge Goethe im zeitgenössischen Urteil,* ed. Peter Müller, 198–201. Berlin: Akademie Verlag.

Meyer-Krentler, Eckhardt. 1982. "'Kalte Abstraktion' gegen 'versengte Einbildung': Destruktion und Restauration aufklärerischer Harmoniemodelle in Goethes 'Leiden' und Nicolais 'Freuden des jungen Werthers.'" *Deutsche Vierteljahrsschrift für Literaturwissenschaft und Geistesgeschichte* 56 (1982): 65–91.

———. 1989. "Die Leiden der jungen Wertherin." In *Zwischen Aufklärung und Restauration: Sozialer Wandel in der deutschen Literatur (1700–1848); Festschrift für Wolfgang Martens zum 65. Geburtstag,* ed. Wolfgang Frühwald and Alberto Martino, 225–48. Tübingen: Niemeyer.

Migge, Walther. 1967. *Goethes "Werther": Entstehung und Wirkung.* Frankfurt am Main: Insel.

Miller, Ronald Duncan. 1981. *The Beautiful Soul: A Study of 18th-Century Idealism as Exemplified by Rousseau's "La nouvelle Heloïse" and Goethe's "Die Leiden des jungen Werthers."* Harrogate, UK: Duchy, 1981.

Möbius, Paul Julius. 1898. *Über das Pathologische bei Goethe.* Leipzig: Barth. Repr. Munich: Matthes & Seitz, 1983.

Mommsen, Momme. 1972. "Goethes Verhältnis zu Christus und Spinoza: Blick auf die Wertherzeit." In *Deutsche Weltliteratur: Von Goethe bis Ingeborg Bachmann; Festgabe für J. Alan Pfeffer,* ed. Klaus W. Jonas. Tübingen.

Müller-Salget, Klaus. 1981. "Zur Struktur von Goethes 'Werther.'" In Herrmann 1994a, 317–37.

Muenzer, Clark. 1984. *Figures of Identity: Goethe's Novels and the Enigmatic Self*. University Park: Penn State UP.

Nelles, Jürgen. 1996. "Werthers Herausgeber oder die Rekonstruktion der 'Geschichte des armen Werthers.'" *Jahrbuch des Freien Deutschen Hochstifts* (1996): 1–37.

Paulin, Roger. 1980. "'Wer werden uns wieder sehn!': On a Theme in 'Werther.'" *Publications of the English Goethe Society* 50 (1980): 55–78.

Phillips, David P. 1974. "The Influence of Suggestion on Suicide: Substantive and Theoretical Implications of the Werther Effect." *American Sociological Review* 39 (1974): 340–54.

Powers, Elizabeth. 1999. "The Artist's Escape from the Idyll: The Relation of Werther to Sesenheim." *Goethe Yearbook* 9 (1999): 47–76.

Prawer, Siegbert. 1984. "Werther's People: Reflections on Literary Portraiture." *Publications of the English Goethe Society* 53 (1984): 70–97.

Pütz, Peter. 1982. "Werthers Leiden an der Literatur." In *Goethe's Narrative Fiction: the Irvine Goethe Symposium,* ed. William J. Lillyman, 55–68. Berlin; New York: de Gruyter, 1983.

Rahmeyer, Ruth. 1994. *Werthers Lotte: Ein Brief, ein Leben, eine Familie; die Biographie der Charlotte Kestner.* Hannover: Fackelträger.

Reiss, Hans S. 1963. *Goethe's Novels*. New York: St. Martin, 1969.

Renner, Karl N. 1985. "'Laß das Büchlein dein Freund seyn': Goethes Roman 'Die Leiden des jungen Werther' und die Diätetik der Aufklärung." In *Zur Sozialgeschichte der deutschen Literatur von der Aufklärung bis zur Jahrhundertwende,* ed. Günter Häntzschel et al., 1–20. Tübingen: Niemeyer.

Rickels, Laurence Arthur. 1996. "Psy Fi Explorations of Out Space: On *Werther*'s Special Effects." In *Outing Goethe and His Age,* ed. Alice A. Kuzniar, 147–73, 264–65. Stanford: Stanford UP.

Riess, Gertrud. 1924. *Die beiden Fassungen von Goethes "Die Leiden des jungen Werthers": Eine stilpsychologische Untersuchung.* Breslau: Trewendt.

Rose, William. 1931. "The Historical Background of Goethe's 'Werther.'" In *Men, Myths, and Movements in German Literature: A Volume of Historical and Critical Papers,* 125–55. New York: Macmillan.

Ryder, Frank G. 1964. "Season, Day, and Hour — Time as Metaphor in Goethe's 'Werther.'" *JEGP* 63 (1964): 389–407.

Saine, Thomas P. 1980. "Passion and Aggression: The Meaning of Werther's Last Letter." *Orbis Litterarum* 35 (1980): 327–56.

———. 1981. "The Portrayal of Lotte in the Two Versions of Goethe's 'Werther.'" *JEGP* 80 (1981): 54–77.

Sauder, Gerhard. 1974. *Voraussetzungen und Elemente:* Vol. 1 of *Empfindsamkeit*. Stuttgart: Metzler.

Sauder, Gerhard. 1987. "'Die Leiden des jungen Werthers.'" In *Johann Wolfgang von Goethe: Sämtliche Werke nach Epochen seines Schaffens,* ed. Karl Richter et al., 770–99. Vol. 1, part 2. Munich: Hanser.

Schaeder, Grete. 1947. *Gott und Welt: Drei Kapitel goethischer Weltanschauung.* Hameln: Seifert.

Scherer, Wilhelm. 1886. *A History of German Literature.* Vol. 2. Trans. F. C. Conybeare. Ed. F. Max Müller. New York: Scribner.

Schmidt, Erich. 1875. *Richardson, Rousseau und Goethe: Ein Beitrag zur Geschichte des Romans im 18. Jahrhundert.* Jena: E. Frommann.

———. 1879. "Aus der Wertherzeit." In *Charakteristiken,* 1:274–86. Berlin: Weidmann, 1901–2.

Schmidt, Hartmut. 1988. "'Werther' oder die Passion des Sturm und Drang." In *Sturm und Drang: Ausstellung im Frankfurter Goethe-Museum,* ed. Christoph Perels, 99–115. Frankfurt am Main: Freies Deutsches Hochstift.

Schöne, Albrecht. 1967. "Über Goethes Brief an Behrisch vom 10. November 1767." In *Festschrift für Richard Alewyn,* ed. Herbert Singer and Benno von Wiese. Cologne, Graz: Böhlau.

Schrader, Erich. 1952. "Johann Jacob Höfler, das Urbild des Gesandten in Goethes 'Werther': Beiträge zum Schicksal Goues und Jerusalems." *Braunschweigisches Jahrbuch* 33 (1952): 118–54.

Schweitzer, Christoph E. 2004. "Who *Is* the Editor in Goethe's *Die Leiden des jungen Werthers? Goethe Yearbook* 12 (2004): 31–40.

Seeger, Lothar G. 1968. "Goethes 'Werther' und der Pietismus." *Susquehanna University Studies* 8 (1968): 30–49.

Siebers, Tobin. 1993. "The Werther Effect: The Esthetics of Suicide." *Mosaic* 26 (1993): 15–34.

Spielhagen, Friedrich. 1871. "Finder oder Erfinder?" In *Beiträge zur Theorie und Technik des Romans,* 3–34. Leipzig: Staackmann, 1883.

Sulzer, Johann Georg. 1771. *Allgemeine Theorie der schönen Künste in einzeln, nach alphabetischer Ordnung der Kunstwörter auf einander folgenden, Artikeln abgehandelt.* 2 vols. Leipzig: Weidmann, 1771–74.

Swales, Martin. 1987. *Goethe: "The Sorrows of Young Werther."* Cambridge: Cambridge UP.

Thorlby, Anthony. 1976. "From What Did Goethe Save Himself in 'Werther'?" In *Versuche zu Goethe: Festschrift für Erich Heller zum 65. Geburtstag am 27.3.1976,* ed. Volker Dürr and Géza v. Molnár, 150–66. Heidelberg: Stiehm.

Trunz, Erich. 1951. "Anmerkungen des Herausgebers zu *Die Leiden des jungen Werther.*" In *Goethes Werke,* 6:514–95. Hamburg: Wegner.

Vaget, Hans. 1982. "Goethe the Novelist: On the Coherence of His Fiction." In *Goethe's Narrative Fiction: The Irvine Goethe Symposium,* ed. William J. Lillyman, 1–20. Berlin; New York: W. de Gruyter, 1983.

Vincent, Deirdre. 1992. *Werther's Goethe and the Game of Literary Creativity.* Toronto: U of Toronto P.

Vollmer, Hartmut. 2003. "'Worte sind hier umsonst': Die Beschreibung des Unbeschreiblichen in Goethes *Werther* und Hölderlins *Hyperion*." *Zeitschrift für deutsche Philologie* 122 (2003): 481–508.

Wagenknecht, Christian. 1973. "Werthers Leiden: Der Roman als Krankheitsgeschichte." *Text & Kontext* 5 (Copenhagen, 1977): 3–14.

Walker, Joyce S. 1999. "Sex, Suicide, and the Sublime: A Reading of Goethe's '*Werther*.'" *Monatshefte* 91 (1999): 208–23.

Weber, Carl Maria. 1928. "Zur Vorgeschichte von Goethes 'Werther.'" *Jahrbuch der Goethe-Gesellschaft* 14 (1928): 82–92.

Wellbery, Caroline. 1986. "From Mirrors to Images: The Transformation of Sentimental Paradigms in Goethe's 'The Sorrows of Young Werther.'" *Studies in Romanticism* 25 (1986): 231–49.

Welz, Dieter. 1973. *Der Weimarer "Werther": Studien zur Sinnstruktur der zweiten Fassung des Werther-Romans.* Bonn: Bouvier.

Wilkinson, Elizabeth M., and Leonard Ashley Willoughby. 1965. "The Blind Man and the Poet: An Early Stage in Goethe's Quest for Form." In *German Studies Presented to Walter Horace Bruford*, 29–57. London: Harrup.

Wilson, W. Daniel. 1989. "Patriarchy, Politics, Passion: Labor and Werther's Search for Nature." *Internationales Archiv für Sozialgeschichte der deutschen Literatur* 14 (1989): 15–44.

Zimmermann, Rolf Christian. 1979. "'Die Leiden des jungen Werthers.'" In *Das Weltbild des jungen Goethe: Studien zur hermetischen Tradition des 18. Jahrhunderts,* 2:167–212, 312–20. Munich: Fink, 1979.

*Etching by Daniel Berger, copied from
Nikolaus Daniel Chodowiecki and printed in Friedrich Himburg's
pirated edition of* Werther *(Berlin, 1775). Courtesy of Goethe-Museum,
Düsseldorf, photograph by Walter Klein.*

6: Lotte, Sex, and Werther

THE LATE TWENTIETH CENTURY'S theoretical concern with the body finds a variety of reflections in *Werther* scholarship. Such studies often begin with Lotte. At one extreme we find inquiries that seek to establish her real self, an entity that has been obscured by Werther's subjectivism. Some of these investigations stress the material, including corporeal, forces that impinge upon or even define her. At the other extreme are critics who start with the assumption that, rather than the self, "The body is the site upon which the various technologies of our culture inscribe themselves, the connecting link to which and from which our medial means of processing, storage, and transmission run" (Wellbery 1990, xiv). Common to all of these approaches is a concern with problems of agency, historicity, and gender, a concern which then extends to the figure of Werther.

It was not always thus. Until relatively recently, critics felt that Lotte's every quality so conforms to traditional, ideal gender norms that she seemed to be a paragon of female virtue, rather than a rounded individual. Even the earliest readers noted this ostensible fact, which they largely welcomed for its inspirational effect (see Meyer-Krentler 1989). Later critics, too, celebrated her status as the ideal woman who uncomplainingly fulfills the roles of submissive wife, nurturing mother, and compassionate caretaker of the sick. Her virtues even take on nationalistic overtones when the times seem to have called for them: in the figure of Lotte, writes Herman Grimm in 1874, Goethe "has so felicitously given the type of true womanhood that every maiden can believe herself a Lotte; and, at the same time, has so individualized her that each must confess that she could never reach this ideal" (1874, 160–61). By "individualized," Grimm means that each of her characteristics represents the ultimate in German female virtue, including a seemly humility: "Lotte is the simplest and most lovely German maiden, of whom nothing special is to be said. She enjoys dancing, she loves poetry, she *can be* enthusiastic; but she only needs to hear the slightest noise in the house, and she leaps down from the heavens into her wonted sphere and is nothing but a housewife (161; see Conger 1986 for a discussion of women's responses to Lotte as a sentimental figure, especially in England from 1785–1805). This judgment has undergone occasional updates: Lilian Furst, for example, writing over 100 years after Grimm, considers Lotte "the pre-figuration, in her blend of tenderness and competence, of a distinctly modern ideal of womanhood" (1982, 26), and H. Carl Finsen offers another, unique interpretation in which he claims that Lotte rises above both class and gender, if only in her appreciation of Klopstock (1977, 33). It is hard to credit these conclusions. Sally Anne Winkle convincingly disputes them, taking "issue with Furst's assertion that Lotte resists Werther's affection due to common sense rather than social values" (1988, 110–11), while also pointing out that the qualities that Finsen attributes to Lotte as an individual in fact conform to established gender norms (108–9). Winkle herself describes Lotte as being torn between two competing idealizations of women that coexisted in the 1770s, evident in "the conflicting images of Lotte by her two admirers, Werther and Albert. Werther's fabulous notion of Lotte's inner harmony and sensitive soul is divorced from the realities of her bourgeois environment, whereas Albert's idealized view of his fiancée concentrates on her common sense, her cheerful acceptance of her obligations as a substitute mother, and her commitment to the perpetuation of bourgeois values within the nuclear family sphere: diligence, obedience, security" (114). At the same time, however, Winkle sees Werther's appeal to Lotte as natural, rather than socially determined: "her sentimental soul and natural inclinations attract her to Werther and assure her eventual discontentment as a wife to a practical, stolid man like Albert, while her sheltered bourgeois background as obedient daughter, sister, and wife eliminates any possibility of transcending those boundaries by embarking on a romantic relationship with Werther" (119). Despite this ambiguity, Winkle's primary point is valid: "the author's criticism against bourgeois society as an obstacle to the development of the human personality is concerned solely with the self-actualization of the *male* character" (115).

Whether or not they approve of her genderedness, most critics assume that Lotte participates in Werther's tragedy only as the passive object of his emotions or even of Goethe's own unresolved incestuous feelings for his sister (Fischer 1986, 204). Like Albert or any of the novel's other figures, she is simply part of Werther's story (Trunz 1951, 546), or, even further removed from selfhood, she represents in his eyes a familial community (Sørensen 1987, 124). Her own, less interesting, sufferings derive from the conflict between her empathy for him and his unreasonable demands on her. That assumption does not, however, lead most of these critics to object that Lotte is no more than a two-dimensional stereotype — for them it literally goes without saying that these qualities would pertain to a woman. Hans Reiss finds her to be a "rounded character" (1963, 45) and feels able to understand the strength and direction of her affections through the editor's reports or, with only slight corrections, through Werther's eyes (for example, 22). Walter Silz, too, confidently applies the evidence at hand to describe Lotte as a somewhat superficial, typically middle-class young woman who is taken unawares by a love for which her upbringing has left her unprepared. He feels sure that she never intends to lead Werther on, and that a bourgeois sense of propriety is what prevents her from intervening in his death. "In her loving sweetness, her helplessness, and her tragedy, Lotte is a true sister of Emilia Galotti, Luise Miller, and Goethe's own Gretchen" (Silz 1972, 129–31). There are, however, exceptions such as Eric Blackall (1976), who infer that a more complex person lies hidden behind Werther's idiosyncratic portrayal. Indeed, her suspiciously perfect congruence with his stated needs is one symptom of his unreliable purchase on the real world. Only recently have critics generally recognized the extent to which both the reader's and Werther's view of Lotte is gendered. As Joyce Walker puts it, "The real Lotte is inaccessible to the reader, for she is embedded and objectified in the male narrative" (1999, 213). Hannelore Schlaffer agrees and compares Lotte to Dulcina, whose image is determined in Don Quixote's imagination, rather than in his experience of her (1987, 216; see also Muenzer 1984, 21).

Ellis Dye is particularly explicit in contrasting the Lotte who has been constructed by "the male imagination" with a real self. What Werther presents of her is a "self-projection" without "authentic otherness" (1988, 494, 504). Here Dye employs the concept of "other" that Simone de Beauvoir introduces in *The Second Sex* (1949), a quality of "autonomy and ascertainable difference from Werther's conception of her" (494). The fictional editor, says Dye, provides us with a more plausible version of Lotte, but "within the limits of his chosen genre he can give us no access to her subjectivity. She is pure object, and in that sense, an 'other' to the reader as well" (504). Yet, Dye claims, this otherness is not so radical that we cease to assume that she has an authentic existence. We have some sense of her, even though we need to accept that our knowledge is incomplete, and that this incompleteness is itself a symptom of Werther's own isolation. That is, in fact, the "novel's central theme — the loneliness and frustration of the human individual in a world in which dreams fail to sustain us and the sharing is always incomplete" (504).

Of course, Lotte is not the only figure to be seen through the lens of Werther's subjectivity. All of the other characters are similarly filtered. Even more important than the distortions of these individuals is the effect that this one-sidedness has on the entire narrative structure. As David Wellbery observes, *Werther* "marks a powerful innovation vis-à-vis its major predecessors." Earlier epistolary novels, with their variety of correspondents, constructed their narratives out of competing perspectives from which the reader could choose. *Werther,* in contrast, "asks the reader not to behold from the outside a drama of tangled motivations and stratagems, but, rather, to listen to . . . and imaginatively reenact the movements of a particular subjectivity" (1994, 180). Few critics are ready to accept this invitation as completely as Wellbery does — see below — but they do turn their attention to the subjective forces that skew the way in which Lotte is presented.

Lotte's objectification has been so generally taken for granted throughout most of the history of *Werther* criticism that Georg Lukács's interpretation of 1936 is one of the first to propose that she is a whole figure in her own right and to offer more wide-ranging speculations about her actual motivations. He maintains "daß Lotte Werther wiederliebt und durch die Explosion seiner Leidenschaft zum Bewußtsein dieser Liebe gebracht wird. Gerade dies bringt aber die Katastrophe hervor: Lotte ist eine bürgerliche Frau, die an ihrer Ehe mit dem tüchtigen und geachteten Mann instinktiv festhält und vor der eigenen Leidenschaft erschreckt zurücktaumelt" (1936, 54; that Lotte loves Werther in return and is made conscious of this love when his passion explodes. This is precisely what brings about the catastrophe: Lotte is a bourgeois woman who instinctively holds firm to her marriage to a capable and respected husband and fearfully lurches away from her own passion.) The novel's tragedy, says Lukács, derives from the necessary conflict between individual love and the socio-economical arrangement that is bourgeois marriage.

For a long time Lukács's approach still remained the exception. It was not until the 1970s that significant numbers of interpreters began to consider Lotte as a truly autonomous character, one with her own individual interests, some of them even less than admirable. After Meno Spann (1972, 83) and Harry Steinhauer (1974, 4) briefly suggested that there is more to her motivations than meets the eye, E. Kathleen Warrick explored "Lotte's Sexuality and Her Responsibility for Werther's Death" (1978). In essence, Warrick accuses Lotte of behaving towards Werther in an "aggressively intimate manner," especially by initiating physical contact that is calculated to inflame his passion. She bears at least some guilt for his suicide by arousing a love that she never intends to satisfy. It is not wholly clear what Warrick thinks motivates this "sexual aggressiveness" (132), whether the sexuality in her study's title refers to Lotte's own urges or only to the source of her power over Werther. Warrick mentions "libidinal desires" (132) and "erotic desire" (134), but she more consistently speaks of Lotte's efforts to "possess" Werther through domination, with no implication that she seeks satisfaction of her own sensual needs. In fact, her manipulation of his desire culminates not in physical union, but in his suicide. In handing over the guns "which she knew Werther would use for his self-destruction . . . she could possess him more passionately and completely than ever before" (134). This might sound as if Werther represented little more than a trophy for her belt, but Warrick also claims that "Lotte's inner struggle to possess Werther . . . became confused with her feelings of grief, pity, selfishness, futility and a genuine love for Albert and the life-style which he represents. A mixture of all these emotions prompted her to hand [over] the guns" (134). However complex her motivations, Lotte's subsequent reaction to Werther's death shows that she is conscious of her guilt.

Later interpreters increasingly see Lotte in this critical light. Benjamin Bennett concludes from the warning that Werther receives on his way to meet Lotte for the first time that she is "a habitual breaker of hearts" who flirts with the newcomer in order to enliven her otherwise dull small-town existence. Werther "is not only a conquest, but also her lifeline to a fuller world" (1980, 65–67). Thomas Saine, in looking at the first version of *Werther*, disputes this characterization, finding that Lotte "is dragged into the catastrophe more by virtue of being who she is, desirable and unattainable, than by anything she has done to encourage Werther's passion for her" (1981, 61). The second version of 1787, however, presents her as "an active participant in Werther's downfall" (77; compare Winkle 1988, 117–18).

Bennett's reading of the famous "Klopstock!" scene exemplifies the hazards of trying to form a definitive picture of Lotte through the filter of Werther's idealizations. With little to go on, Bennett calls her learning into question, suggesting that her invocation of Klopstock's poem "Frühlingsfeier" (Celebration of Spring) is superficial name-dropping. His iconoclastic reading of this scene becomes unconvincingly polemical when he claims that "the best Lotte can manage is to pronounce the poet's not very euphonious surname" (1980, 65) — all poets were called by their last names in this period, and the question of euphony is irrelevant. As Richard Alewyn has already shown in 1979, Lotte's response to the storm is consistent with the late eighteenth century's idea of literary sensibility, and Meredith Lee is right in disputing Bennett's characterization (1990, 4–6; for another interpretation of the invocation of Klopstock, see Gutbrodt 1995, 607–9). Nevertheless, Bennett's main point is valid: *Werther* invites us to approach its text critically. Indeed, in a later study (2001), Bennett advances an interesting, if not always persuasive, argument that the novel, especially in its treatment of Lotte, not only renders transparent the means by which we read aesthetically, but also "co-opts" its readers, implicating them in a process that ultimately subverts the notion of literature (see below; for three differing responses to Bennett's thesis, see MacLeod 2003, Bell 2003, and Kuzniar 2004).

In a somewhat earlier study that looks closely at Lotte as an autonomous individual, Mel D. Faber too accuses her of toying with Werther's affections and ascribes her actions to her own sexual urgings.

> Far from being the romantic ideal into which she is usually transformed, the pure, self-sacrificing, sympathetic creature of the sentimental criticisms and miniature paintings, Charlotte is a very real young woman who finds herself involved in a very real marriage that she does not fully desire, who comes eventually to sense in Werther's ardent, socially unacceptable courtship a powerful assault on her repression, including her repression of strong libidinal energies, and finally, whose conduct toward Werther becomes increasingly aggressive, even vicious, as her anxieties — rooted in her deep ambivalence toward the hero — become increasingly severe. (1973, 270)

Faber then turns Lotte from the traditional, idealized, passive object of a young man's edacious passion into "a neurotic young woman" whose "savage teasing of her unfortunate admirer" unconsciously awakens "his innermost longings with no intention of allowing him to satisfy them" (272–73). Lotte, says Faber, is adept at finding ways to punish Werther for the ambivalent feelings he has aroused in her. She excites him "with an especially seductive performance at the piano" (273; see also Huff 1984) and, in allowing the canary to feed from her lips, even touches "the oral substructure of Werther's tormenting desires" (1973, 272). Faber does not accuse Lotte of intentionally driving her lover to suicide, but he does maintain that, by egging him on and then, in the end, refusing to recognize the signs of his impending death, she has earned the guilt that haunts her afterwards:

> Having resolved her emotional dilemma by behaving in such a way as to permit the suicidal death of her lover, having indulged herself in what current investigators of self-destruction would term an immobilization response to a suicidal communication, Charlotte must now experience the exactions of her conscience, the terrible severity of those same destructive impulses which she formerly directed against her admirer. (275)

Béatrice Dumiche similarly employs a psychoanalytic model to characterize Lotte, who represents her mother not only to Werther, but to herself as well. Torn by her inability to *be* her mother, to join incestuously with her father in the constellation of an idealized family, she tries to use her marriage to Albert, her father's chosen successor, both to break free from this desire and also to restore her childhood innocence by subordinating herself to society's rational morality (1995, 281–82). Within this dynamic, Werther, as a taboo object of her love, becomes a reassertion of her forbidden desire. Both she and Werther equate her with her mother in being the object of his passion, and she tries to justify this attraction with the assurance that her mother might have picked him, had she known him. To arrive at this conclusion, Dumiche relies heavily on Werther's report of September 10, in which Lotte expresses her regret that he has come to Wahlheim too late to know her mother, who was worthy of his acquaintance (282). The emotion that the two lovers display in this scene, says Dumiche, derives from their complicity in displacing the passion that eventually drives him to suicide. When she hands him the means of death, she joins in transcending the barriers that kept her from possessing him. At the same time, she is forced to recognize the responsibility she bears for exploiting Werther in her vain attempt to solve her own conflict. She turns her guilt inward in a psychosomatic disorder that threatens her own life (284–85).

Although Lotte's sexuality has come under discussion only relatively recently, Werther's own such impulses have long been taken for granted, albeit usually subsumed in broader concepts like "passion" (for example,

Schmidt 1875, 158). Reinhart Meyer-Kalkus sums up critics' characterizations of Werther's sexual desire as 'angeborene Leidenschaftlichkeit,' 'genialer Subjektivismus,' 'Absolutismus des Herzens,' und 'unbedingte Subjektivität' " (inherent passionateness, subjectivism of genius, absolutism of the heart, and unfettered subjectivity) — all directed at death (1977, 87). Erich Trunz circumspectly describes Werther's love as "eine Ganzheit" (a totality) that includes both the sacred and profane. Werther sees Lotte as "ein Geschöpf unmittelbar aus Gottes Hand, das zu erleben ihn in religiöse Bereiche führt, aber zugleich ist sie ihm auch eine sehr sinnenhaft geliebte wirkliche Frau" (1951, 547; a creature directly from God's hand, whose presence leads him into religious realms, but she is at the same time to him a very sensually loved, real woman). A modern variant of the terms used to describe Werther's attraction to Lotte, one that includes, but is not limited to sex, is "desire," the urge through which "Werther, in order to escape the forlornness of the self, seeks in the Other the totality that he lacks" (Kuzniar 1989, 22). Such general notions have characterized most descriptions of Werther's feelings throughout the history of *Werther* scholarship, but there have also always been critics who find them too euphemistic. Perhaps the first to insist on describing Werther's carnality was Pastor Johann Melchior Goeze, who in 1775 challenged the claim that Goethe

> seinem Helden nichts weiter als eine *platonische Liebe* zuschreibt, welche sich blos an den Vollkommenheiten des geliebten Gegenstandes ergötzet, und von welcher alle sinnliche Begierden, und das, was man im gewöhnlichen Verstande Wollüste nennet, himmelweit entfernt sind. Diese Entschuldigung könnte vielleicht Kindern scheinbar vorkommen: vernünftige und gesetzte Leute aber muß solche allezeit beleidigen. (. . .) Was ist die platonische Liebe zwischen zwo jungen Personen von beyden Geschlechten? eine leere Abstraction. Und gesetzt sie wäre möglich; so muß derjenige Verfasser seine Leser für elende Dumköpfe ansehen, der von ihnen verlangen kann, daß sie ihm zu gefallen glauben sollen, daß eine platonische Liebe in der Seele eines Menschen wohnen könne, der so denkt, so handelt (. . .). (1775, 119–20)

> [ascribes nothing more to his hero than a *platonic love* that takes delight only in the perfections of its beloved object and stands worlds apart from all sensual desires or what one would normally call lust. This explanation might seem credible to children; reasonable and sedate people, however, will find it insulting. [. . .] What is platonic love between two young people of opposite sexes? An empty abstraction. And even assuming it were possible, any author would have to consider his readers abject blockheads to expect them to be so kind as to believe that a platonic love could reside in the soul of someone who thinks and act thusly [. . .].]

Goeze is trying to emphasize the novel's deleterious effect on society, but more modern critics bring up Werther's sensuality because they cannot imagine a credible description of his motivations that fails to include it.

This is particularly true of the psychoanalytic interpretations discussed in chapter 3, which explain much of Werther's behavior as sublimated eroticism (for example, Schmidt 1968, 17). But sex also has a function in the novel's narrative structure. W. Daniel Wilson is one of several commentators to point out that Werther's "former desire to merge with Lotte's family... contrasts sharply with his sexual desire for an isolated Lotte in the second part of the novel" (1989, 41). Hans Gose, too, stresses the increasing role that Werther's concupiscence plays. At the beginning, says Gose, Werther's love is essentially a satisfying communion of kindred spirits. Especially after Albert's arrival, however, his growing passion increasingly responds to Lotte's physical presence. More and more, her innocent expressions of intimacy and her incidental bodily contact with him arouse his senses. Not only does this carnality displant his moral compunctions, but it also forces him to recognize that what he had imagined to be innocent love was in fact propelled by sexual desire, a disillusionment that helps to bring about his suicide (1921, 40–46, 63). Harry Slochower, referring to the letter of August 21, makes a similar point in maintaining that "Werther's suicide follows largely from his inability to develop beyond an adolescent romanticism which compulsively insists on dreaming its 'way through the world.' (. . .) Werther insists that his love for Lotte is 'pure,' and when this delusion is exposed to him in an erotic dream, Werther decides 'to quit this world'" (1975, 404; on Werther's erotic dreams, see also Goins 1992).

When William Stephen Davis investigates "the intensification of the body" in *Werther*, he is not, as one might first assume, emphasizing Werther's corporeality but, as we saw above, describing the construction of his imagined masculinity. Davis cites Foucault's assertion, in his *History of Sexuality* (1976, 123), that the eighteenth-century bourgeoisie did not repress sex so much as glorify and mystify it, to the effect that this emphasis on the body leads away from it. "Werther's own relation to the body," says Davis, "can be described as an effort to deny the body's physicality, to render it metaphysical, to view the body as pointing away from itself to a hidden realm of meaning" (Davis 1994, 112). In defining Lotte as a projection of the male subject, Davis derives his theoretical underpinnings from Lacan as well as Foucault. Lotte's idealized femininity, he says, does not so much embody Werther's emotional or sexual longings as provide a binary opposition intended to sustain his imagined masculine self. He needs, in other words, her gendered *imago* to justify his own, equally gendered self-definition. It is not sufficient, says Davis, to interpret Werther as a man given to passion, "rather, we must approach him as one who is compelled to see himself as a man of this sort, as someone whose very being depends upon an emotional investment in the feminine" (109). Werther's imagined version of Lotte, whose dark eyes mirror his love, provides the female gaze that he requires to valorize his masculine version of himself. When this strategy founders on her reality, "he commits suicide as a means of transposing his efforts at self-production to a more congenial realm" (115). Albert, too, is an object of Werther's imaginings. Rather than being a real-world hindrance to Werther's fulfillment, he is, says Davis, a projected focus of the hero's castration anxieties, an acknowledgement of the basic insecurity of his constructed masculinity. Werther's letter of July 13 reports that when Lotte speaks of her fiancé, he feels like a dishonored soldier whose sword has been taken away (112). Only in death, where the "apotheosized feminine" will hold sway unimpeded, can he hope to have this sword returned (115).

While Davis finds that Werther clings to a particular notion of masculinity, other interpreters connect his outsider status with feminine qualities. In the novel, Wilhelm, the fictional editor, and Lotte all in one way or another urge Werther to "be a man," and their imperative is echoed by any number of nineteenth-century critics who were appalled by the culture of *Empfindsamkeit* (for example, Hillebrand 1885, 288). The late eighteenth century had of course a different attitude toward sensitive males, and Sally Anne Winkle underestimates their appeal when she makes her otherwise valid point that the Age of Sensibility "was associated with attributes which were usually ascribed to the female sex: compassion, melancholy, sensitivity, reliance on feeling, affiliation with nature, self-denial, and virtue. Werther embodies many of these qualities and thus enjoys an uncommonly good rapport with women and children. It is Werther's adherence to these forbidden feminine tendencies, however, which contributes to his alienation and to the mutual misunderstanding between him and his rational middle class contemporaries" (1984, 109–10).

Gustav Hans Graber is an example of a twentieth-century critic who associates Werther's narcissism with a lack of masculine assertiveness. Werther becomes convinced that Lotte loves him, "Aber wie erwidert der Unglückselige die Liebe? (. . .) Nie würde er sich unterstehen, 'diesen Himmel' aktiv, *männlich* zu erstürmen und in ein sexuelles Lieben einzubeziehen" (1957, 75; But how does this hapless man respond to this love? [. . .] Never would he dare to storm 'this heaven' in active, *manly* fashion and engage in *sexual love*). Consistent with his pathology, Werther chooses to tell about a young girl when he illustrates the case for suicide: "Auch hier wieder die im unbewußten Wiederholungszwang stets neuerliche Identifizierung mit dem Weib, mit seiner Schwäche, Passivität, Leidensbereitschaft und Hingabe (August 12). Auch Lotte vertritt er so intensiviert bei den Kindern, daß sie Essen und Geschichtenerzählen von ihm schon 'fast so gern' annehmen wie von ihr" (76; Here again is the unconscious repetition compulsion to identify repeatedly with the female, with her weakness, passivity, readiness to suffer, and devotion (August 12). He also represents Lotte so intensively to the children that they are 'almost as willing' to receive food and stories from him as from her). Daniel Purdy, on the other hand, argues that Goethe's contemporaries were in fact willing to accept such effeminate, interior qualities, so long as they were offset by countervailing public signs of masculinity, such as the high boots, yellow pants, and blue coat that made up the much-imitated *Werthertracht* (the outfit worn by Werther). "Werther's sentimentalism as it unfolds through the novel's fragmented and private epistolary monologue and the . . . masculinity which was publicly performed . . . constitute the extreme ends of a single interpretive paradigm, one that seeks to correlate knowledge of an interior consciousness with exterior bodily signs" (1996, 125).

Benjamin Bennett, in the context of a much larger deconstruction of the whole enterprise of literature, moves in the opposite direction, ascribing a sexual significance to elements of the novel that critics have generally described in quite different terms. Sex becomes text and vice versa. After provocatively referring to the "Ossian-translation with which Werther clubs Lotte into submission" (2001, 114), Bennett raises the stakes further by claiming that this

> episode is clearly a rape, in the sense that a gesture normally signifying love is used to carry out an act of aggression, violence, hatred. It is in fact a particularly cruel form of rape, in that the victim herself unknowingly provides her attacker with the instrument, the text, that he uses against her (. . .) and that the victim (. . .) apparently does not even know that she has been raped. (. . .) What Werther is aiming at in the attack — especially since his instrument is a piece of text — is in effect the *textualization* of Lotte's body, which would combine the quasi-sexual violation of her privacy as a person with the achievement of her death. (116–18; see also Barton 1999)

This interpretation seems one-sided when we look at Lotte's actual response to Werther's reading, however. Hans Vaget is more persuasive when, like most critics, he sees this scene as a reciprocal, if momentary, union of the two lovers, in which reading substitutes for the sex act (1985, 52–56). Judith Ryan (2004) also acknowledges that Lotte is stirred emotionally, but she argues that Werther and Lotte are in fact responding to different aspects of Ossian's text. He is moved by the mourning lovers, but Lotte's tears are motivated by the described connection between the living and dead, one that echoes her own visions of her deceased mother.

Ehrhard Bahr identifies still another source for Werther's and Lotte's passionate experience of Ossian's text. He maintains that Macpherson's stories of Colma and Daura, with their murderous rivalries, tempt Werther and Lotte with a "barbarische Lösung" (barbaric solution) to their own crisis and shows such a reaction to be consistent with Ossian's general reception in Germany. The reading of Werther's translation ignites their sensuality, and their passion is "desublimated." In the context created by this scene, says Bahr, Lotte's handing over of the pistols seems at one level to be a possible preparation for a duel between Werther and Albert. Society's constraints reassert themselves after this outbreak of "primitivism," however, and Werther turns the murderous impulse back on himself (Bahr 2004, 10–11).

For Bennett, however, Werther's death is yet another assault on Lotte. Additional sexual import accrues to Werther's suicide when Bennett finds particular significance in the statement that "Emilia Galotti lag auf dem Pulte aufgeschlagen" (Emilia Galotti lay opened on the desk). Numerous studies have puzzled over the presence of Lessing's play at Werther's death scene (for example, Feise 1917; Ittner 1942; Dvoretzky 1962; Wilkinson and Willoughby 1965; Leibfried 1977; Meyer-Kalkus 1977; Saine 1980; Duncan 1982; Pütz 1982; Waniek 1982; Burgard 1985; Eyck and Arens 2004), but Bennett is the first to take seriously the double entendre that has long caused winking and nudging among the novel's schoolboy readers. Conjoining the two heroines — "I think it is impossible not to hear the name 'Lotte' in 'Galotti'" — he claims that "we are tempted to hear, as it were from behind the text, the sentence, 'Emilia Galotti (or, cryptically, Lotte) lay on the desk with her legs spread'" (Bennett 2001, 123). Bennett concludes:

> If we are willing to follow this trail of suggestions, the results turn out not to be as outlandish as we might have expected. Werther's suicide, namely, is now understood as the climax of a masturbatory fantasy; and the idea of a textual attack on Lotte's body is given a graphic dimension in the suggested use of that body as a presumably printable pornographic image. To the combination of rape and murder (sexual violence and moral violence), which is the text's relation to Lotte, now corresponds, neatly, the combination of masturbation and suicide, two forms of self-induced climax connected by the well-established metaphorical association of orgasm with death. (123–24)

Stephan Schindler also links Werther's suicide with masturbation via *Emilia Galotti:* Lessing's prince, excited by Emilia's portrait, hopes to spend the morning alone with the painting in private — and, says Schindler, we all know what *that* means. Marinelli's entrance postpones actual masturbation, but the autoerotic fantasies have so taken hold of the prince that he hardly knows how to deal with the real Emilia when he has her in his power. Rather than use his position to force himself on her, he suddenly wants to become her father's son and shifts the location of his sexual satisfaction to the family complex, while, through Emilia's death, the disembodied object of his desire remains available to him. The analogy to Werther, says Schindler, could hardly be more obvious, as the hero fetishizes his "pin-up," Lotte's silhouette, and then, in an autoerotic fantasy, projects the fulfillment of his desires onto the imagined family in heaven (2001, 136–37).

This reading of Werther's death is part of a larger interpretation in which Schindler invokes the concept of "imagined bodies" to characterize a change in sexual discourse during the Age of Goethe. The only officially sanctioned sex of this period, he maintains, limited itself to procreation in marriage, and within these parameters, Werther is clearly a bad match. Apart from having poor employment prospects and identifying himself with social outcasts, he is something of a libertine. His record with other women is anything but respectable: he has, after all, already abandoned two women, broken one heart, initiated a socially inappropriate relationship with Fräulein von B., and finally acted too familiarly with two engaged women in Wahlheim (105). Given his social unacceptability, his interaction with Lotte needs to be confined to a spiritual level, with a truly uniting, corporeal embrace imaginable only in heaven. However, says Schindler, these particular circumstances are not all that cause Werther to spiritualize the body:

> Vielmehr beteiligt sich der Roman an einem vielschichtigen Umwandlungsprozeß, der Sinnlichkeit in ästhetische Sinnhaftigkeit überführt, deren Metaphorik jedoch den Leib wieder sichtbar macht. Werther stiftet eine neue Sexualität, indem er den sexuellen Körper in innerpsychische Bilder übersetzt, die er wieder auf die Wirklichkeit projiziert, um in ihr den in der Phantasie nur versprochenen Genuß einzuklagen. So entsteht der *eingebildete Körper*, der sich in der Realität allerdings nicht wiederfinden läßt und das Subjekt in die Autoerotik stürzt. Radikaler formuliert: Selbst wenn Werther sich mit Lotte der sexuellen Ekstase hingeben würde, würde er nicht mit ihr schlafen, sondern mit dem Körper seiner Phantasie; noch im Moment der körperlichen Vereinigung mit Lotte würde sein Genuß aus der Projektion resultieren, daß er von ihrem 'Ebenbild,' nämlich Lottes Mutter innig umarmt würde. (97–98)

> [The novel participates in a multilayered process of transformation in which sensuality becomes an aestheticized signifier whose imagery in turn makes the body visible again. Werther initiates a new sexuality by translating the sexual body into intra-psychic images that he then projects onto reality in order to bring about there the pleasure that the imagination can only promise. Thus the *imagined body* comes into being, which, however, being unavailable in reality, casts the subject into autoeroticism. In a more radical formulation: even if Werther were to abandon himself to sexual ecstasy with Lotte, he would be sleeping not with her, but with the body from his imagination; even during the moment of physical union with Lotte, his pleasure would result from the projected notion that he was being ardently embraced by Lotte's "image," namely her mother.]

To Schindler, this process is necessarily tied to the concept of masturbation: "Der Roman der Verzweiflung aus unerfüllter Liebe läßt sich somit auch als Roman eines *verzweifelten Onanisten* lesen, der daran leidet, daß er sich der Hoffnung aussetzt, seine erotischen Phantasien würden ihm in der realen Sexualbeziehung den Genuß bereiten, den sie in der Einbildung versprechen" (126–27; The novel about the despair of unfulfilled love can consequently also be read as the novel of the *despairing onanist,* who suffers from making himself vulnerable to the hope that his erotic fantasies would offer him the same pleasure in a real sexual relationship as in his imagination). Schindler is not alone is asserting such a connection. Karl Renner argues that the concept of Werther's body as the site of his pathology can also be taken literally, and that much of the novel corresponds with eighteenth-century psychosomatic medical theory, including the belief that masturbation is an extremely harmful act. Werther, in accordance with eighteenth-century assumptions, displays the symptoms of two extremes: hypochondria and onanism. Each is characterized by a disturbed physical-emotional communication with the world, an unbalanced exchange that is either too stopped up or too profligate. Although Goethe does describe constipation in his parody of Nicolai, "Auf Werther's Grab" (On Werther's Grave, 1775) and actual masturbation, according to Schindler (121–22), in the farce *Hanswursts Hochzeit* (Harlequin's Wedding, 1775), standards of decency of the time would never permit such direct references in a serious novel. Thus Goethe portrays Werther's pathology by means of the conventional medical terms associated with those conditions (Renner 1985, 1–9). Proceeding from this notion of the body as the site of interchange between the mind and physical world, Renner extends his study to elucidate a narrative structure based on the novel's physical spaces. While virtually every study of *Werther* mentions its hero's forays into nature, Renner is unique in dividing the novel into the various such spaces that Werther occupies and in examining his interaction with those environments (9–13).

Although Schindler and Renner do not cite him, their interpretations find some support in Peter Sloterdijk's notion of kynics, symbolized by the figure of Diogenes, who "urinates and masturbates in the marketplace" (1983, 106). Sloterdijk associates the Sturm und Drang and especially the young Goethe with this assertion of the body against inauthenticity. He takes his specific example from Goethe's *Rede zum Schäkespears-Tag* (Speech on Shakespeare's Day, 1771), but the concept could easily be extended to *Werther.* "The young Goethe, more than any other, sensed the vital secret of bourgeois neokynicism and lived it out as art. [. . .] In the Sturm und Drang of early bourgeois art, human beings not of the nobility announce — probably for the first time since antiquity — their claim to a full life, to the embodiment of their sensuousness, to undividedness." Unfortunately, says Sloterdijk, this rebellion is confined to artistic expression and thus kept in check by art's own entanglement with society (106–9).

Masturbation also has metaphorical significance in Friedrich Kittler's study of *Werther.* In exploring the changing status of authorship and forms of reading from medieval times to the eighteenth century, Kittler contrasts the reading experience of Paolo and Francesca in Dante's *Inferno* with Werther's and Lotte's invocation of Klopstock. While the former pair actively breaks a sexual taboo after together reading an anonymously written romance, the latter couple creates a communion of souls by sharing the name of an author that each member has read in isolation. Kittler credits this change in the culture of literacy to developments in print technology and education. Whereas words once had real power over the body, the eighteenth-century experience of the literary text is a closed loop of reading and writing, most tellingly displayed when Werther is so moved by reading aloud his own words in the translation of Ossian (1980, 302–16; see also Kittler 1985, 108–23).

In an approach related to those of Schindler and Kittler, David Wellbery describes Werther's experiences of an imagined — he uses the terms "phantasmatic" and "absolute" — body. Whereas Schindler's process of imagining the body involves a kind of resexualization of an abstraction, Wellbery discovers a "literary rendering of incarnate self-reference" (1994, 181). An examination of Werther's waltz with Lotte, for example, shows "something like a transcendence of human corporeal limitation, a possibility of corporeal movement that would be centered within itself and would course, without resistance, through a boundless space. The dancing couple becomes the transfinite body, isolated because unrelated to any alterity, and yet within this isolation total unto itself" (184). This scene, Wellbery claims, has no metaphorical significance; it is an incident that stands only for itself — a "morphism of the absolute body" (184). What we encounter here is a "linguistic projection" (181); nothing is being represented: "Instead of organizing bodies within a dual system of signifying elements and their correlated fields, the waltz, or at least its fictional version, generates a phantasmatic corporeality that extinguishes representation" (184). Wellbery cites the letter of May 10 as another such morphism. Most critics understand this famous passage as a mystical union with nature, although Reinhart Meyer-Kalkus (1977) considers it an instance of Lacan's mirror-stage. Wellbery disputes both readings and finds it to be an "infinite crossing. Two worlds intersect at the point marked by Werther's subjective position: that of the infinitely small and manifold and that of the infinitely large. Werther's body, then, is felt as being without limitation, as a point of passage where one infinity crosses over into and becomes another. The absolute body is not an object defined by other definite objects; rather, it relates only to the infinitudes whose crossing and equivalence it is" (186–87).

While these morphisms do not stand for anything else, "the experience of this imagined corporeality reactivates aspects of the ontogenesis of bodily experience during early childhood" (182). Wellbery proposes here "the unity of mother and unborn child" (190), which, like the morphisms he describes, is marked by liquid and oral images of self-containment and nourishment. Gustav Hans Graber, whom Wellbery does not cite, has already described the importance of this "primal union" for Werther (1958, 69–84), but as a stage to which the hero regresses. According to Wellbery, however, Werther desires this union only as one variant of the dream of the absolute body, even if it is an extremely evocative one. This distinction is crucial, because Wellbery is offering an interpretation that goes far beyond a psychoanalytic exegesis. It is nothing less than a radical way of reading *Werther,* an experience of a voice of subjectivity *per se,* which struggles against its written form:

> The category of empathy has often been employed to characterize the pragmatics of the novel, but this vague notion of emotional identification misses entirely the psychological, medial, and corporeal dynamics of reading that the text sets into motion. The reader of the novel, I want to say, is drawn into a fantasy scene that is not a scene, not a visual or representational objectification, and not an empathetic actualization of the feelings of a fictional individual. This scene is, rather, the hallucination of the oral-aural circulation of voice within the interior body, the experience of the interior body as dissolved in primordial orality.
>
> This voice, however, only becomes audible intermittently; it is interrupted, checked, fragmented, and suppressed by everything in the novel's language that is not voice, by everything that derives from its *written* character. (204)

According to this interpretation, Werther's Ossian translation represents the "moment when the novel achieves its most radical authenticity. The songs that Werther reads are nothing but an enclosure of voices within voices, each voice recalling and rehearsing the death of voice[, . . .] a kind of ghostly echo-chamber within the novel in which death, without locus or body, reverberates" (208; compare Bennett 2001, 114).

While Wellbery at one point describes Werther's experience of the phantasmatic body as autoerotic, he also sees it as being "pansexual" (185–87) and as including any of a number of possibilities. Other critics interested in the concept of the body extend the notion of Werther's sexuality to include homoeroticism. Several psychologists, as we have seen, posit Werther's sexual attraction to Wilhelm or even Albert (Graber 1958, 75; Eissler 1963; Slochower 1975, 404; Gutbrodt 1995, 621–22). They are joined by more recent theorists who explore this topic in relationship to the broader concept of male identity and desire. Just as Marxists included the early reception of *Werther* as part of the novel's text, these interpreters extend their investigations to the first part of the "Briefe aus der Schweiz" (Letters from Switzerland), a kind of prequel to *Werther* that Goethe wrote in 1796. Of particular interest in this later work is a scene in which the narrator, presumably Werther, reports enthusiastically on watching his friend Ferdinand bathe nude. Inspired by the beauty of his friend's body, he then hires a prostitute to pose naked, and his desire shifts to the woman, although it is not consummated. Robert Tobin concludes from this story that "Homosexuality becomes a phase, albeit also a natural one, through which Werther grows" (1996, 105). Drawing on Wellbery's concept of "the specular moment" (1996), Susan Gustafson finds a broader significance in these incidents: "What these passages from Werther's letters reveal is how the moment of specularity (and the desire it represents) gets 'put into discourse.' Moreover, it is clear throughout Goethe's oeuvre that specular reciprocity is not exclusively reserved for the expression of female-male desire. And, finally, and most significantly, these passages foreground the significance of male same-sex desire. . . . Indeed, . . . viewing a woman may *incite* the poet to form new expressions of his desire, but the *actual process* of poetic formation is contingent upon verbal exchanges between two men who desire one another" (2003, 99). Christoph Brecht, on the other hand, attaches less significance to the undoubted homoeroticism contained in the "Letters" and reads the two scenes as a theoretical consideration of mimesis. The sight of Ferdinand is wholly natural, not because it is homosexually charged, but because it takes place in a natural setting. As a result, it leads immediately to an enrichment of the narrator's imagination, to a metaphorical representation. The socially mediated viewing of the prostitute, in contrast, is more problematic from an aesthetic point of view (1994, 1115–16).

Most recently, Hans Vaget argues that the "Letters" represent Goethe's further attempt to dampen the uncritical ardor of *Werther* enthusiasts. In his voyeuristic encounter with the prostitute, which does not end in a physical coupling, "Werther, the revered embodiment of sentimental love, stands revealed as someone who fails to grasp the centrality of the body in love and in art" (2004, 27).

Works Cited

Alewyn, Richard. 1979. "'Klopstock!'" *Euphorion* 73 (1979): 357–64.

Bahr, Ehrhard. 2004. "Ossian-Rezeption von Michael Denis bis Goethe: Ein Beitrag zur Geschichte des Primitivismus in Deutschland." *Goethe Yearbook* 12 (2004): 1–15.

Barton, Karin. 2001. *Viel Licht, Viel Schatten: Rousseau, Goethe und die Unordnung der Geschlechter; Eine neue Interpretation der "Leiden des jungen Werther."* Diss., U of Toronto.

Bell, Matthew. 2003. Review of Bennett 2001. *MLR* 98 (2003): 1039–40.

Bennett, Benjamin. 1980. "Goethe's 'Werther': Double Perspective and the Game of Life." *The German Quarterly* 53 (1980): 64–81.

———. 2001. *Goethe as Woman: The Undoing of Literature*. Detroit: Wayne State UP.

Blackall, Eric A. 1976. *Goethe and the Novel*. Ithaca: Cornell UP.

Brecht, Christoph. 1994. Commentary to "Briefe aus der Schweiz: Erste Abteilung." In *Johann Wolfgang Goethe, Sämtliche Werke, 1. Abteilung,*

Band 8, ed. Waltraut Wiethölter, 1111–18. Frankfurt am Main: Deutscher Klassiker Verlag.

Burgard, Peter J. 1985. "'Emilia Galotti' und 'Clavigo.' Werthers Pflichtlektüre und unsere." *Zeitschrift für deutsche Philologie* 104 (1985): 481–94.

Conger, Syndy McMillen. 1986. "The Sorrows of Young Charlotte: Werther's English Sisters 1785–1805." *Goethe Yearbook* 3 (1986): 21–56.

Davis, William Stephen. 1994. "The Intensification of the Body in Goethe's *Die Leiden des jungen Werther.*" *The Germanic Review* 69 (1994): 106–17.

Dumiche, Béatrice. 1995. "Lottes Mutterbindung: Ihre Mitschuld an Werthers Selbstmord." *Orbis litterarum* 50 (1995): 278–88.

Duncan, Bruce. 1982. "'Emilia Galotti lag auf dem Pult aufgeschlagen': Werther as (Mis)-Reader." *Goethe Yearbook* 1 (1982): 42–50.

Dvoretzky, Edward. 1962. "Goethe's 'Werther' and Lessing's 'Emilia Galotti.'" *German Life and Letters* 16 (1962–63): 23–26.

Dye, R. Ellis. 1988. "Werther's Lotte: Views of the Other in Goethe's First Novel." *JEGP* 87 (1988): 492–506.

Eissler, Kurt Robert. 1963. *Goethe: A Psychoanalytic Study, 1775–1786.* Detroit: Wayne State UP.

Eyck, John R. J., and Katherine Arens. 2004. "The Court of Public Opinion: Lessing, Goethe, and Werther's *Emilia Galotti.*" *Monatshefte* 96 (2004): 40–61.

Faber, M. D. 1973. "The Suicide of Young Werther." *Psychoanalytical Review* 60 (1973): 239–76.

Feise, Ernst. 1917. "Lessings 'Emilia Galotti' und Goethes 'Werther.'" *Modern Philology* 15 (1917): 321–38.

Finsen, H. Carl. 1977. "Empfindsamkeit als Raum der Alternative: Untersucht am Beispiel von Goethes 'Die Leiden des jungen Werthers.'" *Der Deutschunterricht* 29 (1977): 27–38.

Fischer, Peter. 1986. "Familienauftritte: Goethes Phantasiewelt und die Konstruktion des 'Werther'-Romans." In Schmiedt, 1989a, 189–220.

Foucault, Michel. 1976. *The History of Sexuality.* Trans. Robert Hurley. Vol. 1. New York: Vintage, 1980.

Furst, Lilian R. 1990. "The 'Imprisoning Self': Goethe's Werther and Rousseau's Solitary Walker." In *European Romanticism: Literary Cross-Currents, Modes, and Models,* ed. Gerhardt Hoffmeister, 163–79. Detroit: Wayne State UP.

Goeze, Johann Melchior. 1775. Review of *Werther. Freywillige Beyträge zu den Hamburgischen Nachrichten aus dem Reiche der Gelehrsamkeit* (April 7, 1775). Repr. in *Der junge Goethe im zeitgenössischen Urteil,* ed. Peter Müller, 119–26. Berlin: Akademie Verlag, 1969.

Goins, Scott E. 1992. "Birds and Erotic Fantasies in Catullus and Goethe." *Goethe Yearbook* 6 (1992): 29–40.

Gose, Hans. 1921. *Goethes "Werther."* Halle an der Saale: Niemeyer, 1921. Repr. Walluf bei Wiesbaden: Sändig, 1973.

Graber, Gustav Hans. 1957. "Goethes 'Werther.'" In *Goethe, Psychologie des Mannes,* 178–81. Bern: Huber.

———. 1958. "Goethes Werther: Versuch einer tiefenpsychologischen Pathographie." *Acta psychotherapeutica, pychosomatica et orthopaedagogica* 6 (1958): 120–36. Repr. in Schmiedt 1989a. 69–84.

Grimm, Herman Friedrich. 1874. *The Life and Times of Goethe.* Trans. Sarah Holland Adams. Boston: Little, Brown, 1880.

Gustafson, Susan E. 2003. *Men Desiring Men: The Poetry of Same-sex Identity and Desire in German Classicism.* Detroit: Wayne State UP.

Gutbrodt, Fritz. 1995. "The Worth of 'Werther': Goethe's Literary Marketing." *MLN* 110 (1995): 579–630.

Herrmann, Hans Peter, ed. 1994a. *Goethes "Werther": Kritik und Forschung.* Darmstadt: Wissenschaftliche Buchgesellschaft.

Hillebrand, Karl. 1885. "Die Werther-Krankheit in Europa." In *Völker und Menschen,* 283–320. Strassburg: Trübner, 1914.

Huff, Steven R. 1984. "Lotte's Klavier: A Resounding Symbol in Goethe's *Die Leiden des jungen Werthers.*" *The Germanic Review* 59 (1984): 43–48.

Ittner, R. T. 1942. "Werther und Emilia Galotti." *JEGP* 41 (1942): 418–26.

Kittler, Friedrich A. 1980. *"Autorschaft und Liebe."* In Herrmann 1994a, 295–316.

———. 1985. *Discourse Networks 1800/1900.* Trans. Michael Metteer. Stanford: Stanford UP, 1990.

Kuzniar, Alice. 1989. "The Misrepresentations of Self: Werther versus Goethe." *Mosaic* 22 (1989): 15–28.

———. 2004 Review of Bennett 2001. *Goethe Yearbook* 12 (2004): 270–73.

Lee, Meredith. 1990. "'Klopstock!' Werther, Lotte and the reception of Klopstock's Odes." In *The Age of Goethe Today: Critical Reexamination and Literary Reflection.* ed. Gertrud Bauer Pickar and Sabine Cramer, Houston German Studies 7, 1–11. Munich: Finck.

Leibfried, Erwin. 1977. "Goethes Werther als Leser von Lessings 'Emilia Galotti.'" In *Text — Leser — Bedeutung: Untersuchungen zur Interaktion von Text und Leser,* ed. Herberet Grabes, 145–56. Grossen-Linden: Hoffmann.

Lukács, Georg. 1936. "'Die Leiden des jungen Werther.'" In Herrmann, 1994a, 39–57.

MacLeod, Catriona. 2003. Review of Bennett 2001. *MLQ* 64 (2003): 258–60.

Meyer-Kalkus, Reinhart. 1977. "Werthers Krankheit zum Tode: Pathologie und Familie in der Empfindsamkeit." In Schmiedt 1989a, 85–146.

Meyer-Krentler, Eckhardt. 1982. "'Kalte Abstraktion' gegen 'versengte Einbildung': Destruktion und Restauration aufklärerischer Harmoniemodelle in Goethes 'Leiden' und Nicolais 'Freuden des jungen Werthers.'" *Deutsche*

Vierteljahrsschrift für Literaturwissenschaft und Geistesgeschichte 56 (1982): 65–91.

Muenzer, Clark. 1984. *Figures of Identity: Goethe's Novels and the Enigmatic Self*. University Park: Penn State UP.

Purdy, Daniel. 1996. "The Veil of Masculinity: Clothing and Identity via Goethe's 'Die Leiden des jungen Werther.'" *Lessing Yearbook* 27 (1995): 103–30.

Pütz, Peter. 1982. "Werthers Leiden an der Literatur." In *Goethe's Narrative Fiction: The Irvine Goethe Symposium,* ed. William J. Lillyman, 55–68. Berlin; New York: W. de Gruyter, 1983.

Reiss, Hans S. 1963. *Goethe's Novels*. New York: St. Martin, 1969.

Renner, Karl N. 1985. "'Laß das Büchlein dein Freund seyn': Goethes Roman 'Die Leiden des jungen Werther' und die Diätetik der Aufklärung." In *Zur Sozialgeschichte der deutschen Literatur von der Aufklärung bis zur Jahrhundertwende,* ed. Günter Häntzschel et al., 1–20. Tübingen: Niemeyer.

Ryan, Judith. 2004. "'That day we read no more': Werther, Lotte, and Literary Tradition." Talk delivered at Smith College, Northhampton, MA, September 18, 2004.

Saine, Thomas P. 1980. "Passion and Aggression: The Meaning of Werther's Last Letter." *Orbis litterarum* 35 (1980): 327–56.

———. 1981. "The Portrayal of Lotte in the Two Versions of Goethe's 'Werther.'" *JEGP* 80 (1981): 54–77.

Schindler, Stephan K. 2001. *Eingebildete Körper: Phantasierte Sexualität in der Goethezeit*. Tübingen: Stauffenburg.

Schlaffer, Hannelore. 1987. "'Die Leiden des jungen Werthers.'" In *Johann Wolfgang von Goethe: Sämtliche Werke nach Epochen seines Schaffens,* ed. Karl Richter et al., vol. 2,2:844–53. Munich: Hanser.

Schmidt, Erich. 1875. *Richardson, Rousseau und Goethe: Ein Beitrag zur Geschichte des Romans im 18. Jahrhundert*. Jena: E. Frommann.

Schmidt, Gerhard. 1968. *Die Krankheit zum Tode: Goethes Todesneurose*. Stuttgart: Enke.

Schmiedt, Helmut, ed. 1989a *"Wie froh bin ich, dass ich weg bin!": Goethes Roman "Die Leiden des jungen Werther" in literaturpsychologischer Sicht*. Würzburg: Königshausen & Neumann.

Silz, Walter. 1972. "Werther and Lotte at the Well." In *Traditions and Transitions: Studies in Honor of Harold Jantz,* ed. Lieselotte E. Kurth, 125–31. Munich: Delp.

Slochower, Harry. 1975. "Suicides in Literature: Their Ego Function." *American Imago* 32 (1975): 389–416.

Sloterdijk, Peter. *Critique of Cynical Reason*. Trans. Michael Eldred. Minneapolis: U of Minnesota P, 1987.

Sørensen, Bengt Algot. 1987. "Über die Familie in Goethes 'Werther' und 'Wilhelm Meister.'" *Orbis Litterarum* 42 (1987): 118–40.

Spann, Meno. 1972. "'Werther' Revisited: Two Hundred Years of a Masterpiece." *Mosaic* 5 (1972): 73–83.

Steinhauer, Harry. 1974. "Goethe's 'Werther' after Two Centuries." *University of Toronto Quarterly* 44 (1974): 1–13.

Tobin, Robert D. 1996. "In and Against Nature: Goethe on Homosexuality and Heterosexuality." In *Outing Goethe and His Age*, ed. Alice A. Kuzniar, 94–110. Stanford: Stanford UP.

Trunz, Erich. 1951. "Anmerkungen des Herausgebers zu *Die Leiden des jungen Werther*." In *Goethes Werke*, 6:514–95. Hamburg: Wegner.

Vaget, Hans Rudolf. 1985. "'Die Leiden des jungen Werthers' (1774)." In *Goethes Erzählwerk: Interpretationen*, ed. Paul Michael Lützeler and James E. McLeod, 37–72. Stuttgart: Reclam. Reclams Universal-Bibliothek 8081.

———. 2004. "Werther, The Undead." *Goethe Yearbook* 12 (2004): 17–29.

Walker, Joyce S. 1999. "Sex, Suicide, and the Sublime: A Reading of Goethe's *Werther*." *Monatshefte* 91 (1999): 208–23.

Waniek, Erdmann. 1982. "'Werther' lesen und Werther als Leser." *Goethe Yearbook* 1 (1982): 51–92.

Warrick, E. Kathleen. 1978. "Lotte's Sexuality and Her Responsibility for Werther's Death." *Essays in Literature* 5 (1978): 129–35.

Wellbery, David E. 1990. Foreword to *Discourse Networks 1800/1900*, by Friedrich A. Kittler, trans. Michael Metteer. Stanford: Stanford UP.

———. 1994. "Morphisms of the Phantasmatic Body: Goethe's *The Sorrows of Young Werther*." In *Body & Text in the Eighteenth Century*, ed. Veronica Kelly and Dorothea von Mücke, 181–208. Stanford: Stanford UP.

Wilkinson, Elizabeth M., and Leonard Ashley Willoughby. 1965. "The Blind Man and the Poet: An Early Stage in Goethe's Quest for Form." In *German Studies Presented to Walter Horace Bruford*, 29–57. London: Harrup.

Wilson, W. Daniel. 1989. "Patriarchy, Politics, Passion: Labor and Werther's Search for Nature." *Internationales Archiv für Sozialgeschichte der deutschen Literatur* 14 (1989): 15–44.

Winkle, Sally Anne. 1984. *Woman as Bourgeois Ideal: A Study of Sophie von La Roche's "Geschichte des Fräuleins von Sternheim" and Goethe's "Werther."* New York: Lang, 1988.

Bibliography

Sulzer, Johann Georg. 1771. *Allgemeine Theorie der schönen Künste in einzeln, nach alphabetischer Ordnung der Kunstwörter auf einander folgenden, Artikeln abgehandelt.* 2 vols. Leipzig: Weidmann, 1771–74.

Goethe, Johann Wolfgang von. 1772. "Gedichte von einem polnischen Juden." In *Frankfurter gelehrte Anzeigen vom Jahr 1772,* 461–64. Heilbronn: Henninger, 1882–83.

Anonymous. 1774. Review of *Werther. Frankfurter gelehrte Anzeigen* (November 1, 1774). Repr. in Müller 1969a, 192–94.

Blankenburg, Christian Friedrich von. 1774. *Versuch über den Roman.* Leipzig and Liegnitz: David Siegers Wittwe. Facsimile of the 1st edition, ed. Eberhard Lämmert. Stuttgart: Metzler, 1965.

Claudius, Matthias. 1774. "Die Leiden des jungen Werthers." *Wandsbecker Bote* 169 (October 22, 1774). Repr. in Müller 1969a, 163–64.

Deinet, J. K. 1774. Review of *Werther: Frankfurter gelehrte Anzeigen* (November 15, 1774). Repr. in Müller 1969a, 194.

Heinse, Johann Jakob Wilhelm. 1774. Review of *Werther. Iris* (December, 1774): 78–81. Repr. in Müller 1969a, 208–10.

Herder, Johann Gottfried. 1774. *Übers Erkennen und Empfinden in der menschlichen Seele.* Vol. 8. of *Sämmtliche Werke,* ed. Bernhard Suphan, 236–62. Berlin: Weidmann, 1902.

Schmid, Christian Heinrich. 1774. "Fortsetzung der kritischen Nachrichten vom Zustande des teutschen Parnasses." *Der Teutsche Merkur* (November 1774): 179–83. Repr. in Braun 1883, 61–63.

Schubart, Christian Friedrich Daniel. 1774. Review of *Werther. Deutsche Chronik* (December 5, 1774). Repr. in Müller 1969a, 205–6.

Wieland, Christoph Martin. 1774. " 'Die Leiden des jungen Werthers.' " *Der Teutsche Merkur* (December, 1774): 241–43. Repr. in Müller 1969a, 166.

Anonymous. 1775. "Die Leiden des jungen Werthers — Freuden des jungen Werthers. Leiden und Freuden Werthers des Mannes." *Neueste Critische Nachrichten* (May 20, 1775). Müller 1969a, 162–63.

Blankenburg, Christian Friedrich von. 1775. Review of *Werther. Neue Bibliothek der schönen Wissenschaften und der freyen Künste,* 18 (1775): 46–95.

———. *Theorie und Technik des Romans im 17. und 18. Jahrhundert.* Ed. Dieter Kimpel and Conrad Wiedemann. Vol. 1: Barock und Aufklärung, 138–41. Tübingen, 1970. Deutsche Texte 16. Repr. in Müller 1969a, 168–92.

Breidenbach zu Breidenstein, Karl Wilhelm, Freiherr von. 1775. *Berichtigung der Geschichte des jungen Werthers.* Freystadt, 1775; 2nd ed. Frankfurt and Leipzig, 1775.

Claudius, Matthias. 1775. "Freuden des jungen Werthers: Leiden und Freuden Werthers des Mannes." *Wandsbecker Bote* 15 (1775). Repr. in Müller 1969a, 164–65.

Garve, Christian. 1775. "Aus einem Briefe." In *Der Philosoph für die Welt,* by J. J. Engel, 1. Teil, 2. Stück (1775), 21–33. Repr. in Müller 1969a, 149–53.

Goeze, Johann Melchior. 1775. Review of *Werther. Freywillige Beyträge zu den Hamburgischen Nachrichten aus dem Reiche der Gelehrsamkeit* (April 7, 1775). Repr. in Müller 1969a, 119–26.

Lenz, Jakob Michael Reinhold. 1775. "Briefe über die Moralität der 'Leiden des jungen Werthers.'" In *Werke und Briefe,* ed. Sigrid Damm, 2:673–90. Leipzig: Insel, 1987.

Merck, Johann Heinrich. 1775. Review of *Werther. Allgemeine deutsche Bibliothek* 26 (1775): 102–8. Repr. in Müller 1969a, 198–201.

Nicolai, Friedrich 1775. *Freuden des jungen Werthers: Leiden und Freuden Werthers des Mannes; Voran und zuletzt ein Gespräch.* In Müller 1969a, 130–45.

Schubart, Christian Friedrich Daniel. 1775. Review in *Deutsche Chronik* (March 16, 1775). Repr. in Müller 1969a, 206.

Wieland, Christoph Martin. 1775. "Freuden des jungen Werthers: Leiden und Freuden Werthers des Mannes." *Der Teutsche Merkur* (March, 1775): 282–84. Repr. in Müller 1969a, 167–68.

Ziegra, Christian. 1775. Review of *Werther. Freywillige Beyträge zu den Hamburgischen Nachrichten aus dem Reiche der Gelehrsamkeit* (April 7, 1775). Repr. in Müller 1969a, 126–29.

Merck, Johann Heinrich. 1778. "Ueber den Mangel des epischen Geistes in unserm lieben Vaterlande." In *Johann Heinrich Merck's ausgewählte Schriften zur schönen Literatur und Kunst,* ed. Adolf Stahr, 175–80. Repr. of edition of 1840. Göttingen: Vandenhoeck & Ruprecht, 1965.

Moritz, Karl Philipp. 1778. "Einsame Lektüre." In *Zeichen der Zeit: Ein deutsches Lesebuch,* ed. Walther Killy, 1:140–43. Frankfurt am Main: Fischer, 1962. Also Neuwied: Luchterhand, 1981. Sammlung Luchterhand 351.

Laukhard, Friedrich Christian. 1792. "Werther-Cultus 1776." Excerpt from *Leben und Schicksale,* Halle, 1792. In *Weimarisches Jahrbuch fur deutsche Sprache, Litteratur und Kunst* 6 (1857): 218–19.

Herder, Johann Gottfried. 1796. *Briefe zur Beförderung der Humanität, achte Sammlung.* Vol. 18 of *Sämmtliche Werke,* ed. Bernhard Suphan, 69–140. Berlin: Weidmann, 1877–1913.

Bergk, J. A. 1799. *Die Kunst, Bücher zu lesen: Nebst Bemerkungen über Schriften und Schriftsteller.* Jena. (On Werther: 216–26, 231–34).

Anonymous. 1806. "The Sorrows of Werter." *The Literary Magazine, and American Register* [Philadelphia], 6 (1806): 451.

Goethe, Johann Wolfgang von. 1813. *Dichtung und Wahrheit.* Ed. Erich Trunz. Vol. 9 of *Werke.* Hamburg: Wegner, 1961–64. (This Hamburg edition of Goethe's works is cited in the text as *HA*).

Staël, Madame de (Anne-Louise-Germaine). 1814. *Germany: Translated from the French.* New York: Eastburn, Kirk.

Schlegel, August Wilhelm von. 1818/19. *Geschichte der deutschen Sprache und Poesie: Vorlesungen, gehalten an der Universität Bonn seit dem Wintersemester 1818/19.* Ed. Josef Körner. Berlin: B. Behr (F. Feddersen), 1913.

Heine, Heinrich. 1828. "Beers 'Struensee.' " In *Heines Werke,* ed. Ernst Elster, 7:224–38. Leipzig, Wien: Bibliographisches Institut, 1890.

Menzel, Wolfgang. 1828. *Die deutsche Literatur.* Stuttgart: Gebrüder Franckh, 1828. In English, *German Literature.* Vol. 3. Trans. C. C. Felton. Boston: Hilliard, Gray, 1840.

Eckermann, Johann Peter. 1824. *Gespräche mit Goethe in den letzten Jahren seines Lebens.* Ed. Gustav Moldenhauer. Vol. 3. Leipzig: Reclam, 1884.

Mundt, Theodor. 1834. *Moderne Lebenswirren: Briefe und Zeitabenteuer eines Salzschreibers.* Leipzig: Reichenbach.

Gervinus, Georg Gottfried. 1835. *Geschichte der deutschen Dichtung.* Vol. 4. Leipzig: Engelmann, 1850.

Carlyle, Thomas. 1838. *Lectures on the History of Literature, Delivered by Thomas Carlyle, April to July 1838.* New York: C. Scribner's sons, 1892 (lectures 11 and 12).

Carus, Carl Gustav. 1843. *Goethe, zu dessen näherem Verständnis.* Leipzig: Weichardt, 1843. Repr., ed. Hans Krey, Dresden: Jess, 1949.

Schlosser, Friedrich Christoph. 1843. *Geschichte des achtzehnten Jahrhunderts und des neunzehnten bis zum Sturz des französischen Kaiserreichs mit besonderer Rücksicht auf geistige Bildung.* Vol. 4. Heidelberg: Mohr, 1864.

Engels, Friedrich. 1845. Letter to the editor. *The Northern Star* (Oct. 25, 1845).

Schwenck, Konrad. 1845. *Goethes Werke: Erklärungen von Konrad Schwenck.* Frankfurt am Main: Sauerländer.

Vilmar, August Friedrich Christian. 1845. *Geschichte der deutschen National-Literatur.* Marburg, Leipzig: Elwert, 1877.

Grün, Karl. 1846. *Über Göthe, vom menschlichen Standpunkte.* Darmstadt: Leske.

Engels, Friedrich. 1847. "Karl Grün, *Über Goethe vom menschlichen Standpunkte:* Darmstadt: 1846." In *Karl Marx, Friedrich Engels: Werke,* 4:222–47. Berlin: Dietz, 1969.

Düntzer, Heinrich. 1849. *Zu Goethe's Jubelfeier: Studien zu Goethe's Werken.* Elberfeld und Iserlohn: Baedeker.

Hettner, Hermann. 1850. *Die romantische Schule in ihrem inneren Zusammenhange mit Göthe und Schiller.* Braunschweig: Vieweg.

Eichendorff, Joseph, Freiherr von. 1851. *Der deutsche Roman des achtzehnten Jahrhunderts in seinem Verhältniß zum Christenthum.* Vol. 8, part 2 of

Sämtliche Werke: Historisch-kritische Ausgabe, ed. Wolfram Mauser. Regensburg: Habbel, 1965.

"Goethe and Werther." 1854. *The Living Age*, 43.

Kestner, Georg August. 1854. *Goethe und Werther: Briefe Goethes, meistens aus seiner Jugendzeit, mit erläuternden Dokumenten*. Stuttgart, Tübingen: Cotta.

Düntzer, Heinrich. 1855. *Goethes "Leiden des jungen Werthers": Erläutert*. Jena.

Lewes, George Henry. 1856. *The Life and Works of Goethe: With Sketches of His Age and Contemporaries, from Published and Unpublished Sources*. Boston: Ticknor and Fields.

Prutz, Robert Eduard. 1856. *Goethe, eine biographische Schilderung*. Leipzig: Brockhaus.

Goedeke, Karl. 1859. *Grundriß zur Geschichte der deutschen Dichtung aus den Quellen*. Vol. 4, section 2. Dresden: Ehlermann, 1910.

Prutz, Robert. 1859. *Die deutsche Literatur der Gegenwart: 1848 bis 1858*. Vol. 1. Leipzig: Voigt & Günther.

Scherr, Johannes. 1861. *Allgemeine Geschichte der Literatur: Ein Handbuch*. Stuttgart: Franckh.

Schmidt, Julian. 1861. *Geschichte der deutschen Litteratur von Leibniz bis auf unsere Zeit*. Vol. 2. Berlin: Hertz, 1886–96.

Anonymous. 1862. "Forgotten Novels (Goethe, Werther)." *Littell's Living Age* 73 (1862): 237.

Bernays, Michael. 1866. *Über Kritik und Geschichte des goetheschen Textes*. Berlin: Dümmler.

Jahn, Otto. 1866. "Noch einmal die Wertherbriefe." In *Biographische Aufsätze*. Leipzig.

Biedermann, Karl. 1867. *Deutschland im achtzehnten Jahrhundert*. Vol. 2, part 2. Leipzig: Weber.

Dilthey, Wilhelm. 1867. "Die dichterische und philosophische Bewegung in Deutschland, 1770–1800." In *Gesammelte Schriften*, 5:12–27. Leipzig: Teubner, 1924.

Hettner, Hermann. 1869. *Literaturgeschichte des achtzehnten Jahrhunderts*. Part 3, book 3, 1. Braunschweig: Vieweg, 1894.

Zimmermann, Georg. 1869. "Werthers Leiden und der literarische Kampf um sie." *Herrigs Archiv* 45 (1869): 241–98.

Spielhagen, Friedrich. 1871. "Finder oder Erfinder?" In *Beiträge zur Theorie und Technik des Romans*, 3–34. Leipzig: Staackmann, 1883.

Koberstein, August. 1873. *Grundriss der Geschichte der deutschen Nationalliteratur*. Leipzig: Vogel, 1872–73.

Fontane, Theodor. 1874. "Goethe-Eindrücke: 'Die Leiden des jungen Werther.'" In *Schriften und Glossen zur europäischen Literatur*, ed. Werner Weber, 2:219–20. Zurich, Stuttgart: Artemis, 1967.

———. 1874. "Werthers Leiden." In *Sämmtliche Werke*, ed. Walter Keitel, part 3, 1:464–65. Munich: Hanser. Also in Herrmann 1994a, 21–22.

Grimm, Herman Friedrich. 1874. *The Life and Times of Goethe*. Trans. Sarah Holland Adams. Boston: Little, Brown, 1880.

Bernays, Michael. 1875. Introduction to *Der junge Goethe: Seine Briefe und Dichtungen von 1764–1776,* ed. Salomon Hirzel, 1:iii–xcvii. Leipzig: Hirzel, 1887.

Schmidt, Erich. 1875. *Richardson, Rousseau und Goethe: Ein Beitrag zur Geschichte des Romans im 18. Jahrhundert.* Jena: E. Frommann.

Gesky, Theodor. 1877. "Die Motive zu Goethes Roman 'Werthers Leiden.' Ein literaturgeschichtlicher Rückblick." *Westermanns Monatshefte* 41, no. 246 (March 1877): 657–65.

Viehoff, Heinrich. 1877. *Goethes Leben, Geistesentwickelung und Werke*. Stuttgart: Conradi.

Wille, Ludwig. 1877. *Goethes Werther und seine Zeit: Eine psychiatrisch-litterarische Studie*. Basel. (Oeffentliche Vorträge, gehalten in der Schweiz, vol. 4., book 9.)

Boyesen, Hjalmar Hjorth. 1879. *Goethe and Schiller: Their Lives and Works; Including a Commentary on Goethe's Faust*. New York, Scribner's.

Koenig, Robert. 1879. *Deutsche Literaturgeschichte*. Bielefeld: Velhagen & Klasing.

Schmidt, Erich. 1879. "Aus der Wertherzeit." In *Charakteristiken,* 1:274–86. Berlin: Weidmann, 1901–2.

Taylor, Bayard. 1879. *Studies in German Literature*. New York: Putnam.

Herbst, Wilhelm. 1881. *Goethe in Wetzlar, 1772: Vier Monate aus des Dichters Jugendleben*. Gotha: Perthes.

Koldewey, Friedrich. 1881. "Werther's Urbild." In *Lebens- und Charakterbilder,* 167–202. Wolfenbüttel.

Kurz, Heinrich. 1881. *Geschichte der deutschen Literatur mit ausgewählten Stücken aus den Werken der vorzüglichsten Schriftsteller: Mit vielen nach den besten Originalen und Zeichnungen ausgeführten Illustrationen in Holzschnitt*. Leipzig: Teubner, 1876–81.

Braun, Julius W. 1883. *Goethe im Urtheile seiner Zeitgenossen: Zeitungskritiken, Berichte, Notizen, Goethe und seine Werke betreffend, aus den Jahren 1773–1812*. Berlin: Luckhardt, 1883–85.

Hillebrand, Karl. 1885. "Die Werther-Krankheit in Europa." In *Völker und Menschen,* 283–320. Strassburg: Trübner, 1914.

Hirsch, Franz. 1885. *Geschichte der deutschen Litteratur von ihren Anfängen bis auf die neueste Zeit*. Vol. 2. Leipzig: W. Friedrich, 1883–85.

Scherer, Wilhelm. 1886. *A History of German Literature*. Trans. from the 3rd German edition by Mrs. F. C. Conybeare. Ed. F. Max Müller. Vol. 2. New York, C. Scribner's Sons.

Dilthey, Wilhelm. 1887. *Die Einbildungskraft des Dichters*. In *Gesammelte Schriften,* 6:103–241. Leipzig: Teubner, 1924.

Braitmaier, Friedrich. 1892. *Göthekult und Göthephilologie: Eine Streitschrift*. Tübingen: in Kommission bei G. Fock, Leipzig.

Appell, Johann Wilhelm. 1896. *Werther und seine Zeit: Zur Goethe-Litteratur.* Oldenburg: Schulze.

Viehoff, Heinrich. 1897. *Geschichte der deutschen Literatur von den ältesten Zeiten bis zur Gegenwart* (3 vols.). Leipzig, Wien: Bibilographisches Institut (5 eds. to 1938).

Möbius, Paul Julius. 1898. *Über das Pathologische bei Goethe.* Leipzig: Barth, 1898. Repr. Munich: Matthes & Seitz, 1983. One chapter, "Werthers Leiden," in Schmiedt 1989a, 31–34.

Arnsperger, W. 1900. "Die Entstehung von 'Werthers Leiden.'" *Neue Heidelbergerjahrbücher* 10 (1900): 195–217.

Seuffert, Bernhard. 1900. "Philologische Betrachtungen im Anschluß an Goethes Werther." *Euphorion* 7 (1900): 1–47.

Faust, A. B. 1901. "The Problematic Hero in German Fiction." *PMLA* 16 (1901): 92–106.

Gräf, Hans Gerhard. 1901. *Goethe über seine Dichtungen: Versuch einer Sammlung aller Äußerungen des Dichters über seine poetischen Werke.* Vol. 1. Frankfurt am Main: Literarische Anstalt.

Loewe, Victor. 1901. "Neue Beiträge zur Charakteristik des jungen Jerusalem." *Euphorion* 8 (1901): 72–77.

Meyer, Richard Moritz. 1901. "Goethe als Psycholog." *Goethe-Jahrbuch* 22 (1901): 3*–26*.

Batt, Max. 1902. *The Treatment of Nature in German Literature from Gunther to the Appearance of Goethe's "Werther."* Port Washington, NY: Kennikat, 1969 (Repr. of the 1902 edition).

Haney, John Louis. 1902. "German Literature in England before 1790." *Americana Germanica* 4 (1902): 144–54.

Kluge, Hermann. 1902. *Geschichte der deutschen National-Literatur: Zum Gebrauche an höheren Unterrichtsanstalten und zum Selbststudium.* Altenburg: O. Bonde.

Herrmann, Helene. 1904. *Die psychologischen Anschauungen des jungen Goethe und seiner Zeit.* Diss., Berlin.

Herrmann, Max. 1904. Introduction to *Goethes Sämtliche Werke: Jubiläums-Ausgabe,* 16:v–xli. Stuttgart and Berlin: Cotta.

Wenckebach, Carla. 1905. *Deutsche Literaturgeschichte auf kulturhistorischer Grundlage: For Universities, Colleges and Acadamies.* Boston: D.C. Heath.

Dohrn, Wolf. 1907. *Die künstlerische Darstellung als Problem der Ästhetik: Untersuchungen zur Methode und Begriffsbildung der Ästhetik, mit einer Anwendung auf Goethes "Werther."* Hamburg, Leipzig: Voss.

Engel, Eduard. 1907. *Geschichte der deutschen Literatur: Von den Anfängen bis in die Gegenwart.* Leipzig: Freytag.

Friedell, Egon, and Alfred Polgar. 1908. "Goethe: Groteske in 2 Bildern." In *Wozu das Theater? Essays, Satiren, Humoresken,* ed. Peter Haage, 197–210. Munich: Beck, 1966.

Kaulitz-Niedeck, Rosa. 1908. *Goethe und Jerusalem.* Giessen: Münchow.

Brüggemann, Fritz. 1909. *Die Ironie als entwicklungsgeschichtliches Moment: Ein Beitrag zur Vorgeschichte der deutschen Romantik.* Jena: E. Diederichs. Repr. Darmstadt: Wissenschaftliche Buchgesellschaft, 1976.

Fittbogen, Gottfried. 1910. "Die Charaktere in beiden Fassungen von 'Werthers Leiden.'" *Euphorion* 17 (1910): 556–82.

Francke, Kuno. 1910. *Die Kulturwerte der deutschen Literatur in ihrer geschichtlichen Entwicklung.* Berlin: Weidmann, 1910–28.

Lauterbach, Martin. 1910. *Das Verhältnis der zweiten zur ersten Ausgabe von "Werthers Leiden."* Strassburg: Trübner.

Tornius, Valerian Hugo. 1910. *Die Empfindsamen in Darmstadt: Studien über Männer und Frauen aus der Wertherzeit.* Leipzig, Klinkhardt & Biermann.

Elster, Ernst. 1911. *Prinzipien der Litteraturwissenschaft.* Halle an der Saale: M. Niemeyer, 1897–1911.

Gloël, Heinrich. 1911. *Goethes Wetzlarer Zeit: Bilder aus der Reichskammergerichts- und Wertherstadt.* Berlin: Mittler. Repr. Wetzlar: Will, 1999.

Biese, Alfred. 1912. *Deutsche Literaturgeschichte.* Munich: Beck.

Meyer, Richard Moritz. 1912. *Die deutsche Literatur bis zum Beginn des 19. Jahrhunderts.* Berlin: Bondi, 1920, 1912.

Rank, Otto. 1912. *Das Inzest-Motiv in Dichtung und Sage: Grundzüge einer Psychologie des dichterischen Schaffens.* Leipzig: Deuticke, 1926.

Schmidt, Heinrich. 1912. *Goethe-Lexikon.* Leipzig: Kröner.

Feise, Ernst, ed. 1914a. *"Die Leiden des jungen Werthers," von Johann Wolfgang Goethe.* With a Critical Essay. New York: Oxford UP.

Feise, Ernst. 1914b. "Zu Entstehung, Problem und Technik von Goethes 'Werther.'" *JEGP* 13 (1914): 1–36.

Gerhard, Melitta. 1916. "Die Bauerburschenepisode im 'Werther.'" *Zeitschrift für Ästhetik und allgemeine Kunstwissenschaft* 11 (1916): 61–74. Repr. in Herrmann 1994a, 23–38.

Gundolf, Friedrich. 1916. *Goethe.* Berlin: Georg Bondi, 1920.

Feise, Ernst. 1917. "Lessings 'Emilia Galotti' und Goethes 'Werther.'" *Modern Philology* 15 (1917): 321–38.

Aschner, Siegfried. 1920. *Geschichte der deutschen Literatur.* Berlin: Ebering.

Koch, Max. 1920. *Geschichte der deutschen Literatur.* Berlin, Leipzig: Göschen.

Gose, Hans. 1921. *Goethes "Werther."* Bausteine zur Geschichte der deutschen Literatur 18. Halle an der Saale: Niemeyer, 1921. Repr. Walluf bei Wiesbaden: Sändig, 1973.

Brandes, Georg Morris. 1922. *Goethe.* Berlin: Reiss.

Gloël, Heinrich. 1922. *Goethe und Lotte.* Berlin: Mittler.

Kluckhohn, Paul. 1922. *Die Auffassung der Liebe in der Literatur des 18. Jahrhunderts und in der deutschen Romantik.* Halle an der Saale: Niemeyer.

Marcuse, Herbert. 1922. *Der deutsche Künstlerroman.* Diss. Freiburg. 1922. In *Der deutsche Künstlerroman: Frühe Aufsätze,* Schriften 1:42–51. Frankfurt am Main: Suhrkamp, 1978.

Merker, Paul. 1922. *Neuere deutsche Literaturgeschichte.* Stuttgart-Gotha: F. A. Perthes.

Korff, Hermann August. 1923. *Geist der Goethezeit: Versuch einer ideellen Entwicklung der klassisch-romantischen Literaturgeschichte.* Vol. 1. Leipzig: Weber.

Riess, Gertrud. 1924. *Die beiden Fassungen von Goethes "Die Leiden des jungen Werthers": Eine stilpsychologische Untersuchung.* Breslau: Trewendt.

Brandes, Georg Morris Cohen. 1925. *Wolfgang Goethe.* Trans. from the Danish by Allen W. Porterfield. New York: Frank-Maurice.

Schubert, Hans von. 1925. *Goethes religiöse Jugendentwicklung.* Leipzig: Quelle & Meyer.

Feise, Ernst. 1926. "Goethes Werther als nervöser Charakter." Germanic Review 1 (1926): 185–253. Repr. in *Themes, Forms, and Ideas in German Literature,* by E. F., Xenion, 1–65. Baltimore, 1950. First part also in Schmiedt 1989a, 35–68.

Spiero, Heinrich. 1926. *Deutsche Köpfe: Bausteine zur Geistes- und Literaturgeschichte.* Darmstadt: E. Hofmann.

Springer, Brunold. 1926. *Der Schlüssel zu Goethes Liebesleben: Ein Versuch.* Berlin: Verlag der Neuen Generation.

Kleinberg, Alfred. 1927. *Die deutsche Dichtung in ihren sozialen, zeit- und geistesgeschichtlichen Bedingungen.* Berlin: J. H. W. Dietz.

Pongs, Hermann. 1927. *Versuch einer Morphologie der metaphorischen Formen.* Vol. 1 of *Das Bild in der Dichtung.* Marburg: Elwert.

Bartels, Adolf. 1928. *Geschichte der deutschen Literatur.* Leipzig: Haessel, 1924–28.

Gude, Carl. 1928. *Erläuterungen deutscher Dichtungen: Ausgeführte Anleitungen zur ästhetischen Würdigung und unterrichtlichen Behandlung.* Ed. Ernst Linde. 14th ed. Leipzig: Brandstetter, 1920–28.

Rehm, Walther. 1928. *Der Todesgedanke in der deutschen Dichtung vom Mittelalter bis zur Romantik.* Halle an der Saale: M. Niemeyer.

Weber, Carl Maria. 1928. "Zur Vorgeschichte von Goethes 'Werther.'" *Jahrbuch der Goethe-Gesellschaft* 14 (1928): 82–92.

Goebbels, Joseph. 1929. *Michael: Ein deutsches Schicksal in Tagebuchblättern.* Munich: Eher.

Jenisch, Erich. 1929. *Die Entfaltung des Subjektivismus von der Aufklärung zur Romantik.* Königsberg: Gräfe und Unzer.

Freud, Sigmund. 1930. *Das Unbehagen in der Kultur.* Vienna: Internationaler Psychoanalytischer Verlag.

Heun, Hans Georg. 1930. *Der Satzbau der Prosa des jungen Goethe.* Leipzig, 1930. Repr. New York, London: Johnson, 1967. Palaestra 172.

Eloesser, Arthur. 1931. *Die deutsche Literatur vom Barock bis zur Gegenwart.* Berlin: Cassirer, 1930–31.

Flemming, Willi. 1931. *Der Wandel des deutschen Naturgefühls vom 15. zum 18. Jahrhundert.* Halle an der Saale: Niemeyer.

Robertson, John George. 1931. *A History of German Literature.* New York: Putnam; Edinburgh, London: Blackwood.

Rose, William. 1931. "The Historical Background of Goethe's 'Werther.'" In *Men, Myths, and Movements in German Literature: A Volume of Historical and Critical Papers,* 125–55. New York: Macmillan.

Freud, Sigmund. 1933. Foreword to *Edgar Poe, étude psychoanalytique,* by Marie Bonaparte. In *Gesammelte Werke: Chronologisch geordnet,* ed. Anna Freud et al., 16:276. Frankfurt am Main: S. Fischer, 1968–87.

Klöpzig, Walther. 1933. *Geschichte der deutschen Literatur nach Entwicklungsperioden.* Leipzig: Reclam.

Kluckhohn, Paul, ed. 1934. *Die Idee des Volkes im Schrifttum der deutschen Bewegung.* Berlin: Junker & Dünnhaupt.

Blumenthal, Hermann. 1935. *Zeitgenössische Rezensionen und Urteile über Goethes "Götz" und "Werther."* Berlin: Junker und Dünnhaupt.

Böckmann, Paul. 1935. *Hölderlin und seine Götter.* Munich: Beck.

Hering, Robert. 1935. "Heimatliche Spuren in Goethes Jugenddichtung." *Goethe-Kalender* 28 (1935): 191–202.

Nollau, A. 1935. *Das literarische Publikum des jungen Goethe.* Weimar.

Blumenthal, Herrmann. 1936. "Karl Philipp Moritz und Goethes 'Werther.'" *Zeitschrift für Ästhetik und allgemeine Kunstwissenschaft* 30 (1936): 28–64.

Diez, Max. 1936. "The Principle of the Dominant Metaphor in Goethe's *Werther.*" *PMLA* 51 (1936): 824–41, 985–1006.

Lukács, Georg. 1936. "'Die Leiden des jungen Werther.'" In Herrmann 1994a, 39–57.

Michels, Josef. 1936. *Goethes "Werther": Beiträge zum Formproblem des jungen Goethe.* Diss., Kiel.

Bickelmann, Ingeborg. 1937. *Goethes "Werther" im Urteil des 19. Jahrhunderts. (Romantik bis Naturalismus 1830–1880).* Diss., Frankfurt am Main.

Fricke, Gerhard. 1937. *Die Entdeckung des Volkes in der deutschen Geistesgeschichte vom Sturm und Drang bis zur Romantik: Rede, gehalten bei der Universitätsfeier am 30. Januar, 1937, dem 4. Jahrestag der Begründung des Dritten Reichs.* Hamburg: Hanseatische Verlagsanstalt.

Linden, Walther. 1937. *Geschichte der deutschen Literatur von den Anfängen bis zur Gegenwart.* Leipzig: Reclam.

Müller, Wilhelm. 1938. *Studien über die rassischen Grundlagen des "Sturm und Drang."* Berlin: Junker & Dünnhaupt.

Schöffler, Herbert. 1938. *Die Leiden des jungen Werther: Ihr geistesgeschichtlicher Hintergrund.* Frankfurt am Main: Klostermann. Repr. in Herrmann 1994a, 58–87.

Dzialas, Ingrid. 1939. *Auffassung und Darstellung der Elemente bei Goethe.* Berlin: Ebering. Repr. Nendeln/Liechtenstein: Kraus, 1967.

Kindermann, Heinz. 1939. *Kampf um das soziale Ordnungsgefüge.* Vol. 1. Leipzig: Reclam.

Mann, Thomas. 1939. "Goethes 'Werther.'" In Herrmann 1994a, 85–97.

Beutler, Ernst. 1940. "Wertherfragen." *Viermonatsschrift der Goethe-Gesellschaft* 5 (1940): 138–60.

Blumenthal, Herrmann. 1940. "Ein neues Wertherbild?" *Viermonatsschrift der Goethe-Gesellschaft* 5 (1940): 315–20.

Beutler, Ernst. 1941. "Das ertrunkene Mädchen." In *Essays um Goethe,* 111–20. Wiesbaden: Dieterich, 1947.

Kayser, Wolfgang. 1941. "Die Entstehung von Goethes 'Werther.'" *Deutsche Vierteljahrsschrift für Literaturwissenschaft und Geistesgeschichte* (1941) [Storage PN4 .D4]. Repr. in *Kunst und Spiel: Fünf Goethe-Studien,* by Wolfgang Johannes Kayser, 5–29. Göttingen, Vandenhoeck & Ruprecht, 1961. Also in Herrmann 1994a, 128–57.

Kindermann, Heinz. 1941 "Die Sturm-und-Drang-Bewegung im Kampf um die deutsche Lebensform." In *Von deutscher Art in Sprache und Dichtung,* ed. Gerhard Fricke et al., 4:3–52. Stuttgart, Berlin: Kohlhammer.

Long, O. W. 1941. "'Werther' in America." In *Studies in Honor of John Albrecht Walz,* 86–116. Lancaster, PA: Lancaster Press.

Ittner, R. T. 1942. "Werther und Emilia Galotti." *JEGP* 41 (1942): 418–26.

Clauss, Walter. 1945. *Deutsche Literatur: Eine geschichtliche Darstellung ihrer Hauptgestalten.* Zürich: Schulthess.

Boesch, Bruno, ed. 1946. *Deutsche Literaturgeschichte in Gründzugen.* Bern: Francke.

Meyer, Eva Alexander. 1946. "Goethe und Werther." In *Geistige Welt.* Munich, 1946. (Alternative citation: *Geistige Welt* 1 [*Vierteljahrsschrift für Kultur- und Geisteswissenschaften.* München — only 1–4 (1946/7–1949/51) appeared] (1946/7): H. 3, 15–20.) Also in *Ruperto-Carola* 41 = Jg. 19 (Heidelberg, 1967): 91–94.

Schneider, Hermann. 1946. *Epochen der deutschen Literatur.* Bonn: Universitäts-Verlag.

Beutler, Ernst. 1947. *Essays um Goethe.* 2 vols. Wiesbaden, 1947, 1948.

Clark, Robert T. 1947. "The Psychological Framework of Goethe's 'Werther.'" *JEGP* 46 (1947): 273–78.

Schaeder, Grete. 1947. *Gott und Welt: Drei Kapitel goethischer Weltanschauung.* Hameln: Seifert.

Atkins, Stuart P. 1948. "J. C. Lavater and Goethe: Problems of Psychology and Theology in *Die Leiden des jungen Werther.*" *PMLA* 63 (1948): 520–76.

Brenner, Emil. 1948. *Deutsche Literaturgeschichte.* Wels: Leitner.

Müller, Günther. 1948. *Kleine Goethebiographie.* Bonn: Athenäum, 1947, 1955; Bonn: Universitäts-Verlag, 1948.

Anstett, Jean-Jacques. 1949. "Werthers religiöse Krise." In Herrmann 1994a, 163–73.

Atkins, Stuart. 1949. *The Testament of Werther in Poetry and Drama.* Cambridge, MA: Harvard UP.

Beauvoir, Simone de. 1949. *The Second Sex.* Trans. H. M. Parshley. New York: Knopf, 1953.

Buchwald, Reinhard. 1949. *Goethezeit und Gegenwart: die Wirkungen Goethes in der deutschen Geistesgeschichte.* Stuttgart: Kröner.

Lange, Victor, ed. and trans. 1949. *Johann Wolfgang von Goethe: "The Sorrows of Young Werther"; "The New Melusina"; "Novelle."* New York: Holt, Rinehart & Winston.

Meyer, Eva Alexander. 1949. *Politische Symbolik bei Goethe.* Heidelberg: Winter.

Petry, Karl. 1949. *Handbuch zur deutschen Literaturgeschichte.* Cologne: Pick.

Redslob, Edwin. 1949. *Goethe und seine Zeit: Goethe-Ausstellung der Stadt Berlin veranstaltet von der Freien Universität Berlin; ein Führer.* Berlin: Blaschkerdruck.

Viëtor, Karl. 1949. "La maladie du siècle." In *Goethe: A Collection of Essays,* ed. Victor Lange, 26–32. Englewood Cliffs, NJ: Prentice-Hall, 1968.

Balint, Michael. 1950. "Early Developmental States of the Ego: Primary Object Love." *International Journal of Psycho-Analysis* 30 (1950): 265–73.

Fricke, Gerhard. 1950. "Goethe und Werther." In *Goethe on Human Creativeness and Other Essays,* ed. Rolf King, C. Brown and E. Funke, 29–75. Athens: U of Georgia P, 1950. Also in *Studien und Interpretationen: Ausgewählte Schriften zur deutschen Dichtung,* by Gerhard Fricke, 141–67. Frankfurt am Main: Menck, 1956.

Kayser, Wolfgang. 1950. "Wandlungen im Gebrauch der verbalen Präfixe in der deutschen Sprache des 18. Jahrhunderts." In *Die Vortragsreise: Studien zur Literatur,* 9–38. Bern: Francke, 1958.

Schneider, Heinrich. 1950. "Werther-Jerusalem als Freund Lessings." In *Lessing: Zwölf biographische Studien,* 94–109. Salzburg, 1950; Bern: Francke, 1951.

Trunz, Erich. 1951. "Anmerkungen des Herausgebers zu *Die Leiden des jungen Werther.*" In *Goethes Werke* 6:514–95. Hamburg: Wegner.

Burger, Heinz Otto, ed. 1952. *Annalen der deutschen Literatur: Geschichte der deutschen Literatur von den Anfängen bis zur Gegenwart.* Stuttgart: Metzler.

Ryder, Frank G., ed. 1952. *George Ticknor's "The Sorrows of Young Werter."* Chapel Hill: U of NC P.

Schrader, Erich. 1952. "Johann Jacob Höfler, das Urbild des Gesandten in Goethes 'Werther': Beiträge zum Schicksal Goues und Jerusalems." *Braunschweigisches Jahrbuch* 33 (1952): 118–54.

Staiger, Emil. 1952. *Goethe: 1749–1786.* Zürich: Atlantis.

Storz, Gerhard. 1953. "Der Roman 'Die Leiden des jungen Werthers.'" In *Goethe Vigilien oder Versuche in der Kunst, Dichtung zu verstehen,* 19–41. Stuttgart: Klett.

Boeschenstein, Hermann. 1954. *Deutsche Gefühlskultur: Studien zu ihrer dichterischen Gestaltung.* Bern: Haupt, 1954–66.

Pfeiffer-Belli, Wolfgang. 1954. *Geschichte der deutschen Dichtung.* Freiburg: Herder.

Prinz, Friedrich. 1954. *"Werther" und "Wahlvervandtschaften": Eine morphologische Studie.* Diss., Bonn.

Trunz, Erich. 1954. "Literaturwissenschaft als Auslegung und als Geschichte der Dichtung." In *Festschrift für Jost Trier,* ed. Benno von Wiese and Karl Heinz Borck, 50–87. Meisenheim am Glan: Hain. Also in *Methodenfragen der deutschen Literaturwissenschaft,* ed. Reinhold Grimm und Jost Hermand, 3–46. Darmstadt: Wissenschaftliche Buchgesellschaft, 1973.

Hausmann, Manfred. 1955. *Die Entscheidung: Die Rolle des "Werther" in Goethes Leben und Werk.* Kassel: Goethe-Gesellschaft, 1955; Kassel: Lometsch, 1955. Also in: *Zwiesprache: Begegnungen mit dem Wort und mit großen Leuten,* by Manfred Hausmann. Frankfurt am Main, 1985.

Martini, Fritz. 1955. *Deutsche Literaturgeschichte von den Anfängen bis zur Gegenwart.* Stuttgart: Kröner.

Kollektiv für Literaturgeschichte. 1956. *Erläuterungen zur deutschen Literatur.* Vol. 4: *Klassik.* Berlin: Volk und Wissen.

Schumann, Detlev. 1956. "Some Notes on 'Werther.'" *JEGP* 55 (1956): 533–49.

Friederich, Wolfgang. 1957. *Die Darstellung der Bauern in der Literatur der Sturm und Drang-Zeit.* Diss., Halle.

Graber, Gustav Hans. 1957. "Goethes 'Werther.'" In *Goethe, Psychologie des Mannes,* 178–81. Bern: Huber.

Hass, Hans Egon. 1957. "Werther-Studie." In *Gestaltprobleme der Dichtung: Günther Müller zu seinem 65. Geburtstag,* ed. Richard Alewyn et al., 83–125. Bonn: Bouvier.

Jolles, Matthijs. 1957. *Goethes Kunstanschauung.* Bern: Francke.

Löwenthal, Leo. 1957. "From *Werther* to *Wilhelm Meister.*" In *Literature and the Image of Man: Sociological Studies of the European Drama and Novel,* 136–65. Boston: Beacon, 1957; New Brunswick, NJ: Transaction Books, 1986. Also in *Schriften,* by Leo Löwenthal, ed. Helmut Dubiel, 161–92. Frankfurt am Main: Suhrkamp, 1981, 1990.

Graber, Gustav Hans. 1958. "Goethes 'Werther': Versuch einer tiefenpsychologischen Pathographie." *Acta psychotherapeutica, pychosomatica et orthopaedagogica* 6 (1958): 120–36. Repr. in Schmiedt 1989a, 69–84.

Graefe, Johanna. 1958. "Die Religion in den 'Leiden des jungen Werther': Eine Untersuchung auf Grund des Wortbestandes." *Jahrbuch der Goethe-Gesellschaft* 20 (Weimar, 1958): 72–98.

Hirsch, Arnold. 1958. "'Die Leiden des jungen Werthers': Ein bürgerliches Schicksal im absolutistischen Staat." *Études Germaniques* 13 (1958): 229–50. Repr. in *Sturm und Drang,* ed. Manfred Wacker, 341–67. Darmstadt: Wissenschaftliche Buchgesellschaft, 1985.

Schöne, Albrecht. 1958. *Säkularisation als sprachbildende Kraft: Studien zur Dichtung deutscher Pfarrersöhne.* Göttingen: Vandenhoeck & Ruprecht.

Blackall, Eric A. 1959. *The Emergence of German as a Literary Language, 1700–1775.* Ithaca: Cornell UP, 1978.

Herrmann, Curt. 1959. *Erläuterungen zu Goethes "Die Leiden des jungen Werthers."* Königs Erläuterungen 79. Hollfeld: Bange.

Lernet-Holenia, Alexander. 1959. *Der wahre Werther.* Hamburg: Zsolnay.

Picard, Hans Rudolf. 1959. *Die Stellung des Autors im Briefroman des 18. Jahrhunderts.* Diss., Heidelberg, 1959.

Reiss, Hans S. 1959. "'Die Leiden des jungen Werthers': A Reconsideration." *Modern Language Quarterly* 20 (1959): 81–96.

Burger, Heinz-Otto. 1960. "Die Geschichte der unvergnügten Seele: Ein Entwurf." *Deutsche Vierteljahrsschrift für Literaturwissenschaft und Geistesgeschichte* 34 (1960): 1–20.

Granzow, Hermann. 1960. *Künstler und Gesellschaft im Roman der Goethezeit: Eine Untersuchung zur Bewußtwerdung neuzeitlichen Künstlertums in der Dichtung vom "Werther" bis zum "Kater Murr."* Diss., Bonn.

Mandelkow, Karl Robert. 1960. "Der deutsche Briefroman: Zum Problem der Polyperspektive im Epischen." *Neophilologus* 44 (1960): 200–208.

Tellenbach, Hubertus. 1960. "Gestalten der Melancholie." *Jahrbuch für Psychologie, Psychotherapie und medizinische Anthropologie* 7 (1960): 9–26.

Voss, Ernst Theodor. 1960. *Erzählprobleme des Briefromans, dargestellt an vier Beispielen des 18. Jahrhunderts: Sophie La Roche, "Geschichte des Fräuleins von Sternheim"; Johann Wolfgang Goethe, "DLdjW"; Johann Timotheus Hermes, "Sophiens Reise von memel nach Sachsen"; Christoph Martin Wieland, "Aristipp und einige seiner Zeitgenossen."* Diss., Bonn.

Siegmund, Georg. 1961. "Die Krankheit zum Tode: Goethe–Kierkegaard." *Hochland* 53 (1960–61): 534–42.

Dvoretzky, Edward. 1962. "Goethe's 'Werther' and Lessing's 'Emilia Galotti.'" *German Life and Letters* 16 (1962–3): 23–26.

Graham, Ilse A. 1962. "Minds without Medium: Reflection on 'Emilia Galotti' and 'Werthers Leiden.'" *Euphorion* 56 (1962): 3–24.

Kimpel, Dieter. 1962. *Entstehung und Formen des Briefromans in Deutschland: Interpretationen zur Geschichte einer epischen Gattung des 18. Jahrhunderts und zur Entstehung des modernen deutschen Romans.* Diss., Vienna.

Muchow, Hans Heinrich. 1962. *Jugend und Zeitgeist: Morphologie der Kulturpubertät.* Reinbek bei Hamburg: Rowohlt.

Schultz, Werner. 1962. "Goethes Werther-Erlebnis und der moderne Nihilismus." *Archiv für Kulturgeschichte* 44 (1962): 227–51.

Birznieks, Paul. 1963. *The Two Worlds of Goethe's and Richter's Epistolary Novels.* Diss., Johns Hopkins.

Braemer, Edith (Abel). 1963. *Goethes Prometheus und die Grundpositionen des Sturm und Drang.* Weimar: Arion Verlag.

Eissler, Kurt Robert. 1963. *Goethe: A Psychoanalytic Study, 1775–1786*. Detroit: Wayne State UP.

Hertling, Gunter. 1963. "Die 'Werther'-Kritik im Meinungsstreit der Spätaufklärer." *German Quarterly* 36 (1963): 403–13.

Langen, August. 1963. "Zum Problem der sprachlichen Säkularisation in der deutschen Dichtung des 18. und 19. Jahrhunderts." *Zeitschrift für deutsche Philologie*. Sonderheft zum 83. Band (1964): 24–42.

Maurer, Karl. 1963. "Die verschleierten Konfessionen: Zur Entstehungsgeschichte von Goethes 'Werther.' (Dichtung und Wahrheit, 12. und 13. Buch)." Repr. in *Die Wissenschaft von deutscher Sprache und Dichtung: Methoden, Probleme, Aufgaben; Festschrift für Friedrich Maurer zum 65. Geburtstag*, ed. Siegfried Gutenbrunner et al. Stuttgart: Klett.

Parry, Idris. 1963. "Werther and Lord Chandos." *Publications of the English Goethe Society* 33 (1963): 75–98.

Reiss, Hans S. 1963. *Goethes Romane*. Bern, Munich: Francke. In English: *Goethe's Novels*. London: Macmillan; New York: St. Martin, 1969.

Becker, E. D. 1964. *Der deutsche Roman um 1780*. Stuttgart: Metzler.

Kahn, Ludwig W. 1964. *Literatur und Glaubenskrise*. Stuttgart: Kohlhammer.

Lange, Victor. 1964. "Die Sprache als Erzählform in Goethes Werther." In *Formenwandel: Festschrift zum 65. Geburtstag von Paul Böckmann*, ed. Walter Müller-Seidel and Wolfgang Preisendanz, 261–72. Hamburg: Hoffmann & Campe. Also in Herrmann 1994a, 193–206.

Mann, Otto. 1964. *Deutsche Literaturgeschichte von der germanischen Dichtung bis zur Gegenwart*. Gütersloh: Bertelsmann.

Ryder, Frank G. 1964. "Season, Day, and Hour — Time as Metaphor in Goethe's 'Werther.'" *JEGP* 63 (1964): 389–407.

Fertig, Ludwig. 1965. *Der Adel im deutschen Roman des 18. und 19. Jahrhunderts*. Diss., Heidelberg,

Habermas, Jürgen. 1965. *The Structural Transformation of the Public Sphere: An Inquiry into a Category of Bourgeois Society*. Trans. Thomas Burger. Cambridge, MA.: MIT UP, 1989.

Hebel, Franz. 1965. "Die Erfahrung der Welt als eines sekundären Systems und deren Spiegelung in der Sprache." *Deutschunterricht* 17 (1965): 34–38.

Lämmert, Eberhard. 1965. Afterword to *Friedrich von Blanckenburgs Versuch über den Roman*, ed. Eberhard Lämmert. Leipzig and Liegnitz: David Siegers Wittwe, 1774; Stuttgart: Metzler, 1965.

Merker, Erna, Elisabeth Linke, Isabel Engel et al. 1965. *Wörterbuch zu Goethes Werther*. Berlin: Akademie Verlag, 1965–66.

Müller, Peter. 1965. *Zeitkritik und Utopie in Goethes Roman "Die Leiden des jungen Werther": Analyse zum Menschenbild der Sturm- und Drang-Dichtung Goethes*. Diss. HU, Berlin, 1965; Berlin: Rütten & Loening, 1969.

Roche, Reinhard. 1965. "Skizzen als Interpretationshilfen: Goethes 'Werther.'" *Der Deutschunterricht* 17 (1965): 106–8.

Wellek, René. 1965. *The Later Nineteenth Century.* Vol. 4 of *A History of Modern Criticism: 1750–1950.* New Haven, CT: Yale UP.

Wilkinson, Elizabeth M., and Leonard Ashley Willoughby. 1965. "The Blind Man and the Poet: An Early Stage in Goethe's Quest for Form." In *German Studies Presented to Walter Horace Bruford,* 29–57. London: Harrap.

Grunwald, Stefan. 1966. "Drei romantische Vergangenheitssymbole in Goethes 'Die Leiden des jungen Werther.'" *Germanisch-Romanische Monatsschrift* 16 (1966): 388–91.

Keenan, Randall Hughes. 1966. *Goethe's "The Sorrows of Young Werther."* Monarch Notes and Study Guides. New York: Monarch Press.

Mattausch, Josef. 1966. "Synonymenfelder im alphabetischen Wörterbuch: Zugleich ein Beitrag zur Synonymie in Goethes Werther." *Beiträge zur Geschichte der deutschen Sprache und Literatur* 88 (Halle, 1966): 425–56.

Stenzel, Jürgen. 1966. *Zeichensetzung: Stiluntersuchungen an deutscher Prosadichtung.* Göttingen: Vandenhoeck & Ruprecht, 1966. Palaestra 241. 40–54.

Böschenstein-Schäfer, Renate. 1967. *Idylle.* Stuttgart: Metzler.

Demetz, Peter. 1967. "Zur Situation der Germanistik: Tradition und aktuelle Probleme." In *Methodenfragen der deutschen Literaturwissenschaft,* ed. Reinhold Grimm and Jost Hermand, 162–84. Darmstadt: Wissenschaftliche Buchgesellschaft, 1973.

Lämmert, Eberhard. 1967. "Germanistik — eine deutsche Wissenschaft." In *Germanistik — eine deutsche Wissenschaft: Beiträge von E. Lämmert, W. Killy, O. Conrady, P. v. Polenz,* 9–41. Frankfurt am Main: Suhrkamp, 1967.

Migge, Walther. 1967. *Goethes "Werther": Entstehung und Wirkung.* Frankfurt am Main: Insel.

Müller, Peter. 1967. "Zeitkritik und Utopie in Goethes Roman 'Die Leiden des jungen Werther.'" [Müller's own review of his 1965 dissertation.] *Weimarer Beiträge* 13 (1967): 173–74.

Schöne, Albrecht. 1967. "Über Goethes Brief an Behrisch vom 10. November 1767." In *Festschrift für Richard Alewyn,* ed. Herbert Singer and Benno von Wiese. Cologne, Graz: Böhlau.

Vogt, Guntram. 1967. *Das Thema der Freundschaft in den Romanen der Goethezeit.* Diss., Kiel.

Weisstein, Gotthilf. 1967. "Aus einer Zeitschrift der Sturm und Drang-Periode." *Goethe-Jahrbuch* 3 (Amsterdam, 1967): 361–63.

Doppler, Alfred. 1968. *Der Abgrund: Studien zur Bedeutungsgeschichte eines Motivs.* Graz: Bölau.

Goodheart, Eugene. 1968. "Goethe, Carlyle, and 'The Sorrows of Werther.'" In *The Cult of the Ego: The Self in Modern Literature,* 1–89. Chicago: U of Chicago P.

Heselhaus, Clemens. 1968. "Die Metaphorik der Krankheit." In *Die nicht mehr schönen Künste: Grenzphänomene des Ästhetischen,* ed. Hans Robert Jauß, 417–19. Munich: Fink, 1968.

Holthusen, Hans Egon. 1968. "Vietnam und die Pistolen aus Lottes Hand . . . oder: Die Aktualität eines klassischen deutschen Romans — Anläßlich einer Lektüre von Goethes 'Werther.' " *Die Welt* 77 (30 March 1968): iii.

Lempicki, Zygmunt. 1968. *Geschichte der deutschen Literaturwissenschaft bis zum Ende des 18. Jahrhunderts.* Göttingen: Vandenhoeck & Ruprecht.

Miller, Norbert. 1968. " 'Werther' und der Briefroman." In *Der empfindsame Erzähler: Untersuchungen an Romananfängen des 18. Jahrhunderts,* 135–214. Munich: Hanser.

Schmidt, Gerhard. 1968. *Die Krankheit zum Tode: Goethes Todesneurose.* Forum der Psychiatrie 22. Stuttgart: Enke.

Seeger, Lothar G. 1968. "Goethes 'Werther' und der Pietismus." *Susquehanna University Studies* 8 (1968): 30–49.

Wölfel, Kurt. 1968. *Deutsche Romantheorien: Beiträge zu einer historischen Poetik des Romans in Deutschland.* Ed. Reinhold Grimm. Frankfurt: Athenäum.

Elkhadem, Saad. 1969. "Über 'Werther' als Roman." In *Sechs Essays über den deutschen Roman.* Bern.

Jäger, Georg. 1969. "Moral und Autonomie des Kunstwerks: Die Diskussion um Goethes 'Werther.' " In *Empfindsamkeit und Roman: Wortgeschichte und Kritik im 18. und frühen 19. Jahrhunder,* 93–103. Stuttgart: Kohlhammer.

Kurth, Lieselotte E. 1969. *Die zweite Wirklichkeit: Studien zum Roman des 18. Jahrhunderts.* Studies in the Germanic Languages and Literatures 62. Chapel Hill: U of North Carolina P.

Molnár, Géza von. 1969. "Confinement or Containment: Goethe's 'Werther' and the Concept of Limitation." *German Life and Letters* 23 (1969–70): 226–34.

Müller, Joachim. 1969. "Die Leiden des jungen Werther." In *Neue Goethe Studien* (vol. 1 of Gesammelte Studien), 145–52. Halle an der Saale: Niemeyer.

Müller, Peter. 1969. *Der junge Goethe im zeitgenössischen Urteil.* Berlin: Akademie Verlag.

Alewyn, Richard. 1970. Review of Scherpe 1970. *Germanistik* 11 (1970): 756–57.

Koebner, Thomas. 1970. "Zum Wertungsproblem in der Trivialroman-Forschung: Drei Skizzen." In *Vergleichen und Verändern: Festschrift für Helmut Motekat,* ed. Albrecht Goetze and Günther Pflaum. Munich: Heuber.

Kortum, Hans, and Reinhard Weisbach. 1970. "Unser Verhältnis zum literarischen Erbe: Bemerkungen zu Peter Müllers 'Zeitkritik und Utopie in Goethes *Werther.*' " *Weimarer Beiträge* 16, Heft 5 (1970): 214–19.

Lange, Victor. 1970. "Goethe in pyschologischer und ästhetischer Sicht." In *Psychologie in der Literaturwissenschaft: Amherster Kolloquium zur Modernen Deutschen Literatur (4th: 1970),* ed. Wolfgang Paulsen, 140–56. Heidelberg: L. Stiehm, 1971.

Scherpe, Klaus R. 1970. *"Werther" und Wertherwirkung: Zum Syndrom bürgerlicher Gesellschaftsordnung im 18. Jahrhundert; Anhang: Vier Wertherschriften aus dem Jahre 1775 in Faksimile.* Bad Homburg: Gehlen.

Schiller, Dieter. 1970. "Sozialistisches Erbe und Nationalliteratur." *Weimarer Beiträge* 16, Heft 5 (1970): 117–38.

Stahl, E. L., and W. E. Yuill. 1970. *German Literature of the 18th and 19th Centuries.* New York: Barnes & Noble.

Werner, Hans-Georg. 1970. Review of Peter Müller's "Zeitkritik und Utopie in Goethes 'Werther.'" *Weimarer Beiträge* 16, Heft 7 (1970): 193–99.

Boesch, Bruno, ed. 1971. *German Literature: A Critical Survey.* Trans. Ronald Taylor. London: Methuen.

Fetzer, John. 1971. "Schatten ohne Frau: Marginalia on a Werther Motif." *Germanic Review* 46 (1971): 87–94.

Kaiser, Gerhard. 1971. "Zum Syndrom modischer Germanistik: Bemerkungen über Klaus Scherpe, 'Werther und Wertherwirkung'; Zum Syndrom bürgerlicher Gesellschaftsordnung im 18. Jahrhundert; Bad Homburg v.d.H. 1970." *Euphorion* 65 (1971): 194–99, 185–96.

Kaschnitz, Marie Luise. 1971. "'Werther.'" In *Zwischen Immer und Nie: Gestalten und Themen der Dichtung,* 110–18. Frankfurt am Main: Insel, 1971; Frankfurt am Main: Suhrkamp, 1978.

Kluge, Gerhard. 1971. "Die Leiden des jungen Werthers in der Residenz: Vorschlag zur Interpretation einiger Werther-Briefe." *Euphorion* 65 (1971): 115–31.

Staroste, Wolfgang. 1971. "Werthers Krankheit zum Tode: Zum Aufbau des epischen Vorgangs in Goethes 'Werther.'" In Staroste, *Raum und Realität in dichterischer Gestaltung: Studien zu Goethe und Kafka,* ed. Gotthart Wunberg. Heidelberg: Stiehm.

Atkins, Stuart. 1972. Review of Scherpe 1970. *Germanic Review* 47 (1972): 297–300.

Göres, Jörn, ed. 1972. *Die Leiden des jungen Werthers: Goethes Roman im Spiegel seiner Zeit; Eine Ausstellung des Goethe-Museums Düsseldorf, Anton-und-Katharina-Kippenberg-Stiftung, in Verbindung mit der Stadt Wetzlar; Katalog.* Düsseldorf: Goethe-Museum.

Hohendahl, Peter Uwe. 1972. "Empfindsamkeit und gesellschaftliches Bewusstsein: Zur Soziologie des empfindsamen Romans am Beispiel von *La vie de Marianne, Clarissa, Fräulein von Sternheim,* und *Werther."* *Jahrbuch der Deutschen Schillergesellschaft* 16 (1972): 176–207.

Mannack, Eberhard. 1972. *Raumdarstellung und Realitätsbezug in Goethes epischer Dichtung.* Frankfurt am Main: Athenäum.

Mommsen, Momme. 1972. "Goethes Verhältnis zu Christus und Spinoza: Blick auf die Wertherzeit." In *Deutsche Weltliteratur: Von Goethe bis Ingeborg Bachmann; Festgabe für J. Alan Pfeffer,* ed. Klaus W. Jonas, 1–27. Tübingen: Niemeyer.

Reuter, Hans-Heinrich. 1972. "Der gekreuzigte Prometheus: Goethes Roman 'Die Leiden des jungen Werthers.'" *Goethe-Jahrbuch* 89 (Weimar, 1972): 86–115.

Rothmann, Kurt. 1972. "War Goethes Werther ein Revolutionär? Auseinandersetzung mit Georg Lukács." *University of Dayton Review* 9, no. 1 (1972): 77–90.

Schmidt, Hartmut. 1972. "Goethes 'Werther' als Schule der Leidenschaften: Wertherrezensionen im Horizont der Populärästhetik um 1775." In *"Die Leiden des jungen Werthers": Goethes "Werther" als Schule der Leidenschaften*, ed. Jörn Göres et al., 70–122. Frankfurt am Main: Insel.

Silz, Walter. 1972. "Werther and Lotte at the Well." In *Traditions and Transitions: Studies in Honor of Harold Jantz*, ed. Lieselotte E. Kurth, 125–31. Munich: Delp.

Spann, Meno. 1972. "'Werther' Revisited: Two Hundred Years of a Masterpiece." *Mosaic* 5 (1972): 73–83.

Zabel, H. 1972. "Goethes 'Werther' — eine weltliche Passionsgeschichte?" *Zeitschrift für Religions- und Gesitesgeschichte* 24 (1972): 57–69.

Anderegg, Johannes. 1973. *Fiktion und Kommunikation: Ein Beitrag zur Theorie der Prosa*. Göttingen: Vandenhoeck & Ruprecht.

Faber, M. D. 1973. "The Suicide of Young Werther." *Psychoanalytical Review* 60 (1973): 239–76.

Göres, Jörn. 1973. "200 Jahre Werther." *Insel-Almanach* (1973): 5–22.

Graham, Ilse Appelbaum. 1973. "'Die Leiden des jungen Werther': A Requiem for Inwardness." In *Goethe and Lessing: the Wellsprings of Creation*, 115–36. New York: Barnes & Noble.

Müller, Peter. 1973. "Angriff auf die humanistische Tradition." *Weimarer Beiträge* 19 (1973): Heft 1, 109–27; Heft 3, 92–109.

Neumann, Alfred R. 1973. "Werther the Lawyer." In *Harvesting the Golden Grain: Studies in Honor of Henry W. Nordmeyer*, ed. Luanne T. Frank and Emery E. George, 218–22. Ann Arbor: U of Michigan P.

Plenzdorf, Ulrich. 1973. *Die neuen Leiden des jungen W.*, ed. Richard A. Zipser. New York: Wiley, 1978.

Salm, Peter. 1973. "Werther and the Sensibility of Estrangement." *The German Quarterly* 46 (1973): 47–55.

Schmidt, Hartmut. 1973. "Goethes 'Werther' als Schule der Leidenschaften: Werther-Rezensionen im Horizont der Populärästhetik um 1775." *Insel-Almanach* (1973): 70–122.

Wagenknecht, Christian. 1973. "Werthers Leiden: Der Roman als Krankheitsgeschichte." *Text & Kontext* 5 (Copenhagen, 1977): 3–14.

Welz, Dieter. 1973. *Der Weimarer "Werther": Studien zur Sinnstruktur der zweiten Fassung des Werther-Romans*. Abhandlungen zur Kunst-, Musik- und Literaturwissenschaft 135. Bonn: Bouvier.

Doke, Tadamichi. 1974. "Zur literarischen Methode der 'Leiden des jungen Werther.'" *Goethe-Jahrbuch* 91 (1974): 11–23.

Graham, Ilse Appelbaum. 1974. "Goethes eigener Werther: Eines Künstlers Wahrheit über seine Dichtung." *Jahrbuch der Deutschen Schillergesellschaft* 18 (1974): 268–303. In English: "Goethe's Own Werther: An Artist's Truth about His Fiction." In Graham, *Goethe: Portrait of the Artist*, 7–33. Berlin, New York: de Gruyter, 1977.

Hotz, Karl. 1974. *Goethes "Werther" als Modell für kritisches Lesen: Materialien zur Rezeptionsgeschichte*. Stuttgart: Klett.

Jäger, Georg. 1974. "Die Wertherwirkung: Ein rezeptionsästhetischer Modellfall." In *Historizität in Sprach- und Literaturwissenschaft*, ed. Walter Müller-Seidel, 389–409. Munich: Fink. Also in Herrmann 1994a, 223–31.

Phillips, David P. 1974. "The Influence of Suggestion on Suicide: Substantive and Theoretical Implications of the Werther Effect." *American Sociological Review* 39 (1974): 340–54.

Sauder, Gerhard. 1974. *Voraussetzungen und Elemente*. Vol. 1 of *Empfindsamkeit*. Stuttgart: Metzler.

Scherpe, Klaus R. 1974. "Natürlichkeit und Produktivität im Gegensatz zur 'bürgerlichen Gesellschaft': Die literarische Opposition des Sturm und Drang; Johann Wolfgang Goethes 'Werther.'" In *Grundkurs 18. Jahrhundert: Die Funktion der Literatur bei der Formierung der bürgerlichen Klasse Deutschlands im 18. Jahrhundert*, ed. Gert Mattenklott and Klaus Scherpe, 1:189–215; supporting materials: 2:113–35. Kronberg/Taunus: Scriptor.

Schierenberg, Kurt A. 1974. *Beiträge zu Goethes "Werther."* Wetzlar: Wetzlarer Goethe-Gesellschaft.

Steinhauer, Harry. 1974. "Goethe's 'Werther' after Two Centuries." *University of Toronto Quarterly* 44 (1974): 1–13.

Drews, Jörg. 1975. "Goethe: 'Die Leiden des jungen Werther.'" In *Spektrum der Literatur*, ed. Bettina and Lars Clausen, 176–77. Lexikothek. Gütersloh: Bertelsmann.

Dye, Robert Ellis. 1975. "Man and God in Goethe's 'Werther.'" *Symposium* 29 (1975): 314–29.

Graevenitz, G. von. 1975. "Innerlichkeit und Öffentlichkeit: Aspekte deutscher 'bürgerlicher' Literatur im frühen 18. Jahrhundert." *Deutsche Vierteljahrsschrift für Literaturwissenschaft und Geistesgeschichte* 49. Sonderheft '18. Jahrhundert' (1975): 1–82.

Honnefelder, Gottfried. 1975. *Der Brief im Roman: Untersuchungen zur Erzähltechnischen Verwendung des Briefes im deutschen Roman*. Bonn: Bouvier Verlag H. Grundmann.

Mandelkow, Karl, ed. 1975. *Goethe im Urteil seiner Kritiker: Dokumente zur Wirkungsgeschichte Goethes in Deutschland*. Vol. 1: 1773–1832. Munich: Beck.

Slochower, Harry. 1975. "Suicides in Literature: Their Ego Function." *American Imago* 32 (1975): 389–416.

Stephan, Arndt, and Inge Stephan. 1975. "'Werther' und 'Werther'-Rezeption — Ein Unterrichtsmodell zur Aufarbeitung bürgerlichen

Selbstverständnisses." In *Projekt Deutschunterricht*, 9:146–76. Stuttgart: Metzler.

Wilson, James D. 1975. "Goethe's 'Werther': A Keatsian Quest for Self-Annihilation." *Mosaic* 9/1 (1975): 93–109.

Bennett, Benjamin. 1976. "Werther and Chandos." *MLN* 91 (1976): 552–58.

Blackall, Eric A. 1976. *Goethe and the Novel.* Ithaca: Cornell UP.

Bragg, Marvin. 1976. "The Psychological Elements of 'Werther.'" *South Central Bulletin* 36 (1976): 132–37.

Brinkmann, Richard. 1976. "Goethes 'Werther' and Arnolds 'Kirchen- und Ketzerhistorie': Zur Aporie des modernen Individualitätenbegriffs." In *Versuche zu Goethe: Festschrift für Erich Heller zum 65. Geburtstag am 27.3.1976*, ed. Volker Dürr und Géza v. Molnár, 167–89. Heidelberg: Stiehm.

Elias, Norbert. 1976. *The Civilizing Process: Sociogenetic and Psychogenetic Investigations.* Trans. Edmund Jephcott. Oxford: Blackwell, 2000.

Foucault, Michel. 1976. *The History of Sexuality.* Trans. Robert Hurley. Vol. 1. New York: Vintage, 1980.

Hösle, Johannes. 1976. "Die französische Werther-Rezeption." *Arcadia: Zeitschrift für Vergleichende Literaturwissenschaft* 11 (1976): 113–25.

McCormick, E. Allen. 1976. "Poema Pictura Loquens: Literary Pictorialism and the Psychology of Landscape." *Comparative Literature Studies* 13 (1976): 196–213.

Mog, Paul. 1976. *Ratio und Gefühlskultur: Studien zur Psychogenese und Literatur im 18. Jahrhundert.* Studien zur deutschen Literatur 48. Tübingen: Niemeyer.

Oettinger, Klaus. 1976. "'Eine Krankheit zum Tode': Zum Skandal um Werthers Selbstmord." *Deutschunterricht* 28 (1976): 55–74.

Thorlby, Anthony. 1976. "From What Did Goethe Save Himself in 'Werther'?" In *Versuche zu Goethe: Festschrift für Erich Heller zum 65. Geburtstag am 27.3.1976*, ed. Volker Dürr und Géza v. Molnár, 150–66. Heidelberg: Stiehm.

Ames, Carol. 1977. "Competition, Class, and Structure in 'Die Leiden des jungen Werther.'" *The German Quarterly* 50 (1977): 138–49.

Barthes, Roland. 1977. *A Lover's Discourse: Fragments.* Trans. Richard Howard. New York: Hill & Wang, 1978.

Finsen, H. Carl. 1977. "Empfindsamkeit als Raum der Alternative: Untersucht am Beispiel von Goethes 'Die Leiden des jungen Werthers.'" *Der Deutschunterricht* 29 (1977): 27–38.

Gellinek, Janis. 1977. "Landscape in Werther." In *Symposium on Romanticism: An Interdisciplinary Meeting,* ed. Pierre Deguise and Rita Terras. New London, CT: Connecticut College, 1977.

Hohendahl, Peter Uwe. 1977. *Der europäische Roman der Empfindsamkeit.* Wiesbaden: Athenaion.

Leibfried, Erwin. 1977. "Goethes Werther als Leser von Lessings 'Emilia Galotti.'" In *Text — Leser — Bedeutung: Untersuchungen zur Interaktion von Text und Leser,* ed. Herbert Grabes, 145–56. Grossen-Linden.

Meyer-Kalkus, Reinhart. 1977. "Werthers Krankheit zum Tode: Pathologie und Familie in der Empfindsamkeit." In *Urszenen: Literaturwissenschaft als Diskursanalyse und Diskurskritik,* ed. Friedrich A. Kittler and Horst Turk, 76–138. Frankfurt am Main: Suhrkamp. Also in Schmiedt 1989a, 85–146.

Schings, Hans-Jürgen. 1977. *Melancholie und Aufklärung: Melancholiker und ihre Kritiker in Erfahrungsseelenkunde und Literatur des 18. Jahrhunderts.* Stuttgart: Metzler.

Tellenbach, Hubertus. 1977. "The Suicide of the 'Young Werther' and the Consequences for the Circumstances of Suicide of Endogenic Melancholics." *Israel Annals of Psych. & Related Disciplines* 15 (1977): 16–21.

Tobol, Carol E. W., and Ida Washington. 1977. "Werther's Selective Reading of Homer." *MLN* 92 (1977): 596–601.

Brinckschulte, Eva. 1978. *Erläuterungen zu Johann Wolfgang Goethe, "Die Leiden des jungen Werthers."* Hollfeld/Oberfranken: Bange.

Feuerlicht, Ignace. 1978. "Werther's Suicide: Instinct, Reasons and Defense." *The German Quarterly* 51 (1978): 476–92.

Scharfschwerdt, Jürgen. 1978. "'Werther' in der DDR: Bürgerliches Erbe zwischen sozialistischer Kulturpolitik und gesellschaftlicher Realität." *Jahrbuch der Deutschen Schillergesellschaft* 22 (1978): 235–76.

Thomé, Horst. 1978. *Roman und Naturwissenschaft: Eine Studie zur Vorgeschichte der deutschen Klassik.* Frankfurt am Main: Lang.

Warrick, Kathleen, E. 1978. "Lotte's Sexuality and Her Responsibility for Werther's Death." *Essays in Literature* 5 (1978): 129–35.

Zmegac, Viktor, ed. 1978. *Geschichte der deutschen Literatur vom 18. Jahrhundert bis zur Gegenwart.* Königstein im Taunus: Athenäum-Verlag, 1978–84.

Alewyn, Richard. 1979. "'Klopstock!'" *Euphorion* 73 (1979): 357–64.

Atkins, Stuart. 1979. "Codicils to 'The Testament of Werther in Poetry and Drama.'" In *Literatur als Dialog,* ed. Reingard Nethersole, 195–205. Johannesburg: Ravan.

Blessin, Stefan. 1979. *Die Romane Goethes.* Königstein im Taunus: Athenäum.

Hsia, Adrian. 1979. "Werther in soziologischer Sicht." In *Analecta Helvetica et Germanica: Eine Festschrift zu Ehren von Hermann Boeschenstein,* ed. Achim Arnold et al., 154–69. Bonn.

Irmscher, Johannes, ed. 1979. *Antikerezeption, deutsche Klassik und sozialistische Gegenwart.* Berlin: Akademie-Verlag.

Kaempfer, Wolfgang. 1979. "Das Ich und der Tod in Goethes 'Werther.'" *Recherches Germaniques* 9 (1979): 55–79. Repr. in Herrmann 1994a, 266–94.

Reuter, Hans-Heinrich. 1979. "'Die Leiden des jungen Werthers.'" In Herrmann 1994a, 248–65.

Schmiedt, Helmut. 1979. "Woran scheitert Werther?" *Poetica: Zeitschrift für Sprach- und Literaturwissenschaft* 11 (1979): 83–104. Repr. in Schmiedt 1989a, 147–72.

Skonnord, John. 1979. "Act and Artifact: Narrative Procedure in Werther." *JEGP* 78 (1979): 157–77.

Wapnewski, Peter. 1979. "Zweihundert Jahre Werthers Leiden oder: Dem war nicht zu helfen." In *Zumutungen: Essays zur Literatur des 20. Jahrhunderts*. Düsseldorf: Claassen.

Zimmermann, Rolf Christian. 1979. "'Die Leiden des jungen Werthers.'" In *Das Weltbild des jungen Goethe: Studien zur hermetischen Tradition des 18. Jahrhunderts*, 2:167–212, 312–20. Munich: Fink.

Bennett, Benjamin. 1980. "Goethe's 'Werther': Double Perspective and the Game of Life." *The German Quarterly* 53 (1980): 64–81.

Grimminger, Rolf. 1980. "Roman." In *Deutsche Aufklärung bis zur Französischen Revolution: 1680–1789*, ed. Rolf Grimminger, 635–715. Munich: Hanser.

Kittler, Friedrich A. 1980. *"Autorschaft und Liebe."* In *Austreibung des Geistes aus den Geisteswissenschaften*, ed. Friedrich A. Kittler, 142–73. Paderborn: Schöningh, 1980. Also in Herrmann 1994a, 295–316.

Kreis, Rudolf. 1980. "Die Leiden des jungen Werthers (1774) und die bürgerliche Revolution." In Kreis, *Die verborgene Geschichte des Kindes in der deutschen Literatur: Deutschunterricht als Psychohistorie*, 225–39. Stuttgart: Metzler.

Lange, Sigrid. 1980. *Die Konzeption der Persönlichkeit in Goethes Frühwerk: Untersuchungen zum dramatischen Schaffen und zur Erstfassung des "Werther"-Romans*. Diss., Jena.

Lettau, Reinhard. 1980. "Johann Wolfgang Goethe: 'Die Leiden des jungen Werther.'" In *Die ZEIT-Bibliothek der 100 Bücher*, ed. Fritz J. Raddatz, 109–11. Frankfurt am Main: Suhrkamp, 1980. Also as: "Notizen zum 'Werther,'" in Lettau, *Zerstreutes Hinschauen: Vom Schreiben über Vorgänge in direkter Nähe oder in der Entfernung von Schreibtischen*, 190–93. Frankfurt am Main: Fischer, 1982.

Mandelkow, Karl Robert. 1980. *Goethe in Deutschland: Rezeptionsgeschichte eines Klassikers*. Vol. 1. Munich: Beck.

Mattenklott, Gert. 1980. "Briefroman." In *Zwischen Absolutismus und Aufklärung: Rationalismus, Empfindsamkeit, Sturm und Drang 1740–1786*, ed. Ralph-Rainer Wuthenow, 185–203; vol. 4 of *Deutsche Literatur: Eine Sozialgeschichte*, ed. Horst Albert Glaser. Reinbek bei Hamburg: Rowohlt.

Neuse, Werner. 1980. "Die Anfänge der 'erlebten Rede' und des 'inneren Monologs' in der deutschen Prosa des 18. Jahrhunderts." In *Theatrum mundi: Essays on German Drama and German Literature Dedicated to Harold Lenz on his Seventieth Birthday, September 11, 1978*, ed. Edward R. Haymes, 1–21. Munich: Fink.

Parnell, Peter. 1980. *Sorrows of Stephen: A Comedy*. New York: French.

Paulin, Roger. 1980. "'Wer werden uns wieder sehn!': On a Theme in 'Werther.'" *Publications of the English Goethe Society* 50 (1980): 55–78.

Porter Abbott, H. 1980. "Letters to the Self: The Cloistered Writer in Nonretrospective Fiction". *PMLA* 95 (1980): 23–41.

Rockwood, Heidi. 1980. "Jung's Psychological Types and Goethe's 'Die Leiden des jungen Werthers.'" *The Germanic Review* 55 (1980): 118–23.

Saine, Thomas P. 1980. "Passion and Aggression: The Meaning of Werther's Last Letter." *Orbis litterarum* 35 (1980): 327–56.

Schings, Hans-Jürgen. 1980. *Der mitleidigste Mensch ist der beste Mensch: Poetik des Mitleids von Lessing bis Büchner.* München: Beck.

Wuthenow, Ralph-Rainer. 1980. *Im Buch die Bücher oder Der Held als Leser.* Frankfurt am Main: Europäische Verlagsanstalt.

Assling, Reinhard. 1981. *Werthers Leiden: Die ästhetische Rebellion der Innerlichkeit.* Frankfurt am Main, Bern: Lang.

Dye, Robert Ellis. 1981. "Blanckenburgs Werther-Rezeption." In *Goethezeit: Studien zur Erkenntnis und Rezeption Goethes und seiner Zeitgenossen; Festschrift für Stuart Atkins,* ed. Gerhart Hoffmeister. Bern, Munich: Francke.

Görisch, Reinhard. 1981. *Matthias Claudius und der Sturm und Drang: Ein Abgrenzungsversuch; Vergleiche mit Goethe, Herder, Lenz, Schubart u. a. am Beispiel eschatologischer Vorstellungen im Kontext des Epochenbewußtseins.* Frankfurt am Main: Lang.

Miller, Ronald Duncan. 1981. *The Beautiful Soul: A Study of 18th-Century Idealism as Exemplified by Rousseau's "La nouvelle Heloïse" and Goethe's "Die Leiden des jungen Werthers."* Harrogate, UK: Duchy Press.

Müller-Salget, Klaus. 1981. "Zur Struktur von Goethes 'Werther.'" *Zeitschrift für deutsche Philologie* 100 (1981): 527–44. Repr. in Herrmann 1994a, 317–37.

Pelzer, Wolfgang. 1981. "'Glückliche Revolution': Werthers Leiden; Ein Versuch, sie zu entziffern." *Merkur* 35 (1981): 273–85.

Saine, Thomas P. 1981. "The Portrayal of Lotte in the Two Versions of Goethe's 'Werther.'" *JEGP* 80 (1981): 54–77.

Weber, Evelyn. 1981. "Goethes und Werthers Leiden." In *Dichter Privat,* 21–27. Oberwil bei Zug, Switzerland: Kugler.

Weinstein, Arnold. 1981. *Fictions of the Self: 1550–1800.* Princeton: Princeton UP.

Zons, Raimar Stefan. 1981. "Ein Riß durch die Ewigkeit: Landschaften in 'Werther' und 'Lenz.'" *Literatur für Leser* (1981): 65–78.

Cocalis, Susan L., and Kay Goodman, eds. 1982. *Beyond the Eternal Feminine: Critical Essays on Women and German Literature.* Stuttgart: Akademischer Verlag Hans-Dieter Heinz.

Duncan, Bruce. 1982. "'Emilia Galotti lag auf dem Pult aufgeschlagen': Werther as (Mis)-Reader." *Goethe Yearbook* 1 (1982): 42–50.

Fechner, Jörg-Ulrich. 1982. "Die alten Leiden des jungen Werthers: Goethes Roman aus petrarkistischer Sicht." *Arcadia* 17 (1982): 1–15. Repr. in Herrmann 1994a, 338–59.

Furst, Lilian R. 1982. "The Man of Sensibility and the Woman of Sense." *Jahrbuch für Internationale Germanistik* 14 (1982): 13–26.

Haverkamp, Anselm. 1982. "Illusion und Empathie: Die Struktur der 'teilnehmenden Lektüre' in den 'Leiden des jungen Werthers.'" In *Erzählforschung: Ein Symposium,* ed. Eberhard Lämmert, 243–68. Germanistische Symposien-Berichtsbände 4. Stuttgart: Metzler.

Hillebrand, Bruno. 1982. *Goethes Werther: Ein Deutsches Thema.* Mainz: Akademie der Wissenschaften und der Literatur; Wiesbaden: F. Steiner.

Hübner, Klaus. 1982. *Alltag im literarischen Werk: Eine literatursoziologische Studie zu Goethes "Werther."* Heidelberg: Groos, 1982, 1987.

Jauss, Hans Robert. 1982. *Question and Answer: Forms of Dialogic Understanding.* Trans Michael Hays. Minneapolis: U of Minnesota P, 1989.

Kurz, Gerhard. 1982. "Werther als Künstler." In *Invaliden des Apoll: Motive und Mythen des Dichterleids,* ed. Herbert Anton, 95–112. Munich: Fink.

Martin, Günther. 1982. "Werthers problematische Natur." *Neue deutsche Hefte* 29 (1982): 725–35.

Meyer-Krentler, Eckhardt. 1982. "'Kalte Abstraktion' gegen 'versengte Einbildung': Destruktion und Restauration aufklärerischer Harmoniemodelle in Goethes 'Leiden' und Nicolais 'Freuden des jungen Werthers.'" *Deutsche Vierteljahrsschrift für Literaturwissenschaft und Geistesgeschichte* 56 (1982): 65–91.

Nutz, Maximilian. 1982. "Die Sprachlosigkeit des erregten Gefühls: Zur Problematik der Verständigung in Goethes 'Werther' und seiner Rezeption." *Literatur für Leser* (1982): 217–29.

Prawer, Siegbert. 1982. "Werther's People: Reflections on Literary Portraiture, in Memory of William Robson-Scott." *Publications of the English Goethe Society* 53 (1982–83): 70–97.

Pütz, Peter. 1982. "Werthers Leiden an der Literatur." In *Goethe's Narrative Fiction: The Irvine Goethe Symposium,* ed. William J. Lillyman, 55–68. Berlin; New York: de Gruyter, 1983.

Vaget, Hans Rudolf. 1982. "Goethe the Novelist: On the Coherence of His Fiction." In *Goethe's Narrative Fiction: The Irvine Goethe Symposium,* ed. William J. Lillyman, 1–20. Berlin; New York: W. de Gruyter, 1983.

Waniek, Erdmann. 1982. "Werther lesen und Werther als Leser." *Goethe Yearbook* 1 (1982): 51–92.

Wölfel, Kurt. 1982. "Andeutende Materialien zu einer Poetik des Spaziergangs: Von Kafkas Frühwerk zu Goethes 'Werther.'" In *Zur Geschichtlichkeit der Moderne: Der Begriff der literarischen Moderne in Theorie und Deutung; Ulrich Fülleborn zum 60. Geburtstag,* ed. Theo Elm und Gerd Hemmerich, 69–90. Munich: Fink.

Bell, Michael. 1983. *The Sentiment of Reality: Truth of Feeling in the European Novel.* London; Boston: Allen & Unwin.

Buhr, Gerhard. 1983. "Goethe — 'Die Leiden des jungen Werthers' und der Roman des Sturm und Drang." In *Handbuch des deutschen Romans,* ed. Helmut Koopmann, 226–43. Düsseldorf: Bagel.

Ehrentreich, Alfred. 1983. "An der Peripherie von Goethes 'Werther.'" *Goethe-Jahrbuch* 100 (1983): 266–71.

Herold, Theo, and Hildegard Wittenberg, eds. 1983. *Aufklärung, Sturm und Drang.* Vol. 1 of *Geschichte der deutschen Literatur,* ed. Dietrich Steinbach and Hildegard Wittenberg. Stuttgart: E. Klett, 1983–85.

Hsia, Adrian. 1983. "Zur Werther-Krankheit bei Werther, Wibeau and Schnier." *Colloquia Germanica* 16 (1983): 148–65.

Jilg, Gabriele. 1983. *Die Kollision von Gefühl und Verstand: Vom gesellschaftlichen Charakter des Selbstbewußtseins und der Formen seiner literarischen Dokumentation.* Bern: Lang.

Marhold, Hartmut. 1983. "Prometheus und Werther." *Literatur in Wissenschaft und Unterricht* 16 (1983): 97–108.

Müller, Peter. 1983. "Epochengehalt und nationales Kolorit des deutschen Sentimentalismus in frühen ästhetischen Schriften Goethes und im 'Werther.'" In *Parallelen und Kontraste: Studien zu literarischen Wechselbeziehungen in Europa zwischen 1750 und 1850,* ed. Hans-Dietrich Dahnke, 108–39. Berlin, Weimar.

Muenzer, Clark S. 1983. "Goethe's Werther and Kant's Aesthetics of Failure." *MLN* 98 (1983): 492–99.

Prokop, Ulrike. 1983. "Der Mythos des Weiblichen und die Idee der Gleichheit in literarischen Entwürfen des frühen Bürgertums." In *Feministische Literaturwissenschaft: Dokumentation der Tagung in Hamburg vom Mai 1983,* ed. Inge Stephan and Sigrid Weigel, 15–21. Berlin: Argument-Verlag, 1984.

Sloterdijk, Peter. 1983. *Critique of Cynical Reason.* Trans. Michael Elred. Minneapolis: U of Minnesota P, 1987.

Assel, Jutta. 1984. "Werther-Illustrationen: Bilddokumente als Rezeptionsgeschichte." In Jäger 1984, 57–105, 190–208.

Forget, Philippe. 1984. "Aus der Seele geschrie(b)en?: Zur Problematik des Schreibens (écriture) in Goethes 'Werther.'" In *Text und Interpretation: Deutsch-französische Debatte,* ed. P. Forget, 130–80. Munich: Fink.

Fülleborn, Ulrich. 1984. "'Die Leiden des jungen Werthers' zwischen aufklärerischer Sozialethik und Büchners Mitleidspoesie." In *Goethe im Kontext: Kunst und Humanität, Naturwissenschaft und Politik von der Aufklärung bis zur Restauration; ein Symposium,* ed. Wolfgang Wittkowski, 20–34. Tübingen: M. Niemeyer.

Grathoff, Dirk. 1984. "Der Pflug, die Nußbäume und der Bauerbursche: Natur im thematischen Gefüge des Werther-Romans." *Goethe-Jahrbuch* 102 (Weimar 1985): 184–98.

Herrmann, Hans-Peter. 1984. "Landschaft in Goethes Werther: Zum Brief vom 18. August." In *Goethe im Kontext: Kunst und Humanität, Naturwissenschaft und Politik von der Aufklärung bis zur Restauration; ein Symposium,* ed. Wolfgang Wittkowski, 77–100. Tübingen: M. Niemeyer.

Huff, Steven R. 1984. "Lotte's Klavier: A Resounding Symbol in Goethe's *Die Leiden des jungen Werthers.*" *The Germanic Review* 59 (1984): 43–48.

Jäger, Georg. 1984. *Leiden des alten und neuen Werther: Kommentare, Abbildungen, Materialien zu Goethes "Leiden des jungen Werther" und Plenzdorfs "Neuen Leiden des jungen W."* Munich: Hanser.

Karthaus, Ulrich. 1984. "Goethes 'Werther' und die neuen Leiden." In *Goethe: Vorträge aus Anlaß seines 150. Todestages,* ed. Thomas Clasen and Erwin Leibfried. Frankfurt am Main, New York: Lang.

Meyer-Krentler, Eckhardt. 1984. *Der Bürger als Freund: Ein sozialethisches Programm und seine Kritik in der neueren deutschen Erzählliteratur.* Munich: Fink.

Muenzer, Clark. 1984. *Figures of Identity: Goethe's Novels and the Enigmatic Self.* University Park: Penn State UP.

Nolan, Erika. 1984. "Goethes 'Die Leiden des jungen Werther': Absicht und Methode." *Jahrbuch der Deutschen Schillergesellschaft* 28 (1984): 191–222.

Prawer, Siegbert. 1984. "Werther's People: Reflections on Literary Portraiture." *Publications of the English Goethe Society* 53 (1984): 70–97.

Strack, Friedrich. 1984. "Vater, Söhne und die Krise der Familie in Goethes Werk." *Jahrbuch des Freien deutschen Hochstifts* (1984): 57–87.

Winkle, Sally Anne. 1984. *The Construction of a Bourgeois Ideal of Women as Developed in Sophie von La Roche's "Geschichte des Fräuleins von Sternheim" and Goethe's "Die Leiden des jungen Werther."* Diss., University of Wisconsin. Published as: *Woman as Bourgeois Ideal: A Study of Sophie von La Roche's "Geschichte des Fräuleins von Sternheim" and Goethe's "Werther."* New York: Lang, 1988.

Berghahn, Klaus L. 1985. "From Classicist to Classical Literary Criticism, 1730–1806." In Hohendahl 1985a, 13–98.

Blessin, Stephan. 1985. *Johann Wolfgang von Goethe, "Die Leiden des jungen Werther."* Frankfurt am Main: Diesterweg.

Burgard, Peter J. 1985. " 'Emilia Galotti' und 'Clavigo': Werthers Pflichtlektüre und unsere." *Zeitschrift für deutsche Philologie* 104 (1985): 481–94.

Förster, Jürgen. 1985. "Literatur und Subjektivität: Goethes 'Werther' unter Aspekten der Subjektivitätsdiskussion in Literaturwissenschaft und Literaturdidaktik." *Diskussion Deutsch* 16 (1985): 297–312.

Higonnet, Margaret R. 1985. "Suicide: Representations of the Feminine in the 19th Century." *Poetics today* 6 (1985): 103–18.

Hohendahl, Peter Uwe, ed. 1985a. *Geschichte der deutschen Literaturkritik (1730–1980).* Stuttgart: Metzler.

Hohendahl, Peter Uwe, 1985b. "Literary Criticism in the Epoch of Liberalism, 1820–70." In Hohendahl 1985a, 179–276.

Honolka, Kurt. 1985. *Schubart: Dichter und Musiker, Journalist und Rebell; Sein Leben, sein Werk.* Stuttgart: Deutsche Verlags-Anstalt.

Kittler, Friedrich A. 1985. *Discourse Networks 1800/1900.* Trans. Michael Metteer. Stanford: Stanford UP, 1990.

Klawohn, Lothar. 1985. *Die Vernunft des Geldes und der Kunst: Zur gesellschaftlichen Form ästhetischer Wahrnehmung am Beispiel von "Minnesang" und Goethes "Werther."* Frankfurt am Main, New York: Campus-Verlag.

Klug, Wolfgang. 1985. "Gestaltungslinien in Goethes 'Die Leiden des jungen Werthers': Schema einer Schwerpunktinterpretation." *Anregung* 31 (1985): 155–61.

Redslob, Edwin. 1985. "'Die Leiden des jungen Werthers' 200 Jahre." In Redslob, *Schicksal und Dichtung,* ed. Wieland Schmidt, 21–44. Berlin: De Gruyter.

Renner, Karl N. 1985. "'Laß das Büchlein dein Freund seyn': Goethes Roman 'Die Leiden des jungen Werther' und die Diätetik der Aufklärung." In *Zur Sozialgeschichte der deutschen Literatur von der Aufklärung bis zur Jahrhundertwende,* ed. Günter Häntzschel et al., 1–20. Tübingen: Niemeyer.

Suntinger, Diethard. 1985. *Deutsche Wertheriaden: Beiträge zur Rezeption und produktiven Weiterverarbeitung von Goethes "Die Leiden des jungen Werthers" im Zeitraum von 1774–1787.* Diss., Graz.

Vaget, Hans Rudolf. 1985. "'Die Leiden des jungen Werthers' (1774)." In *Goethes Erzählwerk: Interpretationen,* ed. Paul Michael Lützeler and James E. McLeod, 37–72. Reclams Universal-Bibliothek 8081. Stuttgart: Reclam.

Bennett, Benjamin. 1986. "Werther and Montaigne: The Romantic Renaissance." *Goethe Yearbook* 3 (1986): 1–20.

Conger, Syndy McMillen. 1986. "The Sorrows of Young Charlotte: Werther's English Sisters 1785–1805." *Goethe Yearbook* 3 (1986): 21–56.

Ekmann, Björn. 1986. "Erlebnishaftigkeit und Klassizität: Einfühlung und Verfremdung im 'Werther' Roman." *Text & Kontext* 14 (Copenhagen 1986): 7–47.

Engel, Ingrid. 1986. *Werther und die Wertheriaden: Ein Beitrag zur Wirkungsgeschichte.* St. Ingbert: Röhrig.

Fischer, Peter. 1986. "Familienauftritte: Goethes Phantasiewelt und die Konstruktion des 'Werther'-Romans." *Psyche* 40 (1986): 527–56. Also in Schmiedt 1989a, 189–220.

Hartmann, Horst, ed. 1986. *Werkinterpretationen zur deutschen Literatur.* Berlin: Volk und Wissen.

Mayer, Hans. 1986. *Das unglückliche Bewußtsein: Zur deutschen Literaturgeschichte von Lessing bis Heine.* Frankfurt am Main: Suhrkamp.

Wellbery, Caroline. 1986. "From Mirrors to Images: The Transformation of Sentimental Paradigms in Goethe's 'The Sorrows of Young Werther.'" *Studies in Romanticism* 25 (1986): 231–49.

Bahr, Ehrhard, et al., eds. 1987. *Geschichte der deutschen Literatur: Kontinuität und Veränderung; vom Mittelalter bis zur Gegenwart.* Tübingen: Francke, 1987–1988.

Buck, Theo. 1987. "Goethes 'Werther' und die europäische Romantik." In *De romantiek in de europese roman van de 19e eeuw,* 75–91. Europese reeks: Leuvense cahiers 69. Leuven.

Dawson, John. 1987. "'Pater Abscondicus': Delving into Werther's Neuroses." *AUMLA: Journal of the Australasian Universities Language and Literature Association* 68 (1987): 251–60.

Duncan, Bruce. 1987. "Werther's Reflections on the Tenth of May." In *Exile and Enlightenment: Studies in Honor of Guy Stern,* 1–10. Detroit: Wayne State UP.

Flaschka, Horst. 1987. *Goethes "Werther." Werkkontextuelle Deskription und Analyse.* Munich: Fink.

Husmann, Ina. 1987. *Johann Wolfgang von Goethe, "Die Leiden des jungen Werther": Untersuchungen und Anregungen.* Hollfeld/Oberfranken: Beyer.

Ryder, Frank G. 1987. "Poetic Prose: A Suggested Approach by Way of Goethe's 'Werther.'" *Style* 21 (1987): 427–38.

Sauder, Gerhard. 1987. "'Die Leiden des jungen Werthers.'" In *Johann Wolfgang von Goethe: Sämtliche Werke nach Epochen seines Schaffens,* ed. Karl Richter et al., 1,2:770–99. Munich: Hanse.

Schlaffer, Hannelore. 1987. "'Die Leiden des jungen Werthers.'" In *Johann Wolfgang von Goethe: Sämtliche Werke nach Epochen seines Schaffens,* ed. Karl Richter et al., 2,2:844–53. Munich: Hanser.

Sloterdijk, Peter. 1987. *Critique of Cynical Reason.* Trans. Michael Eldred. Minneapolis: U of Minnesota P.

Sørensen, Bengt Algot. 1987. "Über die Familie in Goethes 'Werther' und 'Wilhelm Meister.'" *Orbis litterarum* 42 (1987): 118–40.

Swales, Martin. 1987. *Goethe: "The Sorrows of Young Werther."* Landmarks of World Literature. Cambridge: Cambridge UP.

Witte, Bernd. 1987. "Casanovas Tochter, Werthers Mutter: Über Liebe und Literatur im 18. Jahrhundert." In *Eros — Liebe — Leidenschaft: Ringvorlesung der Philosophischen Fakultät der RWTH Aachen im SS 1987,* ed. Kaspar H. Spinner and Frank-Rutger Hausmann, 93–113. Bonn, 1988.

Zahlmann, Christel. 1987. "Werther als Tantalus: Zu seiner Angst vor der Liebe." *Text & Kontext* 15 (1987): 43–69.

Aldridge, A. Owen. 1988. "The Japanese Werther of the Twentieth Century." In *The Comparative Perspective on Literature: Approaches to Theory and Practice,* ed. Clayton Koelb and Susan Noakes, 75–92. Ithaca, NY: Cornell UP.

Dye, R. Ellis. 1988. "Werther's Lotte: Views of the Other in Goethe's First Novel." *JEGP* 87 (1988): 492–506.

Mahoney, Dennis F. 1988. *Roman der Goethezeit, 1774–1829.* Stuttgart: Metzler.

Sax, Benjamin C. 1988. "The Sorrow of Finitude: Werther and the Problem of Self-Conception in the 18th Century." In Sax, *Images of Identity*, 1–38. New York: Grove/Atlantic.

Scheff, Thomas J., and Ursula Mahlendorf. 1988. "Emotion and False Consciousness: The Analysis of an Incident from 'Werther.'" *Theory, Culture, and Society* 5 (Cleveland 1988): 57–80.

Schmidt, Hartmut. 1988. "'Werther' oder die Passion des Sturm und Drang." In *Sturm und Drang: Ausstellung im Frankfurter Goethe-Museum*, ed. Christoph Perels, 99–115. Frankfurt am Main: Freies Deutsches Hochstift.

Scholz, Rüdiger. 1988. "Frühe Zerfallserscheinungen des bürgerlichen Selbst." *Jahrbuch der Psychoanalyse* 23 (1988): 213–41.

Walker, Colin. 1988. "Werther, the Good Samaritan and the Pharisees." *German Life and Letters* 41 (1988): 393–401.

Winkle, Sally Anne. 1988. *Woman as Bourgeois Ideal: A Study of Sophie von La Roche's "Geschichte des Fräuleins von Sternheim" and Goethe's "Werther."* New York: Lang.

Boerner, Peter, and Sidney Johnson, eds. 1989. *Faust through Four Centuries: Retrospect and Analysis = Vierhundert Jahre Faust: Rückblick und Analyse.* Tübingen: Niemeyer.

Hasty, Will. 1989. "On the Construction of an Identity: The Imaginary Family in Goethe's Werther." *Monatshefte* 81 (1989): 163–74.

Könecke, Rainer. 1989. *Stundenblätter: Goethes "Die Leiden des jungen Werther" und die Literatur des Sturm und Drang.* Stuttgart: Klett.

Kuzniar, Alice. 1989. "The Misrepresentations of Self: Werther versus Goethe." *Mosaic* 22 (1989): 15–28.

Lange, Victor. 1989. "Erzählformen im Roman des 18. Jahrhunderts." In *Illyrische Betrachtungen: Essays und Aufsätze aus 30 Jahren/zum 80. Geburtstag*, ed. Walter Hinderer und Volkmar Sander, 106–23. Bern, New York: P. Lang.

Meyer-Krentler, Eckhardt. 1989. "Die Leiden der jungen Wertherin." In *Zwischen Aufklärung und Restauration: Sozialer Wandel in der deutschen Literatur (1700–1848); Festschrift für Wolfgang Martens zum 65. Geburtstag*, ed. Wolfgang Frühwald and Alberto Martino, 225–48. Tübingen: Niemeyer.

Schmiedt, Helmut, ed. 1989a. *"Wie froh bin ich, daß ich weg bin!": Goethes Roman "Die Leiden des jungen Werther" in literaturpsychologischer Sicht.* Würzburg: Königshausen & Neumann.

Schmiedt, Helmut. 1989b. "Einleitung: Werther und die Geschichte der Literaturpsychologie." Schmiedt 1989a, 7–29.

Williams, John R. 1989. "'Der die Himmel zusammenrollt wie ein Tuch': Zu einer Werther-Stelle." *Euphorion* 83 (1989): 364–68.

Wilson, W. Daniel. 1989. "Patriarchy, Politics, Passion: Labor and Werther's Search for Nature." *Internationales Archiv für Sozialgeschichte der deutschen Literatur* 14 (1989): 15–44.

Furst, Lilian R. 1990. "The 'Imprisoning Self': Goethe's Werther and Rousseau's Solitary Walker." In Hoffmeister 1990, 163–79.

Hoffmeister, Gerhardt, ed. 1990. *European Romanticism: Literary Cross-Currents, Modes, and Models*. Detroit: Wayne State UP.

Koepke, Wulf. 1990. "Epistolary Fiction and Its Impact on Readers: Reality and Illusion." In *Aesthetic Illusion: Theoretical and Historical Approaches*, ed. Frederick Burwick and Walter Pape. Berlin: De Gruyter.

Koopmann, Helmut. 1990. "Warum bringt Werther sich um?" In *"Stets wird die Wahrheit hadern mit dem Schönen": Festschrift für Manfred Windfuhr zum 60. Geburtstag*, ed. Gertrude Cepl-Kaufmann et al., 29–50. Cologne: Böhlau.

Lee, Meredith. 1990. "'Klopstock!' Werther, Lotte and the Reception of Klopstock's Odes." In *The Age of Goethe Today: Critical Reexamination and Literary Reflection*, ed. Gertrud Bauer Pickar and Sabine Cramer, 1–11. Houston German Studies 7. Munich: Finck.

Packalen, Sture. 1990. "'Trinke meinen Kaffee da und lese meinen Homer': Zu Goethes Homer-Aneignung im Werther." *Studia Neophilologica: A Journal of Germanic and Romance Languages and Literature* 62 (1990): 189–93.

Perels, Christoph. 1990. "Auf der Suche nach dem verlorenen Vater: Das 'Werther'-Evangelium noch einmal." In *Goethe in seiner Epoche*, 49–64. Tübingen: Niemeyer, 1998.

Sonderup, Steven P. 1990. "Wertherism and 'Die Leiden des jungen Werther.'" In Hoffmeister 1990, 163–79.

Wellbery, David E. 1990. Foreword to *Discourse Networks 1800/1900*, by Friedrich A. Kittler, trans. Michael Metteer, vii–xxxiii. Stanford: Stanford UP.

Boyle, Nicholas. 1991. *The Poetry of Desire (1749–1790)*. Vol. 1 of *Goethe: The Poet and the Age*. Oxford: Oxford UP.

Fohrmann, Jürgen. 1991. "Deutsche Literaturgeschichte und historisches Projekt in der ersten Hälfte des 19. Jahrhunderts." In *Wissenschaft und Nation: Zur Entstehungsgeschichte der deutschen Literaturwissenschaft*, ed. Jürgen Fohrmann and Wilhelm Voßkamp, 205–15. Munich: Fink.

Hein, Edgar. 1991. *Johann Wolfgang Goethe, "Die Leiden des jungen Werther": Interpretation*. München: Oldenbourg.

Siepmann, Thomas. 1991. *Johann Wolfgang von Goethe, "Die Leiden des jungen Werther."* Stuttgart: Klett.

Strickland, Stuart Walker. 1991. "Flight from the Given World and Return to the New: The Dialectic of Creation and Escape in Goethe's 'Die Leiden des jungen Werther.'" *The German Quarterly* 64 (1991): 190–206.

Wang, Bingjun. 1991. *Rezeptionsgeschichte des Romans "Die Leiden des jungen Werther" von Johann Wolfgang Goethe in Deutschland seit 1945*. Frankfurt am Main, Bern: Lang.

Abbott, Scott 1992. "The Semiotics of Young Werther." *Goethe Yearbook* 6 (1992): 41–65.

Batley, Edward M. 1992. "Werther's Final Act of Alienation: Goethe, Lessing, and Jerusalem on the Poetry and the Truth of Suicide." *Modern Language Review* 87 (1992): 868–78.

Corbineau-Hoffmann, Angelika. 1992. "'Discours de la passion' als Selbstaussage: Goethe, *Die Leiden des jungen Werther*, Rousseau, *Julie ou la nouvelle Héloïse*, Richardson, *Pamela*." *Colloquium Helveticum* 15 (1992): 27–52.

Goins, Scott E. 1992. "Birds and Erotic Fantasies in Catullus and Goethe." *Goethe Yearbook* 6 (1992): 29–40.

Jenkins, Sylvia P. 1992. "The Depiction of Mental Disorder in 'Die Leiden des jungen Werthers' and 'Torquato Tasso' and Its Place in the Thematic Structure of the Works." *Publications of the English Goethe Society* 62 (1991/92): 96–118.

Rickes, Joachim. 1992. "Das 'Gewittermotiv' in Goethes 'Werther' motivtheoretisch betrachtet: Überlegungen zur Terminologie-Problematik in der Stoff-, Motiv- und Themenforschung." *Wirkendes Wort* 42 (1992): 406–20.

Vincent, Deirdre. 1992. *Werther's Goethe and the Game of Literary Creativity.* Toronto: University of Toronto Press.

Washington, Ida H. 1992. "Werther — Wilhelm — Wolfgang." *Germanic Notes and Reviews* 23 (1992): 11–13.

Batts, Michael S. 1993. *A History of Histories of German Literature, 1835–1914.* Montreal and Kingston: McGill-Queen's UP.

Burwick, Roswitha. 1993. "Goethe's 'Werther' and Mary Shelley's 'Frankenstein.'" *The Wordsworth Circle* 24 (1993): 47–52.

Koebner, Thomas. 1993. *Zurück zur Natur: Ideen der Aufklärung und ihre Nachwirkung.* Heidelberg: Winter.

Schwanke, Martina. 1993. "Aspekte computergestützter Lemmatisierung von Goethes 'Werther.'" *Wirkendes Wort* 43 (1993): 144–56.

Siebers, Tobin. 1993. "The Werther Effect: The Esthetics of Suicide." *Mosaic* 26 (1993): 15–34.

Black, Joel. 1994. "Writing after Murder (and before Suicide): The Confessions of Werther and Rivière." In *Reading After Foucault: Institutions, Disciplines, and Technologies of the Self in Germany, 1750–1830*, ed. Robert S. Leventhal, 233–59. Detroit: Wayne State UP.

Bohm, Arnd. 1994. "Werther's Gravity." In *Analogon rationis: Festschrift fuer Gerwin Marahrens zum 65. Geburtstag*, ed. Marianne Henn and Christoph Lorey, 85–97. Edmonton, Canada: M. Henn and C. Lorey.

Brecht, Christoph. 1994. Commentary to "Briefe aus der Schweiz: Erste Abteilung." In *Johann Wolfgang Goethe, Sämtliche Werke*, part 1, ed. Waltraut Wiethölter, 8:1111–18. Frankfurt am Main: Deutscher Klassiker Verlag.

Dainat, Holger. 1994. "Voraussetzungsreiche Wissenschaft: Anatomie eines Konflikts zweier NS-Literaturwissenschaftler im Jahre 1934." *Euphorion* 88 (1994): 103–22.

Davis, William Stephen. 1994. "The Intensification of the Body in Goethe's *Die Leiden des jungen Werther.*" *The Germanic Review* 69 (1994): 106–17.

Herrmann, Hans Peter, ed. 1994a. *Goethes "Werther": Kritik und Forschung.* Darmstadt: Wissenschaftliche Buchgesellschaft.

Herrmann, Hans Peter. 1994b. "Landschaft in Goethes 'Werther': Zum Brief vom 18. August." In Herrmann 1994a, 360–81.

Koopmann, Helmut. 1994. "Goethes 'Werther': Der Roman einer Krise und ihrer Bewältigung." In *Was soll ein Roman? Tröster, Freudenspender, Religionsersatz: Beiträge einer Tagung der Evangelischen Akademie Baden, 4.-6. März 1994, Bad Herrenalb,* 7–28. Baden: Evangelische Akademie Baden, 1995.

Michéa, René. 1994. "Die Begriffe 'Herz' und 'Seele' im 'Werther': Über die Beziehungen zwischen assoziativem und artikuliertem Denken." In Herrmann 1994a, 207–22.

Nethersole, Reingard. 1994. "Versuch über die Voraussetzungen der Popularität dargestellt an Goethes 'Werther.'" *Acta Germanica: Jahrbuch des Germanistenverbandes im Südlichen Afrika* 22 (1994): 187–202.

Rahmeyer, Ruth. 1994. *Werthers Lotte: Ein Brief, ein Leben, eine Familie: Die Biographie der Charlotte Kestner.* Hannover: Fackelträger.

Schwanke, Martina. 1994. *Lemmatisierter Index zu Goethes Roman "Die Leiden des jungen Werther."* Stuttgart: Heinz.

Wellbery, David E. 1994. "Morphisms of the Phantasmatic Body: Goethe's *The Sorrows of Young Werther.*" In *Body & Text in the Eighteenth Century,* ed. Veronica Kelly and Dorothea von Mücke, 181–208. Stanford: Stanford UP.

Aurnhammer, Achim. 1995. "Maler Werther: Zur Bedeutung der bildenden Kunst in Goethes Roman." *Literaturwissenschaftliches Jahrbuch im Auftrage der Görres-Gesellschaft* 36 (1995): 83–104.

Barnouw, Jeffrey. 1995. "The Cognitive Value of Confusion and Obscurity in the German Enlightenment: Leibniz, Baumgarten, and Herder." *Studies in Eighteenth-Century Culture* 24 (1995): 29–50.

Dumiche, Béatrice. 1995. "Lottes Mutterbindung: Ihre Mitschuld an Werthers Selbstmord." *Orbis litterarum* 50 (1995): 278–88.

Gray, Richard T. 1995. *Stations of the Divided Subject: Contestation and Ideological Legitimation in German Bourgeois Literature, 1770–1914.* Stanford: Stanford UP.

Gutbrodt, Fritz. 1995. "The Worth of 'Werther': Goethe's Literary Marketing." *MLN* 110 (1995): 579–630.

Leistner, Bernd. 1995. "Goethes 'Werther' und seine zeitgenössischen Kritiker." *Goethe-Jahrbuch* 112 (1995): 71–82.

Luserke, Matthias. 1995. *Die Bändigung der wilden Seele: Literatur und Leidenschaft in der Aufklärung.* Stuttgart: Metzler.

Edmunds, Kathryn. 1996. "'Der Gesang soll deinen Namen erhalten': Ossian, Werther, and Texts of/for Mourning." *Goethe Yearbook* 8 (1996): 45–65.

Kuzniar, Alice A., ed. 1996. *Outing Goethe and His Age.* Stanford: Stanford UP.

Nelles, Jürgen. 1996. "Werthers Herausgeber oder die Rekonstruktion der 'Geschichte des armen Werthers.'" *Jahrbuch des Freien Deutschen Hochstifts* (1996): 1–37.

Niggl, Gunter. 1996. "Erzählspiegel in Goethes 'Werther.'" In *Exempla: Studien zur Bedeutung und Funktion exemplarischen Erzählens,* ed. Bernd Engler and Kurt Müller, 199–214. Berlin: Duncker & Humblot.

Purdy, Daniel. 1996. "The Veil of Masculinity: Clothing and Identity via Goethe's 'Die Leiden des jungen Werther.'" *Lessing Yearbook* 27 (1995): 103–30.

Rickels, Laurence Arthur. 1996. "Psy Fi Explorations of Out Space: On Werther's Special Effects." In Kuzniar 1996, 147–73, 264–65.

Tobin, Robert D. 1996. "In and Against Nature: Goethe on Homosexuality and Heterosexuality." In Kuzniar 1996, 94–110.

Wellbery, David E. 1996. *The Specular Moment: Goethe's Early Lyric and the Beginnings of Romanticism.* Stanford: Stanford UP.

Anderegg, Johannes. 1997. "Werther und Ossian." In *Stile, Stilprägungen, Stilgeschichte: Über Epochen-, Gattungs- und Autorenstile, sprachliche Analysen und didaktische Aspekte,* ed. Ulla Fix and Hans Wellmann, 121–33. Heidelberg: Winter.

Brecht, Christoph. 1997. "Werther als Voyeur: Ein Zwischenspiel zu Goethes Romanen." In *Von der Natur zur Kunst zurück: Neue Beiträge zur Goethe-Forschung; Gotthart Wunberg zum 65. Geburtstag,* ed. Moritz Bassler et al., 157–80. Tübingen: Niemeyer.

Farrelly, Daniel. 1997. "Marxist 'Werther' Interpretations Reviewed." In *Schein und Widerschein: Festschrift für T. J. Casey,* ed. Eoin Bourke et al., 54–65. Galway: Galway UP.

Hermann-Huwe, Jasmin. 1997. *"Pathologie und Passion" in Goethes Roman "Die Leiden des jungen Werther."* Frankfurt am Main, Berlin: Lang.

Herminghouse, Patricia, and Magda Mueller, eds. 1997. *Gender and Germanness: Cultural Productions of Nation.* Providence: Berghahn Books.

Lorenz, Annika, and Helmut Schmiedt eds. 1997. *Johann Wolfgang von Goethe: "Die Leiden des jungen Werthers"; Synoptischer Druck der beiden Fassungen 1774 und 1787.* Paderborn: Igel.

Plumpe, Gerhard. 1997. "Kein Mitleid mit Werther." In *Systemtheorie und Hermeneutik,* ed. Henk de Berg and Matthias Prangel, 215–32. Tübingen: Francke.

Pöder, Elfriede. 1997. "Literatur — ein Konstrukt zwischen Fiktionalität und Autorintention? Am Beispiel der 'Wertherwirkung' erörtert." In *Literatur,* ed. Martin Sexl, 175–89. Vienna: Studien Verlag.

Prier, Raymond Adolph. 1997. "Charlotte's Vicar and Goethe's Eighteenth-Century Tale about Werther." In *Narrative Ironies,* ed. A. Prier and Gerald Gillespie. Amsterdam, Atlanta: Rodopi.

Sagarra, Eda. 1997. *A Companion to GermanLiterature: From 1500 to the Present*. Cambridge, MA: Blackwell.

Vazsonyi, Nicholas. 1997. *Lukács Reads Goethe: From Aestheticism to Stalinism*. Columbia, SC: Camden House.

Watanabe-O'Kelly, Helen, ed. 1997. *The Cambridge History of German Literature*. Cambridge, New York: Cambridge UP.

Corngold, Stanley. 1998. *Complex Pleasure: Forms of Feeling in German Literature*. Stanford: Stanford UP.

Große, Wilhelm. 1998. "Kommentar zu Goethe, *Die Leiden des jungen Werthers*." Frankfurt am Main: Suhrkamp.

Auer, Elisabeth. 1999. *"Selbstmord begehen zu wollen ist wie ein Gedicht zu schreiben": Eine psychoanalytische Studie zu Goethes Briefroman "Die Leiden des jungen Werther."* Stockholm: Almqvist & Wiksell.

Brodey, Inger Sigrun. 1999. "Masculinity, Sensibility, and the 'Man of Feeling': The Gendered Ethics of Goethe's 'Werther.'" *Papers on Language and Literature* 35 (1999): 115–40.

Chandler, David. 1999. "'In the End Despondency and Madness': Werther in Wordsworth." *Wordsworth Circle* 30 (1999): 55–59.

Diehl, Christopher, and Hans-Friedrich Foltin. 1999. "Des einen Leid, des andern Freud: Goethes 'Werther.'" In *Lesekultur: Populare Lesestoffe von Gutenberg bis zum Internet,* ed. Petra Bohnsack and Hans-Friedrich Foltin. Marburg: Universität Marburg.

Fetzer, John. 1999. "Threshold Metaphors in Goethe's 'Werther.'" In *Schwellen: Germanistische Erkundungen einer Metapher,* ed. Nicholas Saul et al., 33–45. Würzburg: Königshausen & Neumann.

Kowalik, Jill Anne. 1999. "Pietist Grief, Empfindsamkeit, and Werther." *Goethe Yearbook* 9 (1999): 77–130.

Luserke, Matthias, ed. 1999. *Johann Wolfgang Goethe: "Leiden des jungen Werthers"; Edition der Handschrift von 1786*. Weimar: Böhlau.

Powers, Elizabeth. 1999. "The Artist's Escape from the Idyll: The Relation of Werther to Sesenheim." *Goethe Yearbook* 9 (1999): 47–76.

Sasse, Gunter. 1999. "Woran leidet Werther? Zum Zwiespalt zwischen idealistischer Schwärmerei und sinnlichem Begehren." *Goethe-Jahrbuch* 116 (1999): 245–58.

Walker, Joyce S. 1999. "Sex, Suicide, and the Sublime: A Reading of Goethe's *Werther*." *Monatshefte* 91 (1999): 208–23.

The American Heritage Dictionary of the English Language. 2000. Fourth Edition. New York: www.Bartleby.com.

Brown, Jane K. 2000. "'Es singen wohl die Nixen': 'Werther' and the Romantic Tale." In *Rereading Romanticism,* ed. Martha B. Helfer, 11–25. Amsterdam; Atlanta: Rodopi.

Dollinger, Roland. 2000. "The Self-Inflicted Suffering of Young Werther: An Example of Masochism in the 18th Century." In *One Hundred Years of*

Masochism: Literary Texts, Social and Cultural Contexts, ed. Michael C. Finke and Carl Niekerk, 91–108. Amsterdam: Rodopi.

Gustafson, Susan E. 2000. "From Werther to Amazons: Cross-Dressing and Male-Male Desire." In *Unwrapping Goethe's Weimar: Essays in Cultural Studies and Local Knowledge,* ed. Burkhard Henke et al., 166–87. Rochester: Camden House.

Kennedy, Ellie. 2000. "Rousseau and Werther: In Search of a Sympathetic Soul." In *Material Productions and Cultural Construction/Culture materielle et constructions discursives,* ed. Robert Merrett et al., 109–19. Edmonton: Academic.

Nagl-Docekal, Herta, and Cornelia Klinger, eds. 2000. *Continental Philosophy in Feminist Perspective: Re-reading the Canon in German.* University Park: Pennsylvania State UP.

Barton, Karin. 2001. *Viel Licht, Viel Schatten: Rousseau, Goethe und die Unordnung der Geschlechter; Eine neue Interpretation der "Leiden des jungen Werther."* Diss., U of Toronto.

Bennett, Benjamin. 2001. *Goethe as Woman: The Undoing of Literature.* Detroit: Wayne State UP.

Beutin, Wolfgang, et al. 2001. *Deutsche Literaturgeschichte: Von den Anfängen bis zur Gegenwart.* Stuttgart: Metzler.

Matthias Luserke. 2001. *Goethe nach 1999: Positionen und Perspektiven.* Göttingen: Vandenhoeck & Ruprecht.

Schindler, Stephan K. 2001. *Eingebildete Körper: Phantasierte Sexualität in der Goethezeit.* Stauffenburg-Colloquium 49. Tübingen: Stauffenburg.

Wiethölter, Waltraud, ed. 2001. *Der junge Goethe: Genese und Konstruktion einer Autorschaft.* Tübingen: Francke.

Benthien, Claudia, and Hans Rudolf Velten. 2002. *Germanistik als Kulturwissenschaft: Eine Einführung in neue Theoriekonzepte.* Reinbek: Rowohlt Taschenbuch Verlag.

Luserke, Matthias. 2002. *Medea: Studien zur Kulturgeschichte der Literatur.* Tübingen: Francke.

Steinberg, Holger, and M. C. Angermeyer. 2002. "Two Hundred Years of Psychiatry at Leipzig University: An Overview." *History of Psychiatry* 13 (2002): 267–83.

Bell, Matthew. 2003. Review of Bennett 2001. *MLR* 98 (2003): 1039–40.

Duncan, Bruce. 2003. "Sturm und Drang Passions and Eighteenth-Century Psychology." In *Literature of the Sturm und Drang,* ed. David Hill, 46–68. Rochester, NY: Camden House.

Fuchs, Alfred H., and Katherine S. Milar. 2003. "Psychology as a Science." In *History of Psychology,* vol. 1 of *Handbook of Psychology,* ed. Donald K. Freedheim, 1–26. Hoboken: Wiley.

Gustafson, Susan E. 2003. *Men Desiring Men: The Poetry of Same-Sex Identity and Desire in German Classicism.* Detroit: Wayne State UP.

MacLeod, Catriona. 2003. Review of Bennett 2001. *MLQ* 64 (2003): 258–60.

Vollmer, Hartmut. 2003. "'Worte sind hier umsonst.' Die Beschreibung des Unbeschreiblichen in Goethes *Werther* und Hölderlins *Hyperion*." *Zeitschrift für deutsche Philologie* 122 (2003): 481–508.

Bahr, Ehrhard. 2004. "Ossian-Rezeption von Michael Denis bis Goethe: Ein Beitrag zur Geschichte des Primitivismus in Deutschland." *Goethe Yearbook* 12 (2004): 1–15.

Dye, Ellis. 2004. *Love and Death in Goethe: "One and Double."* 79–96. Rochester, NY: Camden House.

Eyck, John R. J., and Katherine Arens. 2004. "The Court of Public Opinion: Lessing, Goethe, and Werther's *Emilia Galotti*." *Monatshefte* 96 (2004): 40–61.

Kuzniar, Alice. 2004. Review of Bennett 2001. *Goethe Yearbook* 12 (2004): 270–73.

Pike, Burton, trans. 2004. *"The Sorrows of Young Werther," by Johann Wolfgang von Goethe.* New York: Modern Library.

Ryan, Judith. 2004. "'That day we read no more': Werther, Lotte, and Literary Tradition." Talk delivered at Smith College, Northhampton, MA, September 18, 2004.

Schweitzer, Christoph E. "Who *Is* the Editor in Goethe's *Die Leiden des jungen Werthers*"? *Goethe Yearbook* 12 (2004): 31–40.

Vaget, Hans Rudolf. 2004. "Werther, The Undead." *Goethe Yearbook* 12 (2004): 17–29.

Index

Abbott, Scott H. (19–), 50, 66, 118–19, 126, 184
Adler, Alfred (1870–1937), 56, 66
Alewyn, Richard (1902–1979), 77, 91, 93–94, 99, 139, 150, 170, 175
Allgemeine deutsche Bibliothek, 12, 13
Ames, Carol (19–), 86, 99, 174
Analytical Review, The, 21
Anstett, Jean-Jacques (19–), 33, 35, 165
Appell, Johann Wilhelm (1829–1896), 23, 24, 160
Arens, Katherine (1953–), 87, 100, 145, 151, 190
Arnold, Gottfried (1666–1704), 112
Assling, Reinhard (1948–), 62, 96–98, 99, 120–21, 126, 177
Atkins, Stuart P. (1910–1996), 22, 24, 33–34, 35, 46, 49–50, 52–53, 66, 91–93, 99, 110, 115, 126, 164, 165, 171, 175
Auer, Elisabeth (19–), 59, 63–65, 66, 188

Bahr, Ehrhard (19–), 144–145, 150, 190
Balint, Michael (1896–1970), 65, 67, 165
Bancroft, George (1800–1891), 22
Barnouw, Jeffrey (1940–), 30, 186
Barthes, Roland (1915–1980), 29, 64, 67, 121, 125, 126, 174
Barton, Karin (19–), 113, 126, 144, 150, 189
Bassenheim, Graf Johann Maria Rudolf Waltbott von und zu (1731–1772), 109

Batts, Michael S. (19–), 74, 99, 185
Beauvoir, Simone de (1908–1986), 137, 165
Behrisch, Ernst Wolfgang (1738–1809), 116
Bell, Matthew (1964–), 139, 150
Bell, Michael (1941–), 125–26, 179, 189
Bennett, Benjamin (1939–), 82, 99, 110–12, 126, 138–39, 144–45, 149, 150, 174, 176, 181, 189
Berger, Daniel (1744–1824), 106, 134
Berghahn, Klaus (1937–), 23, 24, 180
Bernays, Michael (1834–1897), 76, 100, 110, 124, 126, 158, 159
Beutler, Ernst Rudolf (1885–1960), 31–32, 34, 35, 78, 100, 109, 112, 127, 164
Bickelmann, Ingeborg (19–), 22, 24, 30, 35, 40, 42, 67, 74, 76, 79, 100, 107, 113, 127, 163
Biedermann, Karl (1812–1901), 112, 127, 158
Black, Joel (1950–), 122–23, 127, 185
Blackall, Eric A. (1914–1989), 54, 67, 121, 127, 137, 150, 167, 174
Blankenburg, Christian Friedrich von (1744–1796), 16–19, 20, 24, 155
Blessin, Stefan (19–), 19–20, 23, 24, 92, 100, 175, 180
Blumenthal, Herrmann (1880–), 23, 24, 31, 34, 35, 78, 100, 116, 127, 163, 164
Böckmann, Paul (1899–1987), 78–79, 100, 163

body, the, 135, 142–44, 145–49
Bonaparte, Napoleon (1769–1821), 2
Boyle, Nicholas (1946–), 116, 127, 184
Braemer, Edith (19–), 81–82, 100, 167
Bragg, Marvin (19–), 53, 67, 174
Braun, Julius W. (1843–1895), 23, 24, 27, 159
Brecht, Christoph (19–), 150, 185, 187
Breidenbach zu Breidenstein, Karl Wilhelm Freiherr von (1751–1813), 25, 107–8, 110, 127, 162
Brentano, Maximiliane, née von La Roche (1756–1793), 109, 111
Brentano, Peter Anton (1735–1797), 109
Brinkmann, Richard (1921–2002), 34, 35, 112, 127, 174
Buff, Charlotte. *See* Charlotte Kestner
Buff, Heinrich Adam (1710–1795), 107
Burgard, Peter J. (1957–), 145, 151, 180
Burger, Heinz-Otto (1903–), 165, 167
Burger, Thomas (19–), 4, 168

Carlyle, Thomas (1795–1881), 74, 100, 157
Carter, Patricia A. (19–), 4
Carus, Carl Gustav (1789–1869), 41, 45, 66, 67, 157
Cervantes, Saavedra Miguel De (1547–1616), works by: *Don Quixote*, 137
Chodowiecki, Daniel Nicolaus (1726–1801), 106, 134
Clark, Robert (1906–), 48–50, 67, 164
Claudius, Matthias (1740–1815), 3, 5, 10, 25, 155, 156

Clauer, Johann David Balthasar (17–), 43, 109
Conger, Sydny McMillen (19–), 21, 25, 135, 151, 181
Corbineau-Hoffmann, Angelika (19–), 125, 127, 191
Critical Review, The, 21

Dainat, Holger (19–), 79, 100, 185
Damm, Sigrid (19–), 15
Dante Alighieri (1265–1321), 147
Darmstadter Kreis der Empfindsamen (Darmstadt Circle of Sentimentalists), 109
Deinet, Johann Konrad (1735–1797), 10, 25, 155
Demetz, Peter (1922–), 79, 100, 169
Deutsche Chronik, 9, 13
Dial, The, 22
Diez, Max (18–), 39, 67, 114, 127, 163
Dilthey, Wilhelm (1833–1911), 45–46, 67, 76, 100, 158, 159
Dumiche, Béatrice (1960–), 140, 151, 186
Duncan, Bruce (1942–), 9, 25, 40, 64, 67, 112, 127, 145, 151, 177, 182, 189
Duncan, Walter R. II (1972–), 4
Düntzer, Heinrich (1813–1901), 29–30, 36, 41, 67, 109–10, 123, 127, 157, 158
Dvoretzky, Edward (1930–), 145, 151, 167
Dye, Robert Ellis (1938–), 19, 25, 113, 127, 137, 151, 173, 177, 182, 190

Eckermann, Johann Peter (1792–1854), 39, 67, 157
Edmunds, Kathryn (19–), 62, 67, 120, 127, 186
Eichendorff, Joseph Freiherr von (1788–1857), 40, 67, 157
Eissler, Kurt Robert (1908–1999), 56, 59, 66, 67, 149, 151, 168

Elias, Norbert (1897–1990), 87, 100, 174
Engel, Eduard (1851–1939), 160
Engel, Ingrid (19–), 22, 25, 181
Engel, Johann Jakob (1741–1802), 19
Engels, Friedrich (1820–1895), 74, 76, 81, 100, 157
Erikson, Erik (1902–1994), 56
Erlebnis (experience), 45–46
Everett, Edward (1794–1865), 22
Eyck, John R. J. (19–), 87, 100, 145, 151, 190

Faber, Mel D. (19–), 59–60, 67, 139–40, 151, 172
Farrelly, Daniel (1934–), 84–85, 100, 187
Faust, Albert Bernhardt (1870–1951), 160
Fechner, Jörg-Ulrich (1939–), 113, 127, 178
Feise, Ernst (1884–1966), 56–57, 66, 68, 109, 114, 117, 128, 145, 151, 161, 162
Fertig, Ludwig (1937–), 86, 88, 100, 168
Fetzer, John F. (19–), 118, 128, 171, 188
Feuerlicht, Ignace (19–), 55, 68, 175
Finsen, H. Carl (19–), 112, 128, 135–36, 151, 174
Fischer, Peter (1959–), 55, 66, 68, 87, 100, 112, 124, 128, 136, 151, 181
Fittbogen, Gottfried (1878–1941), 123, 128, 161
Flaschka, Horst (1940–), 7, 9, 15, 25, 35, 36, 50, 68, 77, 78, 98, 101, 108, 110, 111, 116, 128, 182
Fohrmann, Jürgen (1953–), 74, 101, 184
Forget, Philippe (19–), 124–25, 128, 179

Foucault, Michel (1926–1984), 121–22, 128, 142, 151, 174
Frankenstein. *See* Mary Shelley
Frankfurter gelehrte Anzeigen, 10, 49
Freud, Sigmund (1856–1939), 48, 53, 54–56, 64, 68, 125, 162, 163
Freuden des jungen Werthers, 12, 14, 108
Fricke, Gerhard (1901–1980), 78–81, 101, 163, 165
Friedell, Egon (1878–1938), 110, 128, 160
Fuchs, Alfred H. (19–), 66, 68, 189
Fuller, Margaret (1810–1850), 22
Furst, Lilian (1932–), 113, 128, 135, 136, 151, 178, 184

Garve, Christian (1742–1798), 19, 25, 156
George, Stefan (1868–1933), 45
Gerhard, Melitta (1891–1981), 123, 128, 161
Gervinus, Georg Gottfried (1805–1871), 74, 101, 157
Gloël, Heinrich (1855–1940), 109–10, 128, 161
Goebbels, Joseph (1897–1945), 78, 101, 162
Goedeke, Karl (1814–1887), 108, 110, 128, 158
Goethe, Cornelia. *See* Cornelia Schlosser
Goethe, Johann Wolfgang von (1749–1832), works by: "Briefe aus der Schweiz," 23, 149–50; *Dichtung und Wahrheit,* 25, 39, 109, 114–115, 123, 128, 157; *Der ewige Jude,* 34; *Faust,* 45; *Gedichte von einem polnischen Juden,* 25, 115–16, 155; *Götz von Berlichingen,* 9, 116; *Hanswursts Hochzeit,* 111, 147; *Leiden des jungen Werther* (see *Leiden des jungen Werther*); "Prometheus," 32, 81–82; *Rede zum Schäkespears-Tag,* 147; "An Werther," 39; "Auf Werthers Grab," 147

Goeze, Johann Melchior (1717–1786), 11–12, 14, 18, 20, 23, 29, 75, 81, 91, 99, 141, 151, 156
Goins, Scott E. (19–), 142, 151, 185
Göres, Jörn (19–), 2, 5, 171, 172
Gose, Hans (1891–), 30, 36, 47–48, 68, 142, 152, 161
Goue, August Siegfried von [*also:* Goué] (1742–1789), 111
Graber, Gustav Hans (1893–1982), 58–60, 68, 143, 148, 149, 152, 166
Graefe, Johanna (1896–), 33, 36, 166
Graham, Ilse Appelbaum (1914–), 117, 122, 128, 167, 172, 173
Griesbach, Johanna Dorothea, née Rambach (1726–1775), 32
Grimm, Herman Friedrich (1828–1901), 135, 152, 159
Grün, Karl (1817–1887), 75–76, 101, 157
Gundolf, Friedrich (1880–1931), 45–46, 68, 161
Gustafson, Susan E. (19–), 59, 68, 150, 152, 189
Gutbrodt, Fritz (19–), 121–122, 129, 139, 149, 152, 186
Gutzkow, Karl Ferdinand (1811–1878), 74

Habermas, Jürgen (1929–), 4, 5, 9, 25, 168
Haney, John Lewis (1877–1960), 21, 25, 160
Hardin, James N. (19–), 4
Hass, Hans-Egon (1916–1969), 85, 101, 110, 115, 117, 118, 129, 166
Hausmann, Manfred (1898–1986), 113, 129, 166
Haverkamp, Anselm (19–), 24, 26, 178
Heine, Heinrich (1797–1856), 77, 101, 157

Heinse, Johann Jakob Wilhelm (1746–1803), 8, 26, 155
Herbst, Wilhelm (1825–1882), 110, 129, 159
Herd, Elisabet, née Egell (1741–1813), 109
Herd, Phillip Jakob (1735–1809), 109
Herder, Johann Gottfried (1744–1803), 9, 16, 26, 48–49, 68, 81, 83, 101, 118, 119, 155, 156
Hering, Robert (1866–1946), 109–10, 129, 163
Herrmann, Hans Peter (1929–), 3, 5, 101, 152, 180, 186
Herrmann, Helene, née Schlesinger (1877–1944), 46, 50, 68, 160
Herrmann, Max (1865–1942), 39, 46, 68, 160
Hertling, Gunter H. (19–), 11, 12, 26, 168
Heschel, Susannah (19–), 4, 99
Hettner, Hermann (1821–1882), 47, 68, 80, 101, 115, 129, 157, 158
Higgins, Lynn A. (1947–), 4
Hillebrand, Bruno (1935–), 178
Hillebrand, Karl (1829–1884), 40, 68, 74, 81, 101, 143, 152, 159
Himburg, Christian Friedrich (1733–1801), 2, 106, 134
Hirsch, Arnold (1901–1954), 88–89, 101, 166
Hirsch, Franz (1844–1920), 76, 101, 159
Hirzel, Salomon (1804–1877), 110, 126, 159
Höfler, Johann Jakob (1714–1781), 111
Hohendahl, Peter Uwe (19–), 13, 26, 73, 74, 77, 88, 95, 99, 101, 112, 129, 171, 174, 180
Hölderlin, Johann Christian Friedrich (1770–1843), 79
Holthusen, Hans Egon (1913–1997), 99–100, 102, 170

Honolka, Kurt (1913–), 9, 26, 181
Hübner, Klaus (19–), 79, 96, 108, 178
Huffman, Alexia O. (1983–), 4
Hughes, Peter C., Jr (1984–), 4

Innes, Susan (19–), 4
Iris, 8
Ittner, R. T. (1911–), 145, 152, 164

Jacobi, Friedrich Heinrich (1743–1819), 15
Jacobi, Johann Georg (1740–1814), 8
Jäger, Georg (1940–), 23, 26, 170, 173, 180
Jauss, Hans Robert (1921–1997), 20, 26, 77, 95–96, 102, 113, 129, 178
Jenkins, Sylvia P. (19–), 44, 69, 185
Jerusalem, Johann Friedrich Wilhelm (1709–1789), 107
Jerusalem, Karl Wilhelm (1747–1772), 98, 107–11, 114–16, 122–23
Jolles, O. J. Matthijs (1911–1968), 117, 129, 166
Jung, Carl (1875–1961), 57–59

Kaempfer, Wolfgang (19–), 54, 65, 69, 175
Kahn, Ludwig W. (1910–), 34, 36, 168
Kaiser, Gerhard (1927–), 77, 90–91, 93–94, 97, 102, 171
Kant, Immanuel (1724–1804), 51
Kaulitz-Neideck, Rosa (1881–), 110, 129, 161
Kayser, Albert Christoph (1756–1811), 50
Kayser, Wolfgang (1906–1960), 78, 102, 115–16, 129, 164, 165
Kenkel, Konrad O. (1938–), 4
Kennedy, Ellie (19–), 113, 129, 189
Kestner, Charlotte, née Buff (1753–1828), 8, 107–13, 115

Kestner, Georg August (1777–1853), 108–9, 129, 158
Kestner, Johann Georg Christian (1741–1800), 107–12, 116, 123–24
Kindermann, Heinz (1894–1985), 78, 102, 164
Kittler, Friedrich (1943–), 50, 69, 121, 129, 147–48, 152, 176, 181
Klein, Melanie (1882–1960), 63
Klettenberg, Susanna Katharina von (1723–1774), 32, 109
Klopstock, Friedrich Gottlieb (1724–1803), 8–9, 136, 139, 147, 150
Kluckhohn, Paul (1886–1957), 78, 102, 161, 163
Kluge, Gerhard (19–), 85, 102, 171
Kluge, Hermann (1832–1914), 160
Koch, (Frau) (17–), 109
Koch, Max (1855–1931), 161
Kohut, Heinz (1913–1981), 65
Koldewey, Friedrich (1839–1909), 76, 102, 109, 129, 159
Korff, Hermann August (1882–1963), 30, 36, 162
Kortum, Hans (19–), 83, 102, 170
Kowalik, Jill Anne (1943–2003), 51–52, 54, 62, 69, 112, 129, 188
Krey, Hans (19–), 66, 67, 163
Kurz, Gerhard (1943–), 64, 69, 117, 129, 178
Kurz, Heinrich (1805–1873), 159
Kuzniar, Alice (1956–), 62, 69, 139, 141, 152, 183, 187, 190

Lacan, Jacques (1901–1981), 60–62, 125, 142, 148
Lämmert, Eberhard (1924–), 16, 26, 80, 102, 168, 169
Lange, Sigrid (19–), 176
Lange, Victor (1908–1996), 44, 45, 60, 66, 69, 95, 102, 113, 129, 165, 168, 170, 183
Langen, August (19–), 34, 36, 168
Larkin, Maxwell R. (2000–), 4

La Roche, Maximiliane von. *See* Maximiliane Brentano
La Roche, Sophie von (1731–1807), 52, 113
Laukhard, Friedrich Christian (1758–1822), 107, 130, 156
Lauterbach, Martin (18–), 123, 124, 130, 161
Lavater, Johann Caspar (1741–1801), 32, 49–50, 52, 118
Lee, Meredith (1945–), 139, 152, 184
Leibfried, Erwin (1942–), 145, 152, 175
Leiden des jungen Werther, passim; biographical interpretations of, 23, 44–47, 55–57, 64–65, 98–99, 107–113; class conflict in, 78–89, 98; commercial success of, 1–2; editor's role in, 34, 35, 44, 121–22, 136–37, 143; gender roles in, (Lotte) 135–41, (Werther) 143–44; gestation of, 114–21; homoeroticism in, 59, 149–50; illustrations of, 2, 106, 134; literary and philosophical influences on, 20, 30, 34, 48–52, 62, 81, 112–13, 144; Marxist interpretations of, 75–76, 79–85, 87, 92–99; morality of, 1, 10–12, 14–15, 18–22, 34–35, 41, 43, 51–52, 75, 112, 113, 119, 125–26; national-socialist interpretations of, 78–81; political interpretations of, 73–99; psychiatric interpretations of, 40–44; psychoanalytical interpretations of, 53, 54–65, 112, 140, 142; psychological interpretations of, 33–34, 39–65, 95–96; religious interpretations of, 29–35, 75; as *roman à clef,* 13, 32, 107–12; relation to Romanticism, 30, 74, 80; sexuality in, 98, 138–50; relation to Sturm und Drang, 42, 52, 80; translations of, 1–2, 21–22, 29, 60; versions of, 1–2, 123–24; *werkimmanente* interpretations of, 85–87, 91–92. *See also* Werther
Leiden und Freuden Werthers des Mannes, 12, 14, 108
Lenz, Jakob Michael Reinhold (1751–1792), 8, 15–16, 20, 26, 32, 81, 102, 156
Lernet-Holenia, Alexander (1897–1976), 124, 130, 167
Lessing, Gotthold Ephraim (1729–1781), 11, 91
Lessing, Gotthold Ephraim, works by: *Emilia Galotti,* 87, 119, 145; *Miss Sara Sampson,* 11
Lewes, George Henry (1817–1878), 22, 26, 115–16, 130, 158
Lewis, Helen Block (1913–1987), 96
Lichtenberg, Georg Christoph (1742–1799), 61
Linden, Walther (1895–1943), 78, 102, 163
Literary Magazine, The, 21
Littell's Living Age, 22
Loewe, Victor (1871–1933), 110, 130, 160
London Magazine, The, 21
Long, O. W. (1882–), 21–22, 26, 164
Longfellow, Henry Wadsworth (1807–1882)
Lorenz, Annika (19–), 123, 130, 187
Lukács, Georg (1885–1971), 3, 5, 48, 69, 80–83, 85, 87–88, 95–97, 103, 137–38, 152, 163
Luserke, Matthias (1959–), 12, 26, 35, 36, 45, 50, 52, 69, 112, 130, 186, 188, 189

MacLeod, Catriona (1963–), 139, 152, 189
Macpherson, James [*see:* Ossian] (1736–1796)

INDEX ♦ 197

Mahlendorf, Ursula (19–), 96, 104, 183
Mahoney, Dennis F. (1950–), 182
Mandelkow, Karl Robert (19–), 23, 26, 92, 103, 167, 173, 176
Mann, Otto (1898–), 168
Mann, Thomas (1875–1955), 3, 5, 54, 108, 114, 116–17, 130, 164
Massachusetts Magazine, 21
Massenet, Jules (1842–1912), 2
Mattenklott, Gert (1942–), 93, 173, 176
Maurer, Karl (1926–), 113, 119–120, 130, 168
Menzel, Wolfgang (1798–1873), 40, 69, 157
Merck, Johann Heinrich (1741–1791), 13–15, 20, 23, 26, 108, 110, 116, 130, 156
Meyer, Eva Alexander (1874–), 164, 165
Meyer, Richard Moritz (1860–1914), 40, 69, 160, 161
Meyer-Kalkus, Reinhart (19–), 12, 27, 56, 60–62, 69, 141, 145, 148, 152, 175
Meyer-Krentler, Eckhardt (19–), 12, 27, 108, 112, 130, 135, 152, 178, 180, 183
Michels, Josef (1910–), 46–47, 69, 78–79, 103, 163
Migge, Walter (19–), 110, 130, 169
Milar, Katherine S. (19–), 66, 68, 189
Miller, Norbert (1937–), 170
Miller, Ronald Duncan (1915–), 113, 130
Möbius, Paul Julius (1853–1907), 43, 69, 109, 110, 130, 160
Mog, Paul (19–), 33–34, 36, 55, 69, 174
Mommsen, Momme (1907–2001), 111–12, 130, 171
Montaigne, Michel de (1533–1592), 112
Monthly Review, The, 21

Moore, Charles (1743–1811), 21
Moritz, Karl Phillip (1757–1793), 156
Muenzer, Clark S. (19–), 50–51, 62, 69, 120, 131, 137, 153, 179, 180
Müller, Günther (1890–1957), 164
Müller, Joachim (1906–), 170
Müller, Peter (1936–), 12, 27, 32, 36, 82–84, 92–97, 103, 168, 169, 170, 172, 179
Müller, Wilhelm (19–), 78, 103, 163
Müller-Saget, Klaus (1940–), 119, 123, 131, 177
Mundt, Theodor (1808–1861), 74, 76, 103, 157

Nelles, Jürgen (1957–), 121, 137, 187
neuen Leiden des jungen W., Die. See Ulrich Plenzdorf
Neueste critische Nachrichten, 8, 13
Nicolai, Friedrich (1733–1811), 12–15, 27, 41, 50, 77, 83, 91, 108, 147, 156
North American Review, The, 22

Object Relations Theory, 63–65
Ossian [James Macpherson], 31, 61–63, 97, 118, 121, 144, 148, 149–50
Otho, Marcus Salvius (32–69), 114

Parnell, Peter (1953–), 22, 27, 176
Paulin, Roger (1937–), 112, 131, 182
Perels, Christoph (1938–), 34–35, 36, 184
Petrarch [Francesco Petrarca] (1304–1374), 113
Phillips, David P. (1943–), 123, 131, 173
pietism, 30, 32, 34, 51, 109, 112
Pike, Burton (19–), 2, 11, 190
Plenzdorf, Ulrich (1934–), 2, 5, 22, 27, 79, 103, 172

Polgar, Alfred (1873–1955), 110, 128, 160
Pongs, Hermann (1889–1979), 46, 70, 78–79, 103, 162
Powers, Elizabeth (1944–), 109, 112, 131, 188
Prawer, Siegbert (1925–), 114, 131, 178, 180
Prutz, Robert Eduard (1816–1872), 42, 70, 74, 103, 158
Purdy, Daniel (19–), 143–44, 153, 187
Pütz, Peter (1935–2003), 117, 118, 131, 145, 153, 178

Rahmeyer, Ruth (1927–), 108, 131, 186
Rank, Otto (1884–1939), 56, 70, 161
Reik, Theodor (1888–1969), 56
Reiss, Hans (1922–), 33, 36, 53, 70, 85, 103, 123–24, 131, 136, 153, 167, 168
Renner, Karl N. (19–), 40, 64, 70, 97, 103, 112, 131, 147, 153, 181
Reuter, Hans-Heinrich (1926–1978), 82, 103, 172, 175
Rheinische Provinzialblätter, 107
Richardson, Samuel (1689–1761), 113
Riess, Gertrud (18–), 123, 131, 162
Rockwood, Heidi (19–), 57–58, 70, 177
Rose, William (1894–1961), 29, 36, 110, 131, 163
Rothmann, Kurt (1936–), 85, 103, 172
Rousseau, Jean-Jacques (1712–1778), 8, 20, 55, 88, 95; *La Nouvelle Héloïse,* 20, 52, 113
Roussillon, Henriette Alexandrine von (1745–1773), 109
Ryan, Judith (1943–), 144, 153, 190
Ryder, Frank G. (1916–1996), 22, 27, 110, 131, 165, 168, 182

Saine, Thomas P. (1941–), 62, 70, 86, 103, 113, 123, 124, 131, 139, 145, 153, 177
Sauder, Gerhard (1938–), 50, 70, 80, 103, 112, 131, 132, 173, 182
Schaeder, Grete (19–), 32–33, 36, 117, 132, 164
Scharfschwerdt, Jürgen (1938–), 81, 103, 175
Scheff, Thomas J. (19–), 96, 104, 183
Scher, Steven Paul (1937–2004), 4
Scherer, Wilhelm (1841–1886), 76, 104, 113, 132, 159
Scherpe, Klaus (1939–), 11, 23, 27, 66, 70, 89–99, 104, 171, 173
Scherr, Johannes (1817–1886), 76, 104, 158
Schiller, Dieter (19–), 83, 104, 171
Schiller, Friedrich (1759–1805), works by: *Kabale und Liebe,* 11–12, 137
Schindler, Stephan (19–), 145–48, 153, 189
Schings, Hans-Jürgen (1937–), 9, 11, 15, 27, 175, 177
Schlaffer, Hannelore (1939–), 137, 153, 182
Schlesier, Gustav (18–), 74
Schlosser, Cornelia, née Goethe (1750–1777), 56, 64–65
Schlosser, Friedrich Christoph (1776–1861), 74–75, 99, 104, 157
Schmid, Christian Heinrich (1746–1800), 9, 27, 155
Schmidt, Erich (1853–1913), 46, 109, 113, 132, 140–41, 153, 159
Schmidt, Gerhard (1904–), 55, 70, 142, 153, 170
Schmidt, Hartmut (1934–), 13, 27, 110, 132, 172, 183
Schmidt, Heinrich (1874–1935), 161
Schmidt, Julian (1818–1886), 76, 78, 104, 158

Schmiedt, Helmut (1950–), 53–54, 70, 123, 153, 176, 183
Schöffler, Herbert (1888–1946), 30–32, 34, 36, 78, 104, 163
Scholz, Rüdiger (1939–), 66, 70, 96, 104, 183
Schöne, Albrecht (1925–), 29, 34, 36, 116, 132, 167, 169
Schrader, Erich (19–), 110, 111, 132, 165
Schubart, Christian Friedrich Daniel (1739–1791), 9–10, 13, 18, 45, 70, 155, 156
Schubert, Hans von (1859–1931), 30, 36, 162
Schweitzer, Christoph E. (1922–), 121, 132, 190
Schwenck, Konrad (1793–1864), 22, 28, 157
Seeger, Lothar G. (19–), 112, 132, 170
Self-Psychology, 65
Shakespeare, William (1564–1616), 8, 9, 23, 147
Sheehan, Jonathan L. (19–), 99
Shelley, Mary, née Wollstonecraft (1797–1851), works by:
Frankenstein; or, The Modern Prometheus, 1
Shookman, Ellis (1957–), 4
Siebers, Tobin (19–), 39, 70, 74, 104, 121, 123, 132, 185
Silz, Walter (1894–), 136–37, 153, 172
Slochower, Harry (1900–1991), 59, 70, 142, 149, 153, 173
Sloterdijk, Peter (1947–), 147, 153, 179, 182
Sonnenburg, Reinhart (1948–), 4
Sonntag, 82
Spann, Meno (1903–1992), 138, 154, 172
Spielhagen, Friedrich (1829–1911), 115, 132, 158
Sprickmann, Anton Matthias (1749–1781), 44–45

Springer, Brunold (1873–1931), 56, 70, 162
Staël, Anne Louise Germaine de (1766–1817), 157
Staiger, Emil (1908–1987), 85, 104, 165
Stein, Charlotte von (1742–1827), 109, 116
Steinhauer, Harry (1905–), 138, 154, 173
Stephan, Arndt (19–), 79, 95, 104, 173
Stephan, Inge (1944–), 79, 95, 104, 173
Stöber, Anna Elisabeth (1745–1769), 109
Storz, Gerhard (1898–1993), 85, 104, 165
Strack, Friedrich (1939–), 54, 71, 180
Sulzer, Johann Georg (1720–1779), 28, 118, 132, 155
Swales, Martin (19–), 73, 77, 79–80, 86, 104, 124, 132, 182

Taylor, Bayard (1825–1878), 22, 28, 74, 104, 159
Tellenbach, Hubertus (1914–), 43–44, 52, 71, 167, 175
Thorlby, Anthony (19–), 113, 117–18, 122, 132, 174
Ticknor, George (1791–1871), 22, 27, 165
Tobin, Robert D. (19–), 149, 154, 187
Trunz, Erich (1905–2001), 34, 37, 110, 136, 141, 154, 165, 166

Vaget, Hans Rudolf (1938–), 23, 28, 86, 104, 114, 117, 132, 144, 150, 154, 178, 181, 190
Vazsonyi, Nicholas (1963–), 80, 105, 188
Viëtor, Karl (1892–1957), 39, 46, 71, 76, 105, 165

Vilmar, August Friedrich Christian (1800–1868), 74, 105, 157
Vincent, Deidre (1943–), 23, 28, 109, 112, 116, 123, 124, 132, 185
Vollmer, Hartmut (1957–), 120, 133, 190

Wagenknecht, Christian (19–), 108, 133, 172
Walker, Collin (1938), 183
Walker, Jim (1961–), 4
Walker, Joyce S. (19–), 113, 133, 137, 154, 188
Wandsbecker Bote, Der, 3, 5, 10
Waniek, Erdmann (19–), 145, 154, 178
Warrick, E. Kathleen (19–), 138, 154, 175
Weber, Carl Maria (18–), 108–9, 133, 162
Weber, Evelyn (19–), 177
Weisbach, Reinhard (19–), 83, 102, 170
Wellbery, Caroline (19–), 52, 71, 113, 133, 181
Wellbery, David E. (1947–), 39, 50, 71, 135, 137, 148–50, 154, 184, 186, 187
Wellek, René (1903–1995), 37, 39, 45, 71, 169
Welz, Dieter (19–), 123, 133, 172
Werner, Hans-Georg (19–), 83, 105, 171
Werther: as artist, 114, 118–20; as real person/literary figure, 14, 43–48, 51, 55–57, 59, 62, 64–65, 120–22, 124–26; relation to Goethe, 14, 30, 40–47, 55–57, 64–65, 98–99, 113–19, 122–23

Werther-Fieber (Werther-fever), 1
Werther-Krankheit (Werther-sickness, -disease), 1, 73–74, 76, 81
Weygand, Christian Friedrich (17–), 2, 10–11
Wieland, Christoph Martin (1733–1813), 12–13, 16, 28, 155, 156
Wiese, Benno von (1903–1987), 78
Wilhelm I, Kaiser (1797–1888), 76
Wilkinson, Elizabeth Mary (1909–2001), 125, 133, 145, 154, 169
Wille, Ludwig (1834–1912), 42–43, 71, 159
Willoughby, Leonard Ashley (1885–1977), 125, 133, 145, 154, 169
Wilson, James D. (1946–), 33, 37, 74, 105, 174
Wilson, W. Daniel (19–), 86, 105, 124, 133, 142, 154, 183
Winnicott, Donald Woods (1896–1971), 63, 125
Wölfel, Kurt (19–), 16–17, 28, 170, 178
Wordsworth, William (1770–1850), 116

Zabel, Hermann (1935–), 40, 37, 172
Zahlmann, Christel (19–), 65, 71, 182
Zelter, Karl Friedrich (1758–1832), 115
Ziegra, Christian (1719–1778), 11–12, 28, 29, 156
Zimmermann, Georg (1814–1881), 30, 37, 41–42, 71, 77, 105, 158
Zimmermann, Rolf Christian (19–), 34, 37, 112, 133, 176

Wake Tech. Libraries
9101 Fayetteville Road
Raleigh, North Carolina 27603-5696

WAKE TECHNICAL COMMUNITY COLLEGE

3 3063 00138748 8

WN **DATE DUE**

JUL 2007